# Study Skills
# for Business
# & Management

**SAGE** has been part of the global academic community since 1965, supporting high quality research and learning that transforms society and our understanding of individuals, groups, and cultures. SAGE is the independent, innovative, natural home for authors, editors and societies who share our commitment and passion for the social sciences.

Find out more at: **www.sagepublications.com**

**SAGE Study Skills**

# Study Skills for Business & Management

How to Succeed at University and Beyond

Patrick Tissington &
Christos Orthodoxou

Los Angeles | London | New Delhi
Singapore | Washington DC

Los Angeles | London | New Delhi
Singapore | Washington DC

SAGE Publications Ltd
1 Oliver's Yard
55 City Road
London EC1Y 1SP

SAGE Publications Inc.
2455 Teller Road
Thousand Oaks, California 91320

SAGE Publications India Pvt Ltd
B 1/I 1 Mohan Cooperative Industrial Area
Mathura Road
New Delhi 110 044

SAGE Publications Asia-Pacific Pte Ltd
3 Church Street
#10-04 Samsung Hub
Singapore 049483

Editor: Kirsty Smy
Editorial assistant: Nina Smith
Production editor: Sarah Cooke
Copyeditor: Gemma Marren
Proofreader: Nicola Marshall
Indexer: Judith Lavender
Marketing manager: Alison Borg
Cover design: Shaun Mercier
Typeset by: C&M Digitals (P) Ltd, Chennai, India
Printed in Great Britain by Henry Ling Limited at
The Dorset Press, Dorchester, DT1 1HD

**Library of Congress Control Number: 2013939383**

**British Library Cataloguing in Publication data**

A catalogue record for this book is available from
the British Library

ISBN 978-1-4462-6648-9
ISBN 978-1-4462-6649-6 (pbk)

# Contents

# Acknowledgements

Both authors would like to gratefully acknowledge the support of Kirsty Smy at Sage who immediately saw the potential for this book and whose insights and tolerance have made the process as smooth as it could be. We would also like to thank the really helpful comments by the anonymous reviewers as we have learned greatly from their insights. Having said that, any shortcomings in the book are solely the responsibility of the authors.

Pat would like to thank his family (Sally, Dan and Vinny) for their support and tolerance of his disappearing to write in his shed.

Christos would like to thank his parents, Harry and Anthia, and his little brother Giorgio who is now going through university. He is particularly grateful for all the Starbucks his mum and dad bought him whilst he pretended to be a proper writer.

# Introduction

The idea for writing this book came from Chris just after he graduated. He was looking back on his time at university and realised that he had learned not only knowledge and skills directly from his degree, but along the way he had learned how to do well at university (well, he had just got a first!). When he met his former tutor Pat to reflect on this, he discovered that Pat had been thinking of writing some form of study skills book but had shelved the idea when he couldn't see how to make his idea unique. And so, in a coffee shop in Leamington Spa, the idea for this book was hatched. They decided to carry out some research so the book would be based on a broader evidence base rather than just their two experiences of university. So this book has been created by the two authors with the unique slant being that it was written by a student and his lecturer together with their ideas underpinned by research.

In essence, whilst the two authors are separated by an age gap, one thing they definitely have in common is that when they graduated, they wished they had known how to study right from the start. The aim in writing this book is to share these critically important skills with students so they can gain the advantage of knowing how to succeed in their studies. Pat and Chris were further spurred into action when they researched current study guides and discovered the great majority were out of date, irrelevant and not representative of how university life actually works from a student point of view. Combining these reasons they saw the need for a modern and new study guide specifically for business students.

## So who are we?

### Patrick Tissington

At the time of writing Pat was a Reader at Aston Business School who taught Chris in the first year and was later his tutor. Pat had been at Aston for 12 years teaching a very large group of first year Organisational Behaviour students as well as teaching teamworking, leadership and coaching. His motivation as a lecturer has always been to break down the barriers to learning by helping students learn how to learn. His own experience of university was as a mature student (he went to university aged 29) and personally found it very tough going as he tried to find out for himself how best to study. He managed it somehow but was acutely aware that he only really understood how university worked just before his final exams. This book is the result of a long held ambition to help students learn quickly and easily about how to get the best out of university. As of June 2013, he is Professor of Organizational Psychology at Birkbeck, University of London where he continues to teach, research and consult in the areas of teamwork, leadership and other organisational behaviour topics.

### Christos Orthodoxou

Chris graduated from Aston with a first class degree and wanted to share his knowledge with other students. He realised he had developed a number of tactics that any business student could utilise and he wanted to share these with as many students as possible, hence this book.

Chris has moved around a little bit whilst writing this book. He worked at Aston Business School, then went to work at Pepsi and later decided to return to Aston Business School after he realised corporate life wasn't for him and that he had a true passion for working with students. He is now aiming to start a social enterprise that will help students and graduates discover and secure their dream career.

## How to use this book

The book will draw on knowledge and examples from our own experiences, and from current students, recent graduates, business professionals, lecturers, books and academic research to give you a complete and up to date study guide. We have chosen to use examples from academic sources and from working professionals as we aim to provide you with skills that are valuable for university but more importantly way beyond that into your professional working life. Whether you choose to work in an organisation or to become an entrepreneur we guarantee that the skills and knowledge you find in this book will help you for the whole of your life. For example, Mind Maps. Both of us are enthusiastic users of this technique but were encouraged to discover in our research that people with higher degree grades tended to use these whereas those with lower grades did not.

So, we see the main point of this book is to fast track the reader on their way to learning how to do well at university. But we also see that the skills we describe are not only useful at university – they are skills you can use at work in the long term. With this in mind, we have provided information at the end of each chapter on how it applies beyond university.

Ideally this book shall be read by first year business students in order to have the maximum amount of time to practise the suggestions we provide and to generate awareness of one's own strengths and weaknesses. However, this book is valuable to any student on their business degree due to the way it has been written. In terms of degree we personally believe it applies to all business degrees including:

- Marketing
- Business and Management
- International Business
- Information Technology Management/Business Computing
- Innovation, Sustainability and Entrepreneurship
- Logistics
- HRM
- Accounting and Finance
- Operations
- Economics
- Business Economics
- Business and Politics

When writing this book we always kept in mind that these days going to university is a significant cost and our motivation is solely to help students get the best from their days at university. It is doubly important now because we know that you and your family are making sacrifices for you to go to university and we want help you to get the best you possibly can out of the experience. And we do mean 'experience' – not just getting the best grades you can in exams. We firmly believe that you can gain as much from meeting new people, learning new sports, perhaps moving to a new city and having fun as you do from the lectures. But you do need to get the learning done. So we aren't going to tell you how to live your life. But we are providing tools and techniques that we *know* will be of enormous help to you at university. We also believe that all the tools and techniques in this book are just as relevant to work as they are to university so we also show how to use them in your wonderful new job when you graduate – all the chapters have a section about how the ideas can be applied to the workplace.

We realise that not all of you will need every idea contained in the book so each chapter is self-contained to allow you to jump straight to the bits you need. A word of warning though, we have included these chapters after careful research and so we think you will eventually need all the techniques contained within them. But if you are already a superstar essay writer, then perhaps you won't need much from that chapter. We do recommend everyone try using all the skills we describe and in particular, if you have never used Mind Maps before, we strongly recommend you read about them and have a go. Like most of the skills we are describing, it takes some practise but this will pay off in a big way once you master it.

We have read a lot of books and papers that we believe would be of great value to students. Therefore, if you have a particular interest in any of the chapters we have provided a section called our bookshelf and these encompass our recommendations for further reading. By all means follow up on these and if you have any other great examples, then please do let us know. And we love getting feedback so please do get in touch. You can reach us in a number of ways by going to about.me/pat.tissington.

We do hope you find the book a real help and that you have a great time at university!

# 1

# Planning and goal setting

## 1.1 Chapter summary

By the end of this chapter, you should have an idea of the goals you want to achieve at university and a rough plan of how you are going to achieve them. More specifically you should have a list of goals across all areas of your life, the benefits of achieving these and the associated challenges. You will also have devised action plans.

## 1.2 The end goal

What do you want to achieve in your time at university? This is the central question behind this chapter and we hope it is one you have asked yourself already. However, many students go through university without really working out what it is they are trying to achieve. Time at university is actually very short and most of us only ever do a degree once, which means it is crucial to answer this question. Pat went to university late in life – when he was 29. Many friends who went aged 18 said they envied him going when he was older because when they had been at university, they didn't really know why they went and so didn't get anything like what they could have done from the experience. Setting goals is not easy to do and it is even harder to actually achieve them once you do know them. But first, to clarify, our definition of a goal is something you wish to achieve, see the examples given in Figure 1.1:

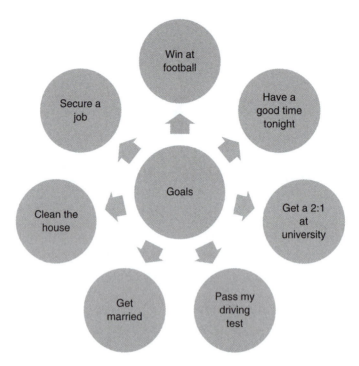

FIGURE 1.1   Examples of goals

These are all examples of goals and a few examples illustrate that we set goals all the time. Sometimes though we need to set more important, larger goals and these are the ones that require the effort of a more thorough approach which this chapter will help to explore.

## 1.3 How do goals work?

> [Goal] theory is based on what Aristotle called *final causality*, that is, action caused by a purpose. (Locke, 1996: 118)

Essentially, goals work by directing what actions somebody needs to take. For example, if somebody wishes to pass their driving test, then they need to take a number of actions such as learn the Highway Code, pass the theory test and undertake lessons. In more detail, 'Goals affect performance by affecting the direction of action, the degree of effort exerted, and the persistence of action over time' (Locke, 1996: 120). However, just like most things, creating goals does have drawbacks:

- Having goals can become daunting and boring.
- You can become too focused on the final result.
- Goals can create a fear of failure by believing that if the goal is not achieved you will be unhappy.

The important thing to highlight is that all these drawbacks can be overcome, which allows goal setting to become a powerful tool. In fact, the immense value of goal setting is well acknowledged. Research has even specifically proven that students who set goals end up with better grades (Zimmerman et al., 1992).

> Backed by years of research data supporting its viability, goal-setting techniques work and work well. (Rubin, 2002: 26)

## 1.4 Creating your goals

Think of it this way: you need to figure out exactly what you want to achieve from university because you are only there for three or four years at the most which is not a lot of time in the grand scheme of things – and these days, in most countries, it will cost you and your family a *lot* of money. So, the pressure is on to make sure you get a good return on this investment. Just as importantly, you need to decide what the meaning of your university life is, what you want to spend your time on and what will make you happy. The absolute key behind goal setting is to *begin with the end in mind*. Stephen Covey explored this really well in his best-selling book, *The 7 Habits of Effective People* (2004), and Pat regularly recommends this as being the most important habit to learn. Just think about it for a moment: what is the ideal situation for you to be in 12 months from now? Tracy (2003) discusses that everybody has great potential within them and writing goals allows them to realise this by focusing their efforts. Without knowing the end in mind, you will never know when you get there (Cairo, 1998).

The most obvious goal is what grade you want to achieve by the time you finish university. From the research we did in preparing for this book – and through a general understanding of students – most aim for a 2:1. It is interesting to highlight from the research that those who achieved a first wished they spent more time socialising; whilst those who achieved a 2:1 wished they worked a little harder to get a first. It seems then that there is a slight dilemma. Do you work your socks off and try to get a first or do you work pretty hard, enjoy yourself and get a 2:1? Deciding upon this comes down to what you want out of university other than the final grade.

## 1.5 Areas to set goals

So how do you get started? Figure 1.2 shows the areas we think you should think of when deciding on your goals. You may well have others, but these form a good starting point.

### 1.5.1 Career and financial – including income, part-time jobs, summer internships

This is the most popular area where goal setting is used, especially as many organisations see the value of creating goals for employees. Undoubtedly, within your career degree, you will have some idea of your career goals. Examples might be:

- secure a placement for the third year of university
- secure a summer job
- network with people in the accounting industry

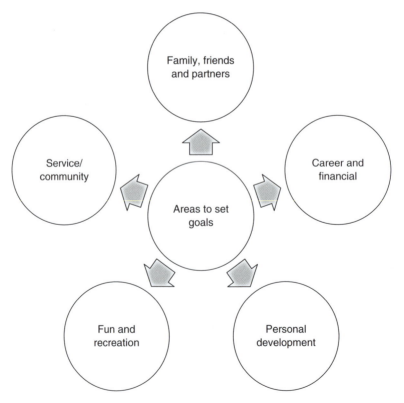

FIGURE 1.2   Areas to set goals

## 1.5.2 Family, friends and partners

This is an area of life where it may seem somewhat strange to set goals, however, most of us do set goals here in a subconscious way. For example, most people will say that they want to have the best possible relationship with their friends and family. The power in this area comes from moving from just having a vague subconscious idea to explicitly thinking about it and writing it down. The fact remains, we are social animals and developing social relationships has been strongly linked to happiness (Myers, 2000), so be sure to make the most out of it. Examples might be:

- make as many friends as possible
- maintain a good relationship with family
- enter into a relationship

Chris recently set himself the goal of spending more time with his family as he realised he was getting too caught up with work and other matters, which resulted in him neglecting precious time with his family.

## 1.5.3 Personal development – including skills, spiritual and mental health

Personal development is absolutely key. Whatever you want to achieve, developing your knowledge and skills will help. Examples might be:

- learn how to write a CV
- keep fit
- become more dedicated to your religion

> I always think that I should aim higher in life to live my mission. My main goal in life is to leave a mark – I am satisfied when someone is inspired by my actions, when I recommend something to them and that changes their life. This desire has driven me to set a number of goals which include getting 70 per cent in my dissertation as part of my wider goal to achieve a first class degree, live at least a year in another country, gain a qualification from the Chartered Institute of Marketing and learn the Russian language in a fluent manner.
>
> Monika J. Čiurlionytė, BSc Marketing

It seems that Monika had a clear set of goals. When you read this, did you think she sounded driven? Focused? We certainly did. And it is no accident that having set out these very specific goals for herself, she achieved them.

### 1.5.4 Fun and recreation – including hobbies, interests, travel and sports

Strategising includes your social life. You will get bored and university is an amazing experience that you will want to enjoy. The techniques in this book will allow you to free up your time to enjoy a social life. Examples might be:

- develop your tennis skills
- establish a new society for students interested in poker
- travel across South America

### 1.5.5 Service/community

We thoroughly recommend students to set goals around service and community. In short, giving something back creates a sense of satisfaction and allows students to develop their skills and realise what areas interest them, e.g. HR or finance. Examples might be:

- establish a new charity
- raise £500 for charity
- become a voluntary youth worker

Charity work has been a large and important part of my life since a young age. Through the years I have been involved in various different social projects and have always tried to set achievable goals in my work. For example, I have recently set myself the goal of helping young homeless people to get back into employment and find their footing again in society. Having lived in Paris where homelessness is a very prevalent problem, I became highly sensitized to it and wanted to do something to help in areas of the UK where homelessness is a major issue. My specific aim is to grow my company, People-Mind, with my business partner in order to create jobs and support specifically for homeless people in the Birmingham area. PeopleMind aims to create products through upcycling and involve homeless people throughout the entire process; from sourcing the materials to making the products, to manufacturing them, to selling them on.

Devon Parker, BSc International Business and French

### 1.5.6 Possessions

This is an area in which a lot of people do set themselves quite high goals, for example, to own a big house or a Lamborghini. However, there is a substantial amount of research to suggest that these goals are not of value (Kasser and

Ryan, 1993). The problem is that possessions do not create happiness because they only provide a short-term buzz and people then want something bigger and better.

You may think it is weird to set goals in some of these areas of your life, what goals can you set around your family and friends? The key is to remember why you are doing so, which is to ensure balance. It is so easy to get caught up in one area of your life and neglect others which are just as important. The balance of achieving these goals should allow you to be happy and just as importantly give you a sense of direction and allow you to nurture relationships with those that are close to you. This is all in the aim of realising your true potential in life and subsequently your satisfaction with life (Ryff, 1989). Balance is also a virtuous circle. For example, if you really want to secure a good degree, then balance in the area of fun and exercise will help you to achieve it. Once you have set goals in these areas of your life, you can then go back to your degree and ascertain what grade to aim for.

Knowing what areas to create goals, how do you actually go about generating them? The general advice is to think about what you wish to achieve and then write it down. This would be fine if everybody knew what they wanted, however, as you probably know, most people do not. This problem is well recognised and so a few methods have been created to help people create goals. We suggest that you maintain an open mind to these methods and have a go at all of them.

## 1.6 How to set goals that work

So, having explored the areas you should focus your goal setting on, we now move on to how you go about actually setting the goals.

### 1.6.1 Envisioning

This method involves defining a vision and working your way back to set manageable goals. By a vision, we mean what would make a perfect life. You can really use your imagination in this approach: if there were simply no limits, what job would you like? Who you would like to be friends with? What would you like your body to be like? For example, to be happy by securing a good education and maintaining fun and healthy relationships with my friends. Taking this example, the goals coming out would include:

- a grade to achieve at university
- what types of fun to have
- a few goals regarding friendship

## 1.6.2 Happiness approach

This involves identifying what makes you happy and going after these to maintain a happy life. Generally, most people aim for happiness in their life and this method gets to the heart of what makes somebody happy. One of the best ways to do this is to list 10 or 20 things over the last month that made you happy, these can be anything from any aspect of your life. Then assess what patterns you notice, are there any common themes? You can then form an idea of what makes you happy and what to set as goals. The trick to this is to list literally whatever has made you happy. Table 1.1 gives an example:

TABLE 1.1  Examples of what made you happy this week

| Received positive feedback | Went for a nice bike ride | Achieved 68% in my essay |
|---|---|---|
| Went bowling with friends | Completed my essay | Went to the gym |
| Read an interesting book | Went to London with family | Went to a nice restaurant |
| Relaxed at home with my family | Completed lifeguard qualification | Saw an old friend |

The example above would suggest development and sociability are important aspects in life and so appropriate goals could include completing a qualification in an area of interest, actively participating in a society and joining the gym.

## 1.6.3 Value-based approach

This is about defining who you are and what you stand for, which ultimately determines your goals. Some helping question here are:

- What things am I proud of?
- What things make me happy in life?
- How would other people describe me?

Pat likes to use the first question when he is coaching executives, as the answers are usually insightful into what really motivates the person. Some of these questions are perhaps a little abstract, which might make you hesitant to use them. Try not to be dismissive, give things a go and if they do not work for you (having really tried), then feel free to scrap them. Hopefully, you will see that they are complementary, some of the goals you see emerging in one technique are similar to those in another.

It is difficult to generate valuable and worthy goals that you will desire to wake up for each morning and achieve. Have a brief go at the techniques and then come back to it later on or even the next day. You may subconsciously be thinking about your goals in the break which is great, be sure to make a note of them. Tracy (2003) recommends people should spend at least one day thinking through their goals and how they are going to achieve them.

## 1.7 Creating the perfect goals

Generating goals can in fact be a relatively easy stage compared to making effective goals. With a push, most people can generate goals and stick to them for a couple of weeks, maybe even a month if they are driven. However, it is easy to lose motivation, which is why it is so important to create effective goals. To test whether or not they are effective, there are three key tests for your goals that we discuss below.

### 1.7.1 Are they challenging enough?

Once you have a complete list of your goals, reread them and think about whether or not they are challenging enough. Are you subconsciously limiting yourself? If you are aiming to get a 2:2 could you challenge yourself to get a 2:1? Do not limit your own potential! An easy to way to assess this is to get your friends and family to review your goals. Do they think you are limiting yourself? Do they believe you can achieve better? If you are too embarrassed to do this, then try to think through their eyes. If they were to see your goals, what would they think?

### 1.7.2 Are they your goals?

This seems like a bit of a stupid question to ask, if you sat down and thought of some goals then they are obviously going to be yours. What we don't sometimes realise is that we have set goals to satisfy others. The most common example of this is family, for example, where students believe they must achieve a certain grade to satisfy their parents. Chris knows this himself, he thought he needed to get a first to make his parents happy until a week before his final exam when his dad said to him he didn't care what grade he got, he would still be happy. Pat's experience is that we are so often trying to please our parents – even late in life – whereas (as a parent himself) he knows for sure that the vast majority of parents simply want their children to be happy. This really highlights

9

that the only source of pressure comes from ourselves, nobody else. So the only person that should be setting your goals is you.

### 1.7.3 Are they SMART?

SMART goals have become universally accepted as a means to make effective goals. However, it is fair to say it has become too simplified and the very words it stands for have become distorted due to hundreds of variations (Rubin, 2002). So what exactly does SMART stand for?

- Specific: your goal must be specific so you know when you achieved it and so you clearly understand what it is you are trying to achieve and how. A common goal is to do your best but this is a rather weak goal due to the fact that nobody knows their 'best'. The lesson is that better performance is often achieved when goals are specified (Locke, 1996).
- Measurable: can you measure what defines success? Without doing so, you will never know if you have succeeded.
- Attainable: is your goal possible with your experience and skills?
- Realistic: is your goal achievable? If a goal is not realistic then you are likely to fail, which can lead to frustration and a sense of disappointment.
- Time based: when should your goal be completed by? Without knowing this, you risk spending longer on a goal then necessary – or worse still, never finish it at all. Specifying a realistic deadline ensures focus.

We do accept the criticisms that SMART goals have generated and we agree that simply making a goal SMART is not going to work in itself, which is why we have included the other information in creating goals. However, it still has value, especially combined with all the techniques we have discussed in this chapter. For example, many students have the aim of obtaining a good degree. If this was to be redefined in the SMART way, it could be to achieve a 2:1 degree by graduation time. Pat has come to the conclusion that the most important way to test whether a goal is useful is to ask yourself whether or not you can tell if you have achieved it. Just by doing this, you will ensure that the goal is specific. Then all you need to do is put a timescale on it. But make sure you are giving yourself enough time – everyone tends to be too optimistic when it comes to working out how long things take. An experienced project manager once told Pat his rule of thumb was to take the worst case scenario for how long every stage of a project would take. Then double it! His projects always came in on time and to high quality. So you should be working to stretch yourself, but give yourself enough time to achieve quality in what you do.

As part of my degree it is mandatory that I complete an International Industrial Placement. Within the first couple of weeks of placement searching, I had heard of what sounded like my dream placement at Mattel Europa and from then on I made it my goal to be working for this company. With Mattel being my superordinate goal I then had to use SMART objectives to reach this final point. These included attending Mattel's Employer Presentation evening to find out more about what the placement encompasses and what Mattel is really all about. I also participated in interview workshops to help me when it came to the interview processes of this placement. All of these little steps eventually led me to the final interview stage of this placement and my passion about the company and setting SMART objectives throughout the course of the process meant that I managed to secure my dream placement.

Lewis Boot, BSc International Business and Management

## 1.8 Planning

Planning is a vital step to achieving your goals. Considering you are currently studying a business degree you will understand that new and existing businesses create plans all the time to achieve what they desire. It is the same for individuals:

Fail to plan, plan to fail.

This quote highlights the absolute importance of planning: without planning, failure is inevitable. Nonetheless, sometimes people do get lucky and without planning still manage to succeed, like the annoying person in every year who leaves everything to the last minute and still gets the top grade. Imagine if these people planned adequately, they could achieve so much more and this is what we want to help you to do. It is by no means easy to set goals and stick to them, as is evident in the fact that a great deal of people never realise their goals. The hard part is to commit to your goals and ultimately achieve them. We hope to provide you with the perfect plan to help you achieve your goals.

## 1.9 The perfect plan

Most advice and thinking around creating a plan revolves around creating a list of goals and actions over the short, medium and long term. This is a crucial part of planning but there is so much more to creating the perfect plan. Our idea of the perfect plan is this:

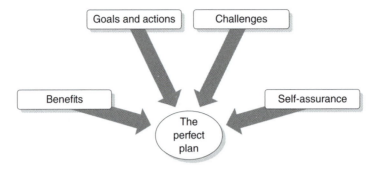

FIGURE 1.3    The perfect plan

## 1.9.1 Goals and actions

This is about breaking your goals down into smaller ones that give specific actions. This is at the core of any plan. It can be very daunting to look at long-term goals that don't transpire into anything today. For example, if your aim is to get a first, then what do you need to do each year or even each term to achieve this?

Keep working your way backwards to reach some steps that you could do right now. The best example to illustrate how to do this is what grade you wish to achieve. Let us take the area of university as an example. First, you need to breakdown each year and ascertain what is expected of you. All this information will be available in your module guidelines. Create a list of all the modules that you are going to be completing throughout the year. Then list how each module is to be assessed and how much that component will contribute to the module mark, i.e. will it include 30 per cent coursework, 60 per cent exam and 10 per cent group work?

We strongly suggest you think about where you want to concentrate your efforts. Clearly, you need to put effort into all your modules but some will require far more effort than others and sometimes you need to be strategic. For example, Chris had a piece of coursework that was worth 15 per cent of a single module. After going through all the modules at the start of the year he made the conscious decision to put little effort into this coursework and instead concentrate elsewhere. In the end, he achieved 52 per cent for the assignment which was one of the lowest marks he ever got. However, in the same week he completed a double module coursework assignment in which he achieved 70 per cent. This might seem a cynical approach to take, but the lecturer is in effect telling you how much effort to put in by varying the marks allocated to each piece of work. Be careful though – some courses require you to reach a certain standard in all the work you do so make sure you really understand the rules of the game by reading the regulations carefully.

Moving further afield from your degree, what other goals have you set yourself and what actions do you need to complete to achieve these? Once you have identified all the necessary actions, we suggest that you place an allocation of time for each step. This will force efficiency and ensure you do not spend unnecessarily longer on any given task. What is more evident is that people are too optimistic about what they can achieve in a given time period (Buehler et al., 1994), be mindful not to fall into this trap, though we will talk more about it in the time management chapter.

Finally, allocate a reward for each sub goal. Little impulse purchases such as some new clothes are good but we recommend more social rewards like going to the cinema or for a night out with friends, which create more lasting memories and happiness. But only do this as a reward to yourself for achieving a particular goal – so often we see students do this sort of thing instead of doing their work. It is never as satisfying and of course the work still needs to be done afterwards!

## 1.9.2 Benefits

Have a think about why it is you want to achieve your goals, i.e. what are the benefits? Without doing this you risk losing motivation when times get tough and easily forgetting why you set the goal in the first place. Samuel illustrates this brilliantly in the example below where he remembered why he wanted to achieve his goal to push him through the challenges.

> I have always been strangely obsessed with entrepreneurship and really enjoy trying new things. Successfully applying to be President of Aston Entrepreneurs, and then subsequently project managing the National Student Enterprise Conference 2012 with NACUE, was a logical goal for me, but this involved managing a large number of unpaid volunteers, roughly my age, with their own individual agendas. The only way I was able to do this with success was to believe in myself and be sure of the reasons why I wanted to put myself in that position (when I was supposed to be dedicating myself to my degree), more than anything else.
>
> Samuel Wilson, BSc International Business and Modern Languages

Try to think beyond the most immediate and obvious benefits, there might be some personal reasons for wanting to achieve your goals and even some tiny benefits that might be generated. Murphy (2010) recommends making them heartfelt, essentially this means putting some emotion into your goals and this is what this stage helps to do. You need to relate the goal to something or somebody you care about. For example, at the start of his final year, Chris wrote out why he wanted to achieve a first class honours degree. There were the immediate benefits such as better career prospects but this really wasn't the key thing in his mind. To Chris, the benefits were more personal – wanting to make his parents proud, to increase his level of confidence, to achieve something which he could be proud of and to be the best in his year. These may seem a bit weird to other people but it worked to motivate him. Here lies a key point: these are your goals and your benefits. Whatever the benefits are for you, write them down – do not be embarrassed, shy or self-conscious. But we do strongly recommend you write them down. Just by doing so you make them more concrete and you will commit to them more than if you just have them in your head. You don't have to show them to anyone else but sometimes it is useful to do so.

To identify the benefits of achieving a goal, you can try to imagine what life would be like if you achieved it. This is the power of visualisation, if people do not envision themselves then they are at serious risk of failing their goals (Murphy, 2010). Truly try to imagine what it would be like to achieve your goals. This can be very motivational and even increase your performance. For example, a study was conducted which illustrated that basketball players performed higher after they visualised scoring shots. The trick here is to really imagine what life would be like if you achieved your goals.

A word about visualisation: it might seem very strange that we are suggesting that you sit down, close your eyes and dream. But this is precisely what we want you to do. There is some great research that shows how athletes who do this can improve their performance massively without any need to go onto the field of play. We want you really to do this. To think deeply and at length about the main goal you have set yourself – the one which you are perhaps not at all sure that you can achieve. Sit quietly and imagine what it is going to be like when you achieve that goal. Do it in detail – what will you be wearing? What will you hear? What smells will there be? Who else will be there? What would happen to you and those around you? What would change?

During the challenges of his PhD, Pat used to do exactly this, imagining of what it would be like to go on to the platform and receive his doctorate. He would then visualise the steps before this (handing in the thesis, going through a viva) and then before this (finishing off chapter after chapter). He would do this often when he wondered whether he would ever finish the thesis or wasn't sure what he was supposed to be doing (and he felt both of these very often indeed!). In the end, he finished his thesis well within the time set and with no corrections apart from spelling mistakes (which is unusual). So, just as research has shown that imagining you are throwing a basket in basketball or shooting for goal in football has some of the same benefits as actually doing it for real, imagining your way to your goal will also help a great deal.

### 1.9.3 The challenges

You must now anticipate the challenges and obstacles that may hinder your ability to achieve your goals and then state how you are going to overcome them. Without doing this, you are at risk of being thrown off your goals too easily once challenges arise. Table 1.2 gives some examples of challenges that you may wish to think about:

TABLE 1.2   Overcoming challenges

| Challenge | Ways to overcome challenge |
| --- | --- |
| Boredom | Join three societies |
| | Regularly adapt study technique |
| | Work on a variety of projects |
| Missing friends | Spend at least an hour a day with friends |
| | Arrange to meet up after setting target workload |
| | Conduct group revision sessions |
| Maintaining health | Take it in turns to cook each day |
| | Go running each morning |
| | Go for a walk when taking breaks from work |

Try to be as specific as possible when thinking of how to overcome challenges. For example, having fun is way too general, think of ways you can have fun such as to play football or go out to eat. A valuable method to help identify how to overcome the challenges and achieve your goals is to think about what resources you have to hand. Who can help you? What can help? What can you give them back in return?

### 1.9.4 Self-assurance

The final step is to create belief that you can achieve your goals, which is known as self-efficacy. Bristol (1985) believes the key to achieving any goal is to believe in yourself and we agree, no matter how good you are at anything, if you don't believe you are good enough then you will make this the reality. It comes back to the idea of:

> If you believe something will happen, you will make it happen.

If you believe you will succeed at university, you will; if you believe you will fail, you will. We are sure you get the idea by now. Pat once interviewed the famous industrialist Sir John Harvey Jones who talked about his poor school exam grades:

> If people tell you often enough that you are stupid, eventually you believe them. That is what happened to me.

He later found confidence in his abilities and rose to be head of one of the biggest firms in the UK and a well-respected thinker on business. But it took a great deal of effort on his part to leave the negative thoughts behind and become confident in his abilities.

A good way to do this is to think about previous times in your life where you have achieved something that illustrates your ability to achieve your current goals. For example, many of you will have completed exams at school and college, which signifies you have the ability to pass your exams at university. Alternatively, you may have previously completed a part-time job, which shows you have the ability to secure a placement or summer internship. Pat often thought about how he had completed the insanely arduous Devizes to Westminster Canoe Race or how he had overcome obstacles during his service in the army as inspiration to help him achieve his current goals.

Each area of planning is crucial. For each goal, you must plan what it is, the benefits, the challenges and create self-assurance. If one area is omitted it will adversely affect the other. For example, you could have many benefits to completing something but then be thrown off course when an unexpected challenge arises. Adversely, you could have anticipated a key challenge but in dealing with it you get too caught up and forget about the benefits and this can squash your level of motivation.

## 1.10 Monitoring your progress

A key argument used by people who do not like planning is that things change all the time and hence any attempt at planning is pointless. We accept the view that life moves at a very fast pace and hence plans will change. This is where the role of monitoring and reviewing comes into play. Each month we recommend you re-read your goals and determine any changes that need to be made. Things change and so do your goals, there is an issue if they are radically changing each week but minor changes are more than acceptable, mostly even desirable. Kayes (2006) really drives this point home, sometimes people are so committed to their goals that they forget to review them, which creates dangerous consequences. Just like his true example of a group of people who aim to climb Mount Everest in the wake of a storm, which should have made them quit. They carried on regardless with disastrous consequences.

Monitoring and reviewing your progress also ensures that you do not forget about your goals. So often, we create amazing goals but then put them away in a drawer or store them on a computer never to be seen again. We suggest that your keep your goals fresh in your mind by:

- Writing them down as it helps to solidify them in the mind (King, 2001) or type them up.
- Using positive language; when writing, reviewing or speaking about your goals, be positive.
- Making your goals public by telling those close to you. This forces commitment as we generally don't want to 'fail' in front of others. It also provides some moral support when times get tough and a gentle push/moral support is needed.
- Reading them aloud each morning. If you find this weird then just read them in your head. The point is to reinforce and remind you of what you wish to achieve each day.
- Placing your goals as your wallpaper or screensaver on your phone and computer.

Goal setting and working towards your goals should not be hard work or feel like a chore. If you find you struggle when you set yourself goals, then you need to re-evaluate your goals or re-evaluate the way you are working towards your goals.

## 1.11 Taking it to work

When you enter your first professional job, you will inevitably have goals set by your line manager. There will also be many phases in your life when you will set yourself new goals, such as complete a Masters degree or PhD or further down the line possibly even start your own business. The techniques we have provided you with will help you achieve whatever goals you wish throughout your life through effective goal setting and planning.

When working in business and running a full service marketing agency, I have to constantly set goals and plan effectively to ensure we can deliver all projects to their desired deadlines. A key part of this is setting deadlines with clients which need to be met and

*(Continued)*

*(Continued)*

matchmaking them with our internal resources. Once we have this information, we create in-depth plans that set out what will be completed when and manage the flow accordingly, this is done across weeks and months to paint a clear picture of the project pipeline. Of course, plans don't always remain static and we appreciate this, that's why we employ a dynamic approach when scheduling the initial work to give us a contingency time buffer. This process allows us to ensure we always meet the deadlines set by clients.

Akmal Saleem, Founder at Brand786

## 1.12 How to get started

### 1.12.1 Professional

- Try each of the goal setting techniques and see if any common goals/themes arise.
- Set yourself three goals that you wish to achieve by the time university finishes.
- Take one goal in your life and come up with a Perfect Plan to achieve it.

### 1.12.2 A little more interesting

- Set yourself one small goal in the area of fun and recreation, friends and family or personal development and follow the process outlined in this chapter to achieve it in the next week. This will help you to become accustomed to the process and realise its potential power.
- If you could be anybody in the world, who would you be? What steps could you take to become more like that person?
- Summarise all your goals in a one sentence vision that is fun and entertaining.

## 1.13 Our bookshelf

Covey, S.R. (2004) *The 7 habits of highly effective people.* London: Simon & Schuster. A great book which has detailed information on how to set goals and more importantly what goals to set for yourself. It is a detailed book and requires you to do a lot of thinking. Overall, it is a great book as proved by its worldwide success. There is quite a lot of information you can get for free from the website: www.stephencovey.com

Murphy, M. (2010) *Hard goals: the secret to getting from where you are to where you want to be.* London: McGraw-Hill.

This is a fantastic book in providing an alternative spin on goal setting and what should be classed as effective goals as opposed to the usual SMART suggestions.

Locke, A.E. and Latham, P.G. (2002) 'Building a practically useful theory of goal setting and task motivation: a 35-year odyssey', *American Psychologist*, 57 (9): 705–717.

This highly readable paper summarises the life's work of these superstars of goal setting research.

## 1.14 References

Bristol, C.M. (1985) *The magic of believing: the science of setting your goal and then achieving it*. New York: Prentice-Hall.

Buehler, R. Griffin, D. and Ross, R. (1994) 'Exploring the "planning fallacy": why people underestimate their task completion times', *Journal of Personality and Social Psychology*, 67 (3): 366–381.

Cairo, J. (1998) *Motivation and goal-setting: how to set and achieve goals and inspire others*. London: Career Press.

Kasser, T. and Ryan R.M. (1993) 'A dark side of the American dream: correlates of financial success as a central life aspiration', *Journal of Personality and Social Psychology*, 65 (2): 410–422.

Kayes, C. D. (2006) *Destructive goal pursuit: the Mount Everest disaster*. London: Palgrave Macmillan.

King, A.L. (2001) 'The health benefits of writing about life goals', *Personality and Social Psychology Bulletin*, 27 (7): 798–807.

Locke, A.E. (1996) 'Motivation through conscious goal setting', *Applied & Preventive Psychology*, 5 (2): 117–124.

Murphy, M. (2010) *Hard goals: the secret to getting from where you are to where you want to be*. London: McGraw-Hill.

Myers, G.D. (2000) 'The funds, friends, and faith of happy people', *American Psychologist*, 55 (1): 56–67.

Rubin, S.R. (2002) 'Will the real smart goals please stand up?', *The Industrial-Organizational Psychologist*, 39 (4): 26–27.

Ryff, D.C. (1989) 'Happiness is everything, or is it? Explorations on the meaning of psychological well-being', *Journal of Personality and Social Psychology*, 57 (6): 1069–1081.

Tracy, B. (2003) *How to get everything you want: faster than you ever thought possible*. London: Berrett-Koehler.

Zimmerman, J.B., Bandura, A. and Pons, M.M. (1992) 'Self-motivation for academic attainment: the role of self-efficacy beliefs and personal goal setting', *American Educational Research Journal*, 29 (3): 663–676.

# 2
# Mind Maps

## 2.1 Chapter summary

Mind Map is a term originally created (and copyrighted) by the author Tony Buzan, which describes a way of presenting information in a diagrammatic format. Sometimes people call them 'spider charts' because they look a little like that. It's a simple idea but one we feel is under used and important because our research showed that those students who got a first or a 2:1 were twice as likely to have used Mind Maps. We can't prove a causal link, i.e. we can't say for sure that by doing Mind Maps you will definitely get a first or a 2:1 but we can say that there is a good chance you will find them really useful. Both Pat and Chris use them all the time and Pat has observed many extremely successful people do too. This chapter tells you what they are, why they help and how to use them.

## 2.2 Overall principle

As we set out in the introduction, this book is intended not only as a resource to help you in your studies at university but also to provide you with tools and techniques which will be invaluable to you at work. Within this chapter we address how Mind Maps have proven be an incredibly effective way of taking notes which we have found to be a great tool for both study and work as well as in many other areas of life. Their use spans wider than simply just note taking and can be used to organise group presentations, help with revision and even organise your thoughts about your career. At first the technique might seem a bit strange, but we have found Mind Maps to be a massively powerful tool in all sorts of situations. As a matter of fact both of us came to Mind Mapping independently and also came to the same conclusions about how brilliant they can be. Perhaps the most famous exponent of this technique is Tony Buzan who has written widely on the topic and some of his books are referenced on the accompanying website. This chapter will give you the essentials for Mind Maps – in fact we think there is everything you need here.

## 2.3 What are they?

A Mind Map is a way of organising thoughts in a diagram (such as the one shown below) rather than in sentences or bullet points. Some people call them spider diagrams or even concept charts. Mind Maps can be drawn by hand or created on a computer using specialist (but often free) software. The key to their effectiveness seems to be the way we read things. When you started to read this page, you started at the top and worked down. You might have skipped a bit and looked at the headings but essentially you will naturally have been drawn to following the text in order down the page. If you saw a Mind Map of this page, you could take in all the sub-headings in one go and easily assimilate the information much quicker.

This entire book was planned using Mind Maps and in fact both of us use them in our everyday life. Pat uses them in research, taking notes during meetings with business, planning lectures, structuring ideas, planning what tasks to do during the day and many more applications. Chris uses them to prepare for interviews, take notes in meetings, plan projects, revise for exams and to plan his voluntary work. We both noticed how quickly we came to rely on them as a great way of organising our thoughts on a huge range of daily tasks. Figure 2.1 shows the actual Mind Map we

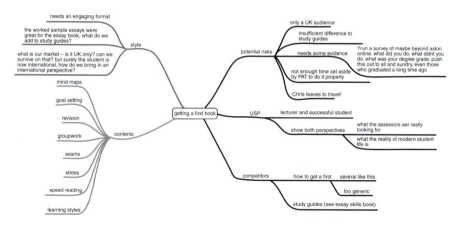

FIGURE 2.1   First ideas for the book

used when we first started thinking about writing this book. You will see that we did it on a computer – more about that later. You will also see that some of it changed before publication and there was only sketchy information on most of it. We used it as a way of clarifying our thoughts and making sure we both had the same understanding of what we were trying to achieve.

Mind Maps are about helping you to organise your thinking. The name is perhaps misleading as it seems to suggest something to do with the way the brain works and indeed the main proponent of this, Tony Buzan, uses claims such as these to justify their effectiveness. Much of what is claimed in terms of Mind Maps accessing some untapped brain resource is baloney. But, we do know that Mind Maps will:

- help organise thoughts
- make it easier to remember material for exams
- make note taking in lectures more effective and efficient

Perhaps the most persuasive argument for using Mind Mapping at university is that our research showed that more successful students tended to have used them and the less successful ones didn't. In other words, we feel strongly that there is no individual who would not benefit from using them – it isn't a matter of individual preference depending on personality. We recommend *everyone* should use them. As with all techniques in this book, it might take a little practise at first, but after a while you will wonder how you ever did without them. It took Chris six months to get used to Mind Mapping. He constantly thought that it must not be the thing for him, but after much practise, he has never looked back and constantly uses the technique in all aspects of his life. He even recently planned a weekend trip with his girlfriend using a Mind Map to ensure he didn't forget anything.

## 2.4 When can you use them?

As Chris demonstrates, Mind Mapping can be applied to a huge number of the things you need to do. Before we go into detail about how to Mind Map, we want to show just how many different ways this simple technique can help your studies – and beyond.

### 2.4.1 Lecture notes

As this is a book on succeeding at university, perhaps the most obvious use for the technique is taking notes in lectures. Despite advances in online resources, the stock in trade of most university learning experiences is still the lecture. The basic format for these has remained pretty well unchanged for hundreds of years – the lecturer speaks (hopefully interestingly and with relevant facts, explanations, theory, research, etc.) whilst students listen and take notes. The successful student will have the PowerPoint slides printed off but will also make notes using Mind Maps as well as adding to the printed slides. In this way you will make more sense of the lecture and, when you come to revise the material, you will be able to understand the concepts from the lecture quicker and more fully. Mind Mapping enables you to get the key information down on paper for future reference without taking up time. As we will see in Chapter 12, physically writing things down has a major impact on remembering. The key to making notes in any lecture, seminar or meeting of any kind is to make sure you are writing as little as you can because it isn't possible to write and listen at the same time. So when you are writing, you aren't listening so you might be missing the next point. Mind Maps are great ways to make sure you have noted things efficiently so you can keep listening.

### 2.4.2 Exam revision

Aside from the lecture, the other unchanging feature of university life is the exam and Mind Maps are a great way to aid revision. We have found that it is possible to do different levels of maps which really help structure in your mind what the key points about the topic are and what theories you need to remember. You can plan out the key topic areas for a module with main nodes for the topics covered and sub-nodes showing key points and the theories you need to remember. You can then do individual Mind Maps for all the topics. Usually this would mean you have one Mind Map for the whole module with perhaps a dozen main topics each with three or four points – perhaps theories, perhaps key researchers. Then each of these topics might have a Mind Map of its own – especially if you think it is going to be asked about in detail in the exam. By having the entire topic represented graphically on the page, there is a massively increased chance you will be able to recall them when you need them in the exam hall. More about this in Chapter 12.

Figure 2.2 is an example which shows a student (Jenna Bonfiglio) using the technique to show all the topics in a module she was taking. She remembers that this simple diagram helped her understand where she was during revision and also to remind her when writing assignments how all the topics fitted together. You will notice that perhaps it doesn't completely conform to the strictest ideas of a Mind Map but we would say that the way things are organised on the page needs to make sense to the person who needs to understand it. This worked for her so therefore is the right thing to have

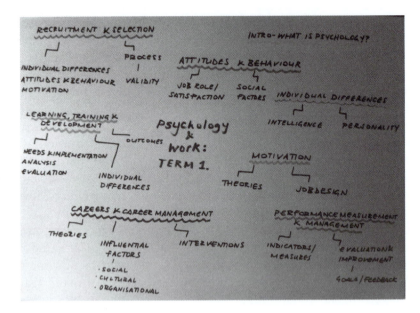

FIGURE 2.2   Jenna's Mind Map

done. Other examples in this chapter show a range of styles and you need to experiment a bit to find what works for you.

We found a really interesting study which showed a possible 10 per cent increase in exam marks through the use of the technique (Farrand et al., 2002) which is an impressive statistic! So, it's worth spending a bit of time working out how to do Mind Maps and what style works for you personally.

### 2.4.3 In exams

Mind Maps are also useful for organising thoughts and the exam hall is a place where you need to be really focused. As we will discuss in Chapter 12, you should take some time to plan your answers in exams and Mind Mapping is the way to do this really quickly and effectively. The key here is once you have read the questions through (and for essay and short answer exams, always read all the questions before you write anything) you use part of your answer book to sketch out the main points you want to make in your answer. You will very quickly realise whether you have enough material to include in your answers so you can then decide which question to answer (assuming there is a choice). Then, having drawn a Mind Map, very often you will be able to add to it as you go along as things come back to you. If you have revised using Mind Maps, you might be able to reproduce close copies of the maps you used in revision but be careful – make sure you are answering the question and not simply reproducing everything you know about a topic! The Mind Map serves as a way of ordering your thoughts when planning the answer but it also keeps you on track so you know where you are taking the reader. In other words, use it as a map in a real sense where you are following a route you have planned out. There is always time to plan even when the exam puts you under a lot of time pressure.

## 2.4.4 Essay plans

As we will discuss later on, essay plans are crucial to writing a well-structured essay and Mind Maps can work perfectly to help you do this. After you have done all of the reading, you can create a simple Mind Map which will include basic points about your introduction, discussion and conclusion. Then you can flip points around to where you see best, for example, moving a topic from one section of the essay to the other. The best thing about using a Mind Map for your essay plan is that you can change things as you go along, which the example from Devon Parker below brings to life.

One of the most important essays I've written to date was my placement essay. It was a lot of hard work and since it was worth 10 per cent of my degree, planning it properly was essential in order to be as successful as possible. The way I always approached planning the essay was through the use of a Mind Map. That way, I found it easier to identify all of the issues that I needed to address in the essay. Once all of my ideas were down in the Mind Map, I could then go about organising my ideas to ensure my argument was logical and coherent. I viewed the plan as a preliminary structure to my essay, because once I started actually writing the essay, I had to adapt the plan in line with my research. Indeed, following feedback from my placement essay supervisor, I also made several alterations.

Devon Parker, BSc International Business and French

## 2.4.5 Individual presentations

As we keep saying, Mind Maps are great for structuring your thoughts and we are seeing more and more modules that require students to give presentations. It's a great skill to have when you go to work – despite many finding them tough going at least at first. Whenever Pat writes a new lecture, he always sets out the key points on a Mind Map before he even opens PowerPoint to write the slides. And sometimes he will take the Mind Map to lectures to use as his own quick reference notes. It is useful to see what is coming next and to make sure all points have been covered. In terms of writing the presentation, it is often really hard to know where to start and what to include. Drawing a Mind Map of all the things you think might be included in the presentation is a great way of organising your thoughts on paper. Once it is all in front of you, it is really easy to work out what the order is going to be, what to include and what to leave out.

### 2.4.6 Groups

It is becoming more and more common for students to be assessed through group work and this can be stressful! Students talk about problems with getting some of their fellow students to turn up to meetings, and perhaps there are language and cultural differences. Again the ability of Mind Maps to organise thoughts can be really helpful. We have seen Mind Maps used effectively from the very start of group work. The key to using Mind Maps in groups is that everyone in the group uses one single Mind Map. This is how you achieve agreement on what the project is and (the critical part of any project) the '3Ws' – **w**ho needs to do **w**hat by **w**hen. There are several ways of doing this – you can work from a large piece of paper (such as a flipchart) or perhaps an A3 sheet on a table. Perhaps you have access to a digital projector or a large flat screen (at our university students can book rooms which have this facility and many universities do the same) so you might work from a computerised Mind Map which everyone can see. Perhaps in groups of about four you could just huddle round a single screen. The key advantage of working from a computer is that the end product can be saved and circulated to all the members of the group so there is no argument about what was decided. Each set of tasks can be allocated on the Mind Map and even given dates for when they are due.

### 2.4.7 Notes in meetings

When you are in a meeting, you need to be able to write notes of the important points to remind you later. Pat often visits businesses that are interested in having a general conversation about working with the university. In these meetings it is vital to keep a record of the ideas discussed and items to follow up. He always uses a Mind Map to do this. An additional tip is to have the questions for a potential client drawn out on a Mind Map and then add notes from the answers to the questions on each node. Using Mind Maps in a meeting can really help you to stand out. Chris's Mind Maps frequently get commented upon in meetings, with comments such as, 'You are very creative' or 'I love your Mind Map'.

This might be done initially using software, printing out the core map and then adding notes in pencil during the meeting. These can then be added on to the computer later. Opening a laptop in a meeting can look rather unfriendly but the iPad or similar tablet provides less of a barrier between people and there is some great software for the iPad which can be used to note down items quickly without disturbing the flow of conversation. More on software later.

## 2.5 Other aspects of university

### 2.5.1 Goal setting

We have spoken in detail about goal setting and Mind Mapping is a very powerful tool in aiding this process. You can use them to help generate your goals. Once done, you can use them to create the perfect plan as we have done in Figure 2.3.

As you can see, it is a great way to summarise all your goals on one page.

### 2.5.2 Securing a job

Mind Maps are great for every part of the recruitment process. When putting your CV together, you can write everything you have ever done on a giant Mind Map and then use it as the basis to organise and write your CV. The same can be done for cover letters and competency based questions. If you have an assessment centre or interview, Mind Maps are great for researching organisations. You can get all the information down in one place and constantly expand it when you need to, rather than writing a new page of notes all the time.

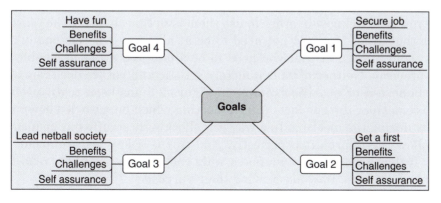

FIGURE 2.3   Example of a goal setting Mind Map

FIGURE 2.4    Pat's job interview presentation Mind Map

Figure 2.4 shows an example that Pat did recently when making a presentation as part of a job interview.

Now most of this will make no sense to anyone apart from Pat. And that doesn't matter at all because the aim was to capture the ideas he had before opening Prezi (presentation software) and actually writing the presentation.

### 2.5.3 Organising your life

Mind Maps can be used for any aspect of your life and we truly do mean it:

- shopping lists
- planning a night out
- weekend away
- thinking of a gift to buy

## 2.6 How to do Mind Maps

There are lots of books available on Mind Mapping – indeed there is a list of them at the end of this chapter. We feel strongly that they are almost all too complicated. Mind Mapping is really easy to learn and pretty much everything you need to know in order to use them is in this chapter. The reason for this is that Mind Maps do not need to be at all fancy whereas many of the books seem to suggest that you need to be a talented artist to be able to do them properly. Neither of us is remotely artistic and yet we use them all the time. Believe it or not, the example in Figure 2.5 has been really useful for Pat to remember the key facts from a meeting which he scrawled down really quickly during the meeting. In a way it is shockingly scruffy but he insists he can follow the information perfectly. And this is a key feature about Mind Maps: if they are for your own notes, only you need to be able to read them. As long as you can, they are serving their purpose.

Contrast this with the set of notes in Figure 2.6 which Pat made as part of preparation for a research project on the topic of courage. In this case, what

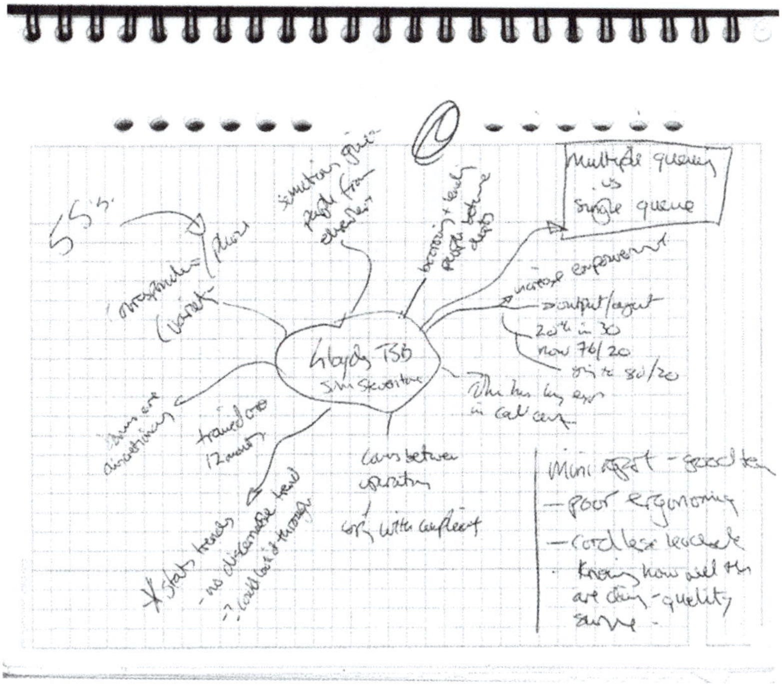

FIGURE 2.5   Example of a meeting recorded using a Mind Map

was needed was a summary of key points from previous research for a litera-ture review. The initial planning was made using a Mind Map but then the detailed note taking moved to a more traditional format, the reason being that the eye would follow the progress of the notes easily and, because there were headings, it is easy to jump to the right place. More detail was needed here than is possible in a Mind Map. There is more on reading and note tak-ing in Chapter 3.

The Mind Map, as can be seen in Figure 2.5, can be a very simple diagram using only one colour and very rough lines and notes. Some people really like embellishing their Mind Maps by using multiple colours, pictures and doo-dles. This is fine if that's the way your mind works but those of us who don't have that artistic flair, plain single colours and simple lines do not detract at all from the effectiveness of recording ideas and concepts.

## 2.7 How to make a Mind Map

You will need paper – the ideal is blank or squared – and something to write with. We also recommend A4 paper – smaller is restricting and A3 is often

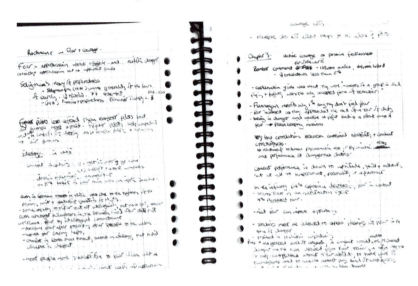

FIGURE 2.6   Example of notes not using a Mind Map

too cumbersome. We would suggest a B or 2B pencil so you can rub out mistakes easily but anything will do. Turn the paper so it is landscape (i.e. the longest side is horizontal) and write something in the middle of the page which describes what you are going to make notes on. So, perhaps the subject of the lecture or the name of the person you are meeting with and possibly the date. Now draw a circle or a sort of wobbly cloud shape round it and you are ready to take notes.

Let's say you are making notes in a lecture on Financial Accounting. You will have the slide pack on the desk in front of you as well as the Mind Map. The lecturer opens with a piece of information about the exam. So you draw a line from the centre circle, write 'exam', then add lines coming off. The lecturer discusses the essay so you add another node stating 'essay'. You again write all the key points about the essay. Next you add in other nodes and sub-nodes until you have recorded everything you need.

## 2.8 Mind Maps to get you unstuck

The key thing about Mind Maps is that they allow you to record some main concepts on paper in a loose way. With their free flowing structure, your eye can wander around the page (or screen) without needing to follow across the lines of the page from top to bottom, left to right, as it does with conventional writing. Mind Maps use key words rather than sentences and your memory adds the detail. Using these features you can find ways out of sticky situations. For example, some time ago Pat was in a panic as many of his ideas for projects had suddenly come off at the same time. Whilst it is always great to have lots to do, he became really worried that he wouldn't be able to deliver on all of them. He wheeled a flipchart into his office and drew a large Mind Map of all the things he needed to do. He then took a long hard look at all the projects and tasks he had and decided that several had to go, one or two could be given to other people to do, others were priorities and some could perhaps be fitted in between other things. He remembers the feeling of relief that what seemed an unmanageable amount of stuff to do became less scary and more manageable when organised on paper. One by one he crossed off the projects and tasks as they were completed. Nowadays he is more likely to do this on his laptop or iPad but the concept is the same.

Another example of someone doing just this sort of thing came from a contact of Pat's. Realising his job role consisted of a very large number of different elements, David wanted to map out everything he was expected to do. The result was a picture of all the different tasks but in a format where he could see at a glance what he needed to do. Having put everything into this Mind Map, he felt in control and far more confident that he was on top of everything he needed to do. Figure 2.7 shows the very map that he drew.

We really like this example as it shows how Mind Maps do not need to be fancy or full of different colours and pictures, you can really dump all your ideas onto paper and structure them in front of your eyes. You can use this for all the topics you are studying at university or later on when you are at work, to give an overview of all the projects you are working on. These days it will be definitely more than one at once! Just by putting down on paper in a Mind Map the names of the things you have to do, you can easily tell which to work on right away, which can wait until later and which you should ditch.

## 2.9 Creating Mind Maps on computers or tablets

In many situations, it is only possible to make notes on paper but other scenarios it is possible to work from a computer as you have seen with some examples in this chapter. There are benefits and drawbacks to this. One of the key issues is that it is not regarded as acceptable to make notes on a laptop when in most business meetings. For example, when going to meet a potential client, you will need to record all the information you can about the meeting for future reference and to brief others. It might be easiest for you if you could record notes on your laptop and then email them out afterwards but this would be a major breach of etiquette. However, making notes of some sort is essential and the accepted format is on paper. One exception which

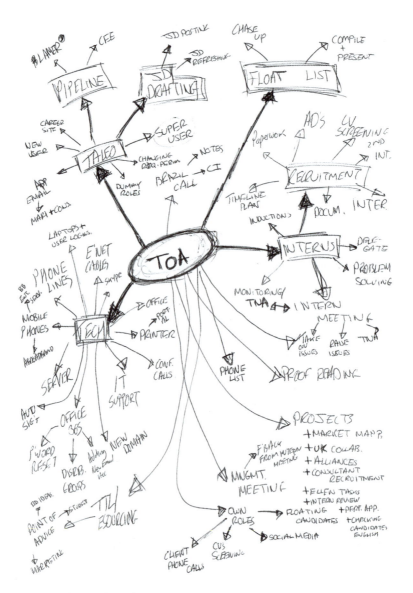

FIGURE 2.7   Goodwin job tasks

has become prevalent recently is the use of small hand held tablet computers which are becoming more common in meetings. Indeed when Pat started his new job, the first thing he was issued with was an iPad as they have proved so valuable to senior academics at the university.

A further use for computerised Mind Maps is when you are working in a group to solve a problem. By connecting your laptop to a projector or large

TV, the whole group can become involved in recording ideas. Indeed, there are sophisticated techniques for problem solving that used to be high tech and based in labs which used this idea, whereas now it is widely available. The advantage of this technique is that everyone is able to follow the creation of the Mind Map so there is a greater shared understanding and everyone can read a copy of the document after the meeting. Pat has used this technique to organise very large amounts of complex information and, with the ubiquitous projectors in lecture rooms these days, it is a really useful tool which in our experience people don't use enough.

## 2.10 Which computer package?

There is no one agreed best package for Mind Mapping and there are a great many available. In fact, many of them are free or virtually free so you can download and try them out without worrying about the cost. Pat works on a Mac so this restricts the number of packages available. He has been using MindNode (www.mindnode.com) for some years which has the advantage of being available on the iPad as well as Mac platforms so he can create and edit on whichever machine is most convenient. However, MindNode is not currently available on PC so if you are a Mac user and need to collaborate with PC users, another package is probably better. Having said that, there are a number of times when it is only you that needs to be able to look at the Mind Map so this might be suitable. The website has some really cool ideas about how to use Mind Maps so it is worth looking at anyway. Pat is currently working on a project where inter-operability is important because he is working with people who only use PCs and the Mind Map is crucial to the project. So he is now also using Freemind which (as the name suggests) is also free and is now available for use on both platforms. Interestingly, Freemind documents can be read immediately on MindNode which suggests some form of standardisation is under way and vice versa. One thing you do need to be sure of is that your finished Mind Maps can be exported as pdf or jpeg files so anyone can read them.

The big name in Mind Mapping is Tony Buzan who created the term and has been working with the technique for decades. His company has its own software which is available from www.thinkbuzan.com. Since there are free or virtually free packages available, I'm afraid we haven't used it ourselves but many people have found it to be really helpful.

If you are seeking some very fancy software we suggest Mindjet. This is something Chris uses and he loves it. Many large organisations use the software and so it comes with many advanced features. It can be used on any mobile device or computer which all integrate together to form a one stop shop for your Mind Maps. You can also use it to create very fancy Mind Maps so, for example, you can embed anything you wish like a video or picture and have automatically calculated branches – you could total up the cost of a project from all the different branches.

## 2.11 Taking it to work

When you get out into the world of work, you will need to make notes all the time. Nothing will annoy your manager more than you sitting in a meeting and not writing things down. Working without notes is a sure fire way of forgetting things, getting things wrong and generally annoying people. So, keep a note book, organise it and always, always have it with you! One important way of keeping things in order is to note the date of the meeting and who is chairing it in the centre of the Mind Map together with perhaps a title. Then when you come to look back over your notes you can tell which meeting they come from. Pat often finds people comment that they are Mind Mappers too and others are intrigued by the technique. It is a great ice breaker sometimes! In the workplace then we recommend that you use Mind Maps to organise your priorities, structure presentations and facilitate group discussions. The technique is the same as at university – only the topic changes.

> I came to discover Mind Maps a few years ago and have used them ever since. At work, I use them to take notes in meetings, plan large scale projects and organise my diary when I get too busy. I even taught Chris how to Mind Map.
>
> Haden Mills, Systems Analyst, National Grid

Here is a further example of a Mind Map which was created by a Doctoral Researcher supervised by Pat. The researcher, Frank Watt, has been an enthusiastic Mind Mapper for years and it was in fact him who put Pat onto the technique years ago. He has used it to scope out a 4 year research project.

And finally, to show that you can create Mind Maps in many ways, here is one which was created just using standard Microsoft PowerPoint using shapes and colours to map out the skills a graduating student had acquired so he could think more clearly about what jobs to apply for and what he could offer.

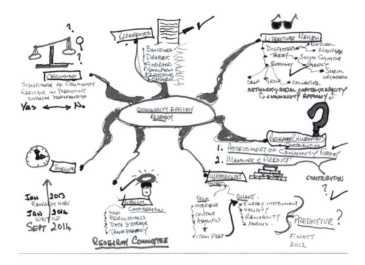

FIGURE 2.8    Mapping out a research project

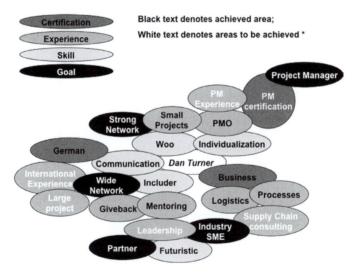

FIGURE 2.9    Assessing your skills on a Mind Map

## 2.12 How to get started

### 2.12.1 Professional

- Mind Map your next essay plan.
- Mind Map your goals from Chapter 1 along with a plan for each of them.
- Teach a friend to Mind Map.

35

### 2.12.2 A little more interesting

- Mind Map your holiday plans – possible destinations, who might come, etc.
- Mind Map your shopping list, into different categories or aisles of things you need to purchase.
- Plan your next weekend using a Mind Map. Main nodes for each day and sub-nodes for activities, friends you plan to see and how much it will cost.

## 2.13 Our bookshelf

Buzan, T. (2002) *How to Mind Map: the ultimate thinking tool that will change your life.* London: Harper-Collins.
A single resource for those interested in Mind Mapping. Pat is critical of some of the 'science' in it but the technique is without doubt shown really clearly. Most people only need the basics so we wouldn't expect you to need to read it all in detail. Great examples throughout.

Buzan, T. and Griffiths, C. (2009) *Mind Maps for business.* London: BBC Books.
This book applies the Mind Map ideas to work and gives examples as to how they can help your career.

## 2.14 References

Farrand, P., Hussain, F. and Hennessy, E. (2002) 'The efficacy of the "Mind Map" study technique', *Medical Education*, 36 (5): 426–431.

# 3

# Effective and efficient reading

## 3.1 Chapter summary

It might seem odd to include a chapter on reading since it is obviously something that all students can do. But reading at university is a skill of itself and needs to be approached in a particular way. If you read in the way you would read a novel or a newspaper, you will find it really hard to get through the material you need to cover. So, the focus of this chapter is to learn how to be highly selective about what you need to read whilst developing your own system of making memorable notes. In combination, these tips will considerably reduce the amount of time devoted to reading and will serve you well when you leave university as many jobs require the absorption of large amounts of information. And this is the skill we are discussing in this chapter. Separate advice will also be given on how to tackle the use of academic journals in terms of reading them, critiquing them and using them effectively because of their importance in achieving a high degree grade.

## 3.2 Reading at university

Many students (Pat and Chris included!) find that there is a moment of panic when presented with a module reading list for the first time. Pat remembers seeing there were so many books on the list he couldn't possibly read them all – so decided to read none of them! This tactic was of course a disaster so he started to ask around to find out how on earth everyone managed. He soon discovered that (a) the lecturers didn't expect students to read *everything* on the list and (b) nobody got anywhere near to reading everything. He remembers meeting someone in his second year who confessed to never reading entire books. This came as a complete shock to Pat who had up to then been trying to read complete works from start to finish. He then started to be far more targeted and selected just relevant chapters or even parts of chapters to read. The research carried out before writing this book showed that he is far from being alone: those who did best at university eventually learned to target particular parts of texts and found ways to identify which of them were going to be the most valuable before even starting to read. So this is where we will begin – how do you know what to read and what not to?

## 3.3 Reasons for reading

Many lecturers set a certain amount of reading each week. Pat's experience is that students are reluctant to do the reading as it seems to be one of those things you can put off until you are revising for the exam or writing the assignments, and you are likely to get away without doing the reading and not be 'found out'. But the reading has been set for specific reasons. The most important one is that we know it is a better way of learning. If you read a topic before the lecture, when you get to the lecture, you will have already gone some way to understanding the topic even as the lecturer speaks. You don't need to have read very carefully before the lecture, just read it quickly. Perhaps you can note particular things that don't seem to make sense to you. Look out for explanations of these in the lecture and if it is an interactive session, ask about it during the lecture. Or you can approach the lecturer afterwards or make an appointment to discuss. These days there is often the option of posting questions and ideas on a Virtual Learning Environment such as Blackboard or Moodle. You should definitely use these and post as many questions as you need answering.

Aside from set reading, there are essentially two reasons for you to be reading: in order to prepare assignments or to revise for exams. Techniques are similar for both but we have specific advice for both types of reading.

## 3.4 Targeting your reading effort

The majority of courses are run in a modular form where a topic is taught in a block. The topic for each lecture will be available to the student and most often there will be essential reading set for each lecture. Many (if not most) universities will struggle to have enough copies of core texts in the library for all students so it might be a good idea to look at this well ahead of time and get the core texts out even before the term starts. Either that or look to buy copies – sites such as Amazon sell second hand copies which can be significantly cheaper than new (but make sure you are buying the right edition as you might find you have an out of date copy). Ideally, this core text should be the minimum amount of reading for the module and so you should take this as just the start point for your exploration of the topic.

Sometimes lecturers will set a large amount of reading and if this is the case, you need to become picky. First, if the book or journal set on the list isn't stocked in your library, it is unlikely to be important. It is extremely poor lecturing practise to do this but sadly it does happen sometimes. So, you can focus your attention on the material that is actually available (and probably a good idea to point out the error to the lecturer – see Chapter 4 on managing your lecturer). Beyond this, if you see more than about 50 pages per week set as essential reading, it's quite likely that you don't need to read it all – especially if there is more than one text set. There is likely to be an overlap. How can you tell this? By going to the library and flicking through the book in question. If it is a journal article, you should be able to find it through the electronic resources in the library which in all probability you will be able to access remotely from your computer.

Here we get to a really important thing you should avoid at all costs. Do not look at a reading list, ignore it and bash some words into Google (or similar search engine) and work with whatever comes up on the first screen of responses. Your lecturer will be working from the appropriate resources and your search may well be returning work of dubious quality. By all means consult widely – even with Wikipedia (but never ever cite it as a source – use it to understand then go to the academic texts). If you don't understand a particular theory, by all means look for other descriptions or explanations of it – perhaps there is a university with some free online lecture material, for example. But you absolutely have to use the proper type of material in the end – in other words, academically rigorous material from respected sources. Essentially this is the list of text books and journal articles your lecturer will provide you with plus other work you find for yourself.

If you are ever unsure of what you should and shouldn't read, book an appointment with your lecturer. Explain that you do not believe you have the time to read everything and you want to know where to concentrate your efforts. Chris once did this for his economics module when the lecturer set a 10 page reading list. The lecturer explained that it would be good to read all the material but pointed out the absolute must-reads and the nice to haves.

Your aim here is to discover exactly this, what is crucial to read and what is a nice to have. This is particularly the case with modules that are maybe worth less in relative terms to others or where you believe you do not have the strongest chance of getting a high mark. Conversely, if you are doing well in a particular module then you will want to read all the texts and may go above and beyond to maximise your marks where you can.

## 3.5 Learning the language

Added to the sheer volume of reading set on some modules is the problem of getting used to the style of writing. Academic writing is pretty tough to get used to – in fact students sometimes tell us that they can read a sentence and whilst they have understood the meaning of every individual word in the sentence, they have absolutely no idea what the whole sentence means! Don't worry at all if this also applies to you – it actually means you are normal! Pat was recently talking to a student who had exactly this feeling when he started his course but Pat could see him become far more confident as he grew accustomed to the style. Academic writing is a particular style of English which on the one hand could be described as compact but this also means it can be found to be un-intelligible at first. Pat's experience over many years is that students who work at this find that they suddenly 'get' the skill of understanding the academic style and never look back. The only way to do this is by practise. But we have also seen that it is best to approach academic reading in a very tactical way and the best students quickly learn how to get the most out of the time they spend reading. Our first point then is that you shouldn't confuse reading at university for 'normal' reading. You will need to work at it, but this chapter shows the way it should be done to be both effective (understanding the material) and efficient (doing it quickly). If you follow these rules, you will understand more and spend less time doing it.

To help learn the language it is a good idea to keep an online/paper dictionary nearby when you are reading academic material. You will often come across words you do not understand when reading academic material so if you learn them when you first come across them you will understand next time round. However, it is likely that having established the meaning of a word just once, you will not remember it, so when you do come across an unknown word, check the meaning and note it down. Next time you come across the word you can just look it up in your list. Chris did exactly this in his final year due to the sheer amount of journals he had to read. Every time he did not understand a word, he would look up the meaning and note it down in his own personal dictionary. Then once a word was firmly in his mind, he would delete it to keep it constantly up to date.

The main rule about the language is that there is only one way to get used to it: practise. You need to plough on regardless of how dispirited you might find it or how much you are convinced that you will never understand it. We have all been through this and nobody can do it for you. Sometimes you may have to read through the same page twice over or even three times before you understand it. If you still don't get it, move on. Sometimes you may even find that you struggle with the whole chapter or paper and it may be a good idea to discuss it with your lecturer. You really do need to keep the faith, you have been accepted on to a university course and this means that with time and effort, you will be absolutely fine.

## 3.6 Generating a pool of papers and chapters for reading

You gain marks for going beyond the set reading list but this can appear a daunting task at first. There is a danger that you try putting a key word into the electronic search engine in the library and either have literally hundreds of results or none at all. By all means take this approach but only after you have been through a process that Pat calls a 'daisy chain', as shown in Figure 3.1.

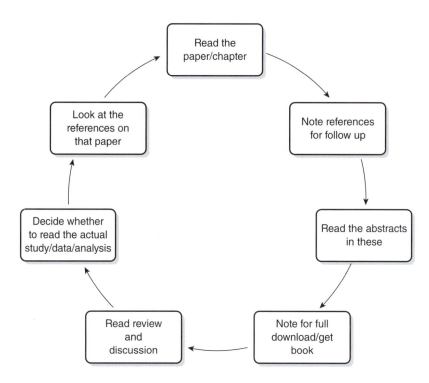

FIGURE 3.1   The reading daisy chain

### 3.6.1 Read the paper/chapter

With any luck, your lecturer will have indicated what the basic set reading is. If so, start with that. If this isn't provided, use the techniques in Chapter 4 to find out from your lecturer what the best grounding text is. Hopefully this will be some sort of summary of the theory you need to follow through. If this doesn't deliver, then you can ask students who have done the course previously and there is also a lot to be gained from talking to the librarian or even finding the shelf where the books are and browsing. Having spent time getting to grips with the basics, then you need to follow up.

### 3.6.2 Note references for follow up

Go to the reference list for the chapter or paper and look for likely ones which will enhance your knowledge or give you more detail on the theory. Make a note of these – perhaps if you have a printed copy of the paper, highlight them. Then hunt these down. Not all will be available in your library but don't get side-tracked into getting inter-library loans of obscure papers. If it isn't in the library, the likelihood is that it won't help you all that much. By all means if you are convinced it is crucial to your arguments then see if you can get hold of it. But be aware this process can take quite some time!

### 3.6.3 Read the abstracts in these

Having assembled the likely papers, don't read the entire paper right away. Read the abstract/summary first – is it still looking useful? Many times you will find that it isn't quite what you expected and needs to be discarded. In fact, you should be able to read the abstract without even having to download the entire paper. So glance at it quickly to check whether it is worth some further reading. If it is then make a note of it for later.

### 3.6.4 Note for full download

Online resources are becoming more user-friendly but it is still often quite a hassle getting hold of the full paper. It is usually easier to do this on university computers even if you have remote access. Again, if the full text of a paper is not available, ask yourself whether you really do need to have it in full. Sometimes just reading the abstract is enough if the paper isn't central to your work. But for the important papers, you will need a full copy to read.

### 3.6.5 Read review and discussion

Now you have the full papers to read, you don't just read the whole paper. Start with the literature review. This is often really helpful in terms of grasping an overview of what the latest thinking is in the field you are researching. Beware of the date of the paper though – something which was topical in 1980 might be irrelevant now. Then read the discussion section. This is where the findings of the study are compared with the literature. At this point, you may have enough information. But if you need to, you can then go and read the rest of the paper – usually the method, data and analysis.

### 3.6.6 Decide whether to read the actual study/data/analysis

To be honest, for most undergraduate purposes, there is no real need to read these sections. Unless of course you are about to use the paper as the basis of research you plan to carry out yourself, in which case these sections will be very important indeed! But often these sections are very complicated and only of relevance to other researchers. In particular, don't be put off complicated looking statistics. If you really need to understand these for your own research, then dive into it. Otherwise, glance at it and move on.

### 3.6.7 Look at the references on that paper

Now here's the clever bit. Every time you read a paper – even if only the abstract – you should look through the references to see if there are any other interesting papers. So the process begins again.

> In the beginning, I would always try to at least look at everything from the module's recommended reading lists, including a large amount of journals. It took me a while to get used to skim reading them effectively. Now, I usually read the abstract and the conclusion to make sure the journal suits the subject I am interested in, then if so, I try to find the killer points in each paragraph. After you read journals, you realise that they have a certain pattern, starting with an abstract, then the theory used, the methods of research and explaining the findings, sometimes even limitations of research.
>
> Alexandra Cojanu, BSc Business and Management

Having discussed the means of collecting papers together, we now move on to how you use these in practice.

## 3.7 Reading for assignments

Whether it is an essay, presentation or some form of group work, the concept is the same. You should be building on the reading you do every week as part of what you need to do in lectures (see Chapter 4 for more information on how to get the most out of your lectures). The reason you are set reading is to give you information which isn't completely covered in lectures. Most modules don't have enough lecture time allocated to be able to cover the whole topic area so many lecturers pick the most central or the most difficult to understand theories to discuss and illustrate in the lectures.

You need to fully understand the topics you are going to be covering using the system illustrated in Figure 3.2 before you start the essay because you need to have this knowledge before you start to plan your answer. Essays at university are not about just showing that you understand an area, they are about showing you have *mastery* of them and can build logical arguments.

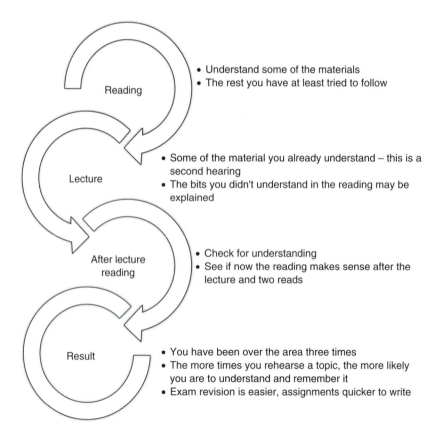

FIGURE 3.2    Links between reading, lectures and learning

This preparation work is designed to give you a good basis to start planning your essay. Incidentally these steps will also leave you better prepared for exams and other coursework too so we recommend you get into the habit of doing this all the time you are at university and you will get a lot more out of your course as a whole.

We approach reading and note making as being closely linked activities and recommend you follow the steps shown in Figure 3.3, which we will describe in detail.

### 3.7.1 Make notes before lecture

In order to get the best out of your lectures, you need to put in a little bit of preparation time. This needn't take long but will pay off in terms of you understanding the material better and quicker. Most lecturers these days will make their slides available to be printed off before the lecture (and if they don't – ask them!). Once you have printed them off, you now have the basis for your notes on the topic – and with most of the information printed, you won't have to write down loads of information during the lecture. If you have the option to choose a format for printing, we often find that having the slides three to a page is useful as it leaves you room next to them to make notes. So print your lecture slides well in advance of the lecture and find out

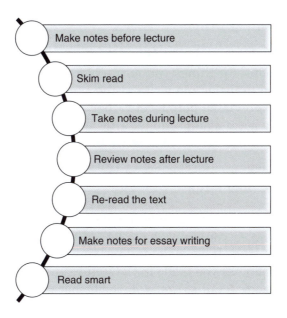

FIGURE 3.3    Note making process

what the relevant reading for the lecture is going to be (there are more details on how to do this in Chapter 4 on lectures and lecturers).

### 3.7.2 Skim reading

You now need to spend a few minutes reading with your slide print-offs close at hand. The idea is for you to very quickly read through just the material which is to be covered in the lecture and note down any key points you don't understand. You will always get better results if you arrive at lectures with at least some idea what the topic is so that when you hear the models and theories presented by the lecturer, it will not be for the first time. Reading before the lecture is probably the most important step for you to take on board from this section – experience also tells us it is the step you are most likely to omit. If you have read the material first, you can then use the lecture to clarify the areas you don't understand and to reinforce the areas you are happier with. But don't worry about reading thoroughly – we are saying you should 'skim read', where you read through very quickly and don't stop when you don't understand something. Just the act of reading the words will be helping you to understand once the lecturer covers the area. You should not take very long over this and as you become well practised, you might be able to do this in about 15 minutes or so – a very worthwhile investment of your time.

### 3.7.3 Take notes during lecture

Take your notes to the lecture and follow the points in the lecture on them. Make very short notes for things you now understand or for follow up later on. It is really hard to listen and write at the same time so try to keep your writing to much abbreviated note form rather than long sentences. You are going to look at the notes again straight after the lecture so you only need to remind yourself of things rather than write them out in full.

### 3.7.4 Review notes after lecture

Before you forget what you were thinking about in the lecture, go over your notes again. As long as you didn't have lots of things to follow up on, this shouldn't take too long. It is so important you make sure that you have understood the brief notes you made in the lecture and write any notes which are very brief in more detail so you will remember them later. If you leave this for more than a couple of hours, you will forget, so make sure you do this before disappearing for coffee with friends.

I know that I am an active learner; therefore I find that I retain the most information when I have a copy of the slides or information in front of me. This allows me to annotate around the lecturer's slides so that my notes are more detailed when it comes to revision. I also retain more information by physically writing out the notes rather than typing as it holds my concentration for longer periods of time. I find that even circling key words or concepts that the lecturer has highlighted forces me to engage with the information and so I gain at least a basic knowledge of the topic during each lecture rather than worrying about copying all the notes down before the slide changes.

Eilish Beeby, LLB Law with Management

### 3.7.5 Re-read the text

Before the next lecture, you need to sit down again and re-read the set chapter. Again, have your notes to hand so you can further build on them. This time you should read more slowly and thoroughly – but do skip sections which don't seem relevant to the course you are taking. This should take a bit longer than the first skim read but by now you should be fairly sure of the material. Make some attempt to understand sections you didn't follow until now but don't get hung up on them. If you are still stuck, make a note of what you don't understand and move on. You can get help on this by asking your fellow students, looking up other texts books on the topic (sometimes reading another author's description can really help) or contacting your lecturer. Many courses these days use an online discussion board so try posting your question on that.

### 3.7.6 Make notes for essay writing

Now you have made notes on the topics, you need to move on to preparing for the essay. You will find that following the steps before this stage will make the process of planning and writing your essay so much easier. The next set of notes you need to make is the first steps towards writing your essay. The first notes you need to make are concerning the essay question itself. As described in Chapter 1, questions often have more than one part to them so you should note what your answer needs to contain. Jot down some theory you could include – referring to your lecture notes to make sure you have included everything you are likely to need. Now go back to the text. Read through this again but this time with the essay question in mind. Likely quotes should be noted with full references to enable their use in the essay.

### 3.7.7 Read smart

It is a good idea to go beyond the set text – in fact many lecturers insist on it. Use the set reading as a start point then follow up promising references and search using your library catalogue. Do not necessarily read whole books or complete academic papers. Look at abstracts/summaries/introductions/ conclusions to ascertain their relevance. Focus on what you need to extract from the books and journals.

In our experience, lecturers will work from a chapter of a key text for each lecture, which they publicise in advance of the lecture. If this information is not provided, contact the lecturer to find out what reading you should be doing. Be wary of very long reading lists – you can't be expected to read everything. Perhaps some of the references you are given are duplicates of similar sorts of books, so don't feel you have to read all the set texts. If you have read a section and feel you have got a good understanding of the material, leave it at that.

## 3.8 Reading for revision

Whilst you are reading, think critically about what the author is saying. By this we mean you should get into the habit of having some key questions in mind when reading:

- What are the main findings?
- Has the author provided strong evidence to support claims?
- Have any other researchers pointed out particular weaknesses in the theory?
- Are you convinced by the arguments presented? If not, think of what logical argument you can present for saying you are not convinced.
- If you think the theory is strong, show why you think so.
- For each article or book you read, develop the habit of recording the information you will need for your reference list. In fact, you will save yourself a lot of time later if you record this in full in the format it will be needed in later (see Chapter 6 for full information on how to format references), i.e. author, title, date, publisher, place of publication. Some students use software to help them do this – the standard programme is called EndNote but it isn't essential to use this as it is more for advanced researchers who have to organise hundreds of references.

A few very important points about technology:

- Switch off your email when writing because having messages pop up will interrupt your train of thought. Likewise your social media – we know that students use this a lot. But you need to focus your attention fully on writing. By all means take a short break every hour or so and check what your friends are up to. Indeed, we have seen research that shows this can be really helpful.

- Notes are much more useful if they are written by hand rather than typed. There is more flexibility this way and you can easily carry round a few sheets of paper and have these next to the computer when you start to write.
- A very useful idea is to use a Mind Map – and don't think you need to be able to draw. Just a series of lines and bullet points is fine. Or you can do this on your computer – Chapter 2 shows you how to do it.

## 3.9 Advanced reading skills

The best way to get better at reading is to practise. There isn't a short cut to the skill but investing time in this and others skills at an early stage will really pay dividends later on. We would recommend the following:

- become faster at reading
  - o speed reading
- targeting
  - o read broad
  - o read deep
- advanced note taking

### 3.9.1 Become faster at reading

By the time you reach university, you will have already developed your own style and pace of reading. Some people naturally read faster than others but regardless of how fast you read when you arrive at university, you will certainly benefit from learning how to make yourself read faster. In principle, the concept is to move from reading word by word (or even letter by letter) to scanning your eye across the page and gaining an overall sense of what material is there before focusing into more precise (and slow) reading. If you have had the experience of showing your essay to an academic, you will find that many of them can take what appears to be a cursory look at your carefully crafted work and immediately tell you what you have and have not done. Academics are people who virtually read for a living so they have become used to it somehow. You need to learn it more deliberately as a skill. Work towards being able to drift your eye down the middle of the page and avoid reading individual words. Can you get any sense of what the author is saying? Keep thinking about almost de-focusing your eye so you are not reading the words, just absorbing the overall message as if through some sort of sixth sense. Once you have established a vague idea of what is in a section or chapter, you can decide whether you want to read it in more detail. See if you can get to a stage of reading more than a page in a minute – even for dense texts on large pages this is possible! The idea is that you can very quickly get to know whether or not you want to invest time in reading a chapter in detail. Once you have this skill, it will come in useful for the rest of your working life so the investment of time practicing it is well worthwhile.

### 3.9.2 Speed reading

This is a concept that you can train yourself to read faster whilst also learning from texts. There are lots of free online resources which could help you with this as well as many, many books. The website www.readingsoft.com is interesting because it offers a free reading speed test so you can see how fast you are reading at the moment. We have some concerns about these techniques – not least because our research showed that the people we surveyed who said they used speed reading tended to end up with worse degrees than those who did not. We think this is because people using it thought it was a short cut to actually doing the work. Our book is all about being efficient and effective but we never suggest that there is a substitute for hard work. We want students to direct their effort – not save it!

That said, you might be someone who reads extremely slowly and it might be holding you back, so some practise of the techniques of speed reading could be really useful. Though do be warned that the techniques do seem a bit weird at first. Chris remembers the first time he tried to train himself to speed read and he found it extremely weird and difficult. What worked for him and what we recommend for you, is to stick with it. After enough practise, you will get used to it. Pat has always been an extremely fast reader but this became a disadvantage at university as he would read so fast he sometimes missed important information. After university, this has again become extremely useful as he can get through large swathes of written information in his management role much faster than many other people. He has also learned that he might miss things so he goes back over important material several times and forces himself to slow down.

For most people, the very prastise of reading a lot at university is enough to speed them up to the right pace where they can get through the material without missing too much.

### 3.9.3 Targeting

Now you are building an ability to read quickly, you have made yourself more time so use this skill wisely by first reading widely and then drilling down into the detail. Think of it as being a T shape – skim across the surface of a topic – rather like a jet ski skimming over the waves of a topic. Once you work out in which areas you need to gain more depth you can drill down into them in more detail.

### 3.9.4 Read broadly

As we have said already, lecturers give reading lists to accompany their lectures and we described how Pat once decided not to read any of them. A far better attitude would be to see how many of the books were available in the library and then at least get them off the shelf to have a glance at them in the library. Having used your speed reading skills to get some sense of the value of the different books, you can then take out only the ones you think are going to be of use to you. With journal articles, you can search for these online and look at the abstract and ask yourself, 'Does it look useful/interesting?'. This is the jet ski part of reading. Just literally flicking through the relevant chapter. You should ask yourself these questions:

- Is this relevant to me?
- Is it written in a way I can understand?
- Does it cover the topic completely?
- Are there useful references to follow up?

Then you can borrow (or buy) the books which you absolutely need and download only the papers you are pretty sure are going to help you. You then can 'daisy chain' from the book or paper you begin with to move to other sources.

### 3.9.5 Read deeply

Having assembled the reading you think is going to be useful, now is the time to read deep. You still don't need to start from the beginning of a text book nor do you even need to read complete research papers. Just focus in on the bits you think are going to be relevant then settle yourself in a comfortable place to read slowly. For those of you who naturally read quickly, this requires a conscious effort to slow down and read every single word. One useful way of slowing down is to read through once fairly quickly, then go back over the relevant sections taking notes. Which brings us neatly on to the next advanced tip.

### 3.9.6 Advanced note taking

There are different sorts of notes for you to be making – are you writing a coursework essay or revising for an exam? For the former, you need to be noting likely looking quotes from the text as you go along – but do make sure you record the place you are quoting from (paper or book) with page number. This means you can use the notes directly when writing your essay. Some people refer to this process as being a sort of treasure hunt where you are searching for nuggets of treasure that will help you answer the essay question. You should be ruthless in only reading the parts of the text which are going to help in your quest of writing the particular essay set. Even if other sections look interesting, perhaps make a note of them for reading another time. For exam revision, you are quite unlikely to be expected to give precise quotes so it is better to note down useful summaries of theories, write down author and date and the name of the theory if there is one. Try to note down short summaries as you work through the reading so when you come back to your notes you no longer need to read the text again as everything you need from it, you have already extracted.

## 3.10 Summary

- Take your module reading list as a starting point for your reading.
- Be prepared to only read the papers and chapters you really need.
- Learn to skim read to get the sense of a paper.
- Then go back over promising sections and read slowly making notes of useful quotes.
- Finally, always follow up using the 'daisy chain' method.

## 3.11 Taking it to work

Many managers have large amounts of reading to do – indeed the more senior you get, the more reading you will need to do. Typically documents will come with an executive summary so you can decide whether to read particular sections in more depth. But if a large document comes without this, you can use the skimming method to get the sense of a document and of particular sections. You can then dive into more depth in the areas that seem interesting or important.

## 3.12 How to get started

### 3.12.1 Professional

- Try scan reading three chapters of a book in just ten minutes, then see if you can manage the next three chapters in five minutes.

- Ease into academic reading with an easy book first, then move on to journals later.
- Next time you go to read a textbook or paper, switch off your phone and computer.

### 3.12.2 A little more interesting

- Apply the scan reading idea to your favourite magazine. Pick an article and as you read it note down the key points using a Mind Map.
- Practise speed reading an online article using your mouse as a pointer on your screen.
- See how fast you can read a broadsheet newspaper. Skim over the bits you aren't interested in and glean the key points from the articles you are interested in.

## 3.13 Our bookshelf

Metcalfe, M. (2012) *Reading critically at university*. London: Sage.
A detailed work about what being critical means. It is a little heavy going in places but if you are struggling to figure the whole university reading thing out, this has the answers. But you will need to work at it!

Sutz, R. and Weverka, P. (2009) *Speed reading for dummies*. Hoboken, NJ: Wiley.
Does what it says on the tin really – some great tools and techniques.

# 4

# Lectures and lecturers

## 4.1 Chapter summary

This chapter is about the whole concept of lectures and especially how they are different from lessons. This includes how they are run, different expectations of students and lecturers and how different teaching styles can be tackled by the student. We go further and give the inside track on what makes lecturers tick so a key part of this chapter will be our take on how to develop valuable relationships with lecturers and why it is important to do so. Also, a specific technique of dealing with PowerPoint slides will be covered since these are ubiquitous. In order to understand lectures, first you should know something about the rather odd people giving them – lecturers.

## 4.2 Introduction

Many business courses are very large – especially in the first year. And it can be really hard to get to know a lecturer. The trouble is your lecturers probably went to university in a time when they got to know their lecturers because they saw them frequently in a small group such as a tutorial or seminar. However, this is now rare and students are usually in large groups of over 50 and frequently in groups of several hundred. However, if you do have the opportunity to go to tutorials where you can interact with your lecturers more closely, we strongly recommend you take this opportunity whenever possible as there is a huge benefit in doing so. Otherwise, you need to find ways of getting more out of your lecturer because it can start to look like the sort of experience you would get from watching videos of lectures and then working alone. It doesn't have to be like this – even if you are on a very large course and sit in lectures with several hundred other students.

## 4.3 The big secret

Most students hardly ever ask their lecturer anything. This means that despite appearances, your lecturer does potentially have time for you because the majority of your fellow students only talk to them when their assignments are due. And time spent with your lecturer can be incredibly valuable, both in terms of gaining extra subject knowledge and gaining an insight into what the lecturer expects of you in the assessments. The lecturer is an expert in the subject, an expert in the assessment and should be treated as a valuable source of knowledge. You should therefore consider them like a resource for you to get the best use out of – in the same way you would want to get the best out of any resource at your disposal. The more time you spend with them, the more you will learn. And the more you learn, the more value you are getting out of university. Further down the line, there is also great value to having the lecturer know who you are when it comes to getting a job when you leave university. For example, many lecturers are asked by employers to recommend a good student and if you are one of the students the lecturer remembers, maybe you can benefit from the lecturer's network and their links to employers. You must also remember that your lecturer is just a person, and so they can be fun and entertaining to get to know. You may even share the same passions or interests as them.

A word of caution. Your degree is the most important thing in your life at university. But you as an individual student are one of many who the lecturer has and you need to be careful you don't become known as a pest.

## 4.4 From the lecturer's point of view

To get the best out of lecturers, first you need to understand them. They probably appear rather remote, aloof or strange. But once you understand some important things about them, you will find it much easier to figure out how to get the best out of them as a 'resource'. At many universities – and this is definitely true for the top rated universities – lecturers careers are determined not only by the quality of their lectures, but largely by the quality and quantity of their research. In fact, traditionally, the quality of teaching didn't matter at all and from time to time this culture shows through. This is because not all that long ago going to university was paid for by the state which meant lecturers sometimes took the attitude that students will get whatever it is they decide to give them and they had better be grateful too! It is a great development that this attitude has largely changed but you might come across it from time to time. The current movement is towards students being customers just like any organisation has customers. Lecturers *hate* this idea and you won't help if you refer to it! It is true that a general level of customer service is expected from lecturers but for your own sake, don't *ever* remind them of this to their face. If something goes badly wrong – your lecturer not responding to repeated emails over an extended period of time – there are formal redress processes available to you usually through the student representative system. In fact, a legitimate complaint of this type is taken more seriously than students might think. In general lecturers think of students as being products rather than customers – although hopefully they will also think of you as being human too!

This means that at any one time they will have research projects running – and it is worth realising that these might be at least as interesting to them as their lectures! In fact at some universities, lecturers will have as little as 40 per cent of their time allocated to lecturing, with the rest focused on research and management. They will also be under pressure from their managers to produce papers for peer reviewed journals and to generate research funding. Even if your lecturer is not 'research active', they will have many modules they are teaching apart from your particular one and have Masters dissertations to supervise, marking to complete and lectures to plan – all this on top of dealing with universities' famously bureaucratic administration systems. For the majority of lecturers though, the student who books a time slot for a discussion, turns up on time, is prepared and is polite is extremely warmly welcomed. Lecturers are fascinated by their subject and having a discussion about it will be a welcome part of their day and not an intrusion. But very few lecturers will welcome you turning up unannounced as it cuts in to the other tasks they have planned. For example, Pat has a management role at the university that involves meeting with executives from external business partners which takes him out of the office frequently. He also writes journal articles (and this book of course!). Sometimes students email him annoyed that he wasn't available when they turned up without an appointment at his office. His diary is filled several weeks ahead because he tries to get the most out of his work day by planning in advance. This is like any job and it is useful for students to become accustomed to it – work is like that! Perhaps more importantly, you need to become organised yourself which is why we focus on this skill in Chapters 1 and 6.

Finally, try to see it from their point of view. Lecturers are the kids who did exceptionally well at university. So they are all very bright and extremely well clued up on the subject. Sometimes this means that they forget how difficult it is to understand concepts and theories for the first time. You need to allow for this even if they don't.

# 4.5 Preparing to meet your lecturer

Having established that you need to get the best out of your lecturer's time, it is a really good idea to prepare for your meeting. This needn't take very long but just showing that you have thought about things properly will predispose your lecturer to be more likely to help. It also means you will make more effective use of your time. Table 4.1 gives a quick summary of what you need to do in preparation – and what not to!

We know many students do not meet with their lecturer at all. Perhaps they don't know what do discuss, why they would go or indeed whether the lecturer would be helpful. We believe every student should meet with their lecturers because it is a great way of adding value to the knowledge you gain in the lecture and also can be a great help in your experience of university in general. It is also a good habit to get into – that of learning from feedback. Figure 4.1 shows what successful people do.

In other words, they are constantly seeking feedback, learning from it, trying new things and seeking further feedback. This should be something you

TABLE 4.1    The loves and hates of lecturers

| Things lecturers hate | Things lecturers respond well to |
| --- | --- |
| Not turning up to appointments | Politeness (sadly many students aren't, so if you are nice you stand out and they will spend more time with you – a life lesson!) |
| Talking in lectures – even if it's about the subject. To the lecturer it looks rude and they assume you are talking about them – and not in a good way! | Showing a real interest in their subject by actively listening and responding to questions asked by lecturers |
| Asking questions they have already answered. It shows a lack of attention and lack of understanding to others | Showing you have listened to what they have said in the lectures |
| Students who haven't tried – have questions but nothing to show about the thinking and work they have done to try and solve the question for themselves | Doing the homework – showing that you have really tried to understand the reading/a task but have some questions |
| Students who have questions which show they haven't done the reading | Even if you don't really understand what an essay/piece of work is requiring you to do, you have tried and bring it along for comment |
| Missing obviously presented help like links on virtual learning environments, questions that have been answered on the discussion board | Being present at lectures and tutorials |
| Students who have missed lectures without good reason but want the lecturer to recite the lecture for them alone | Attending lectures, participating in tutorials |

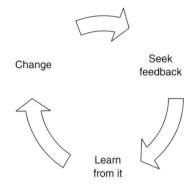

Change                    Seek
                          feedback

Learn
from it

FIGURE 4.1    The process of learning from feedback

are doing all the time. It is how we can develop and learn new skills. We should be learning all the time. For example, Pat realised that after three years in a particular role, he wasn't really learning anything new. This is when he decided to change jobs and he is now learning new things again.

## 4.6 What to discuss with your lecturer

You need to have a trusted source to provide feedback and this is where your lecturer comes in. So here are our suggestions on what you could ask your lecturer.

### 4.6.1 Assignments

Chapter 9 on coursework gives our take on the various assignments that you might be set. Hopefully your lecturer will have already given clear guidance on what is expected from you. What you can gain in addition from a meeting is to see if you have interpreted this guidance correctly. The best plan is to draft out what you intend to do with notes about the various sources you are going to use and what your outline is. Then make an appointment with the lecturer and take this to the meeting. In this way you will show that you have been thinking about the assignment and the lecturer can then indicate if you are on the right lines with your work. This can be very motivating for you as too often students spend a lot of their time at university wondering what they are supposed to be doing or whether they are doing the 'right' thing. Once you have this confirmation, you can really get on with the work happy in the knowledge that you are putting your effort into the right things.

Chris did this for one of his final year economics assignments and it worked out very well for him. He did some research on the assignment which was about the energy sector (not very exciting) and thought about what he was going to write. He booked a meeting with the lecturer and was gobsmacked at how much help he received. The topic Chris had chosen was a passion of the lecturer and he spoke to Chris for ages about research in the energy sector. Chris then discussed what he planned to write and the lecturer reassured him he was on the right track and told him to read about a couple of theories. The result was Chris has plenty of research to read and ideas of where he could develop his essay to make it stronger. Most importantly, he knew he was on the right track and could write the essay without worrying whether or not he was doing the right thing.

If you do choose to discuss an assignment with a lecturer, which we definitely recommend that you do, you should of course make sure that you do so early – there is no point coming to the lecturer with this at the last minute. It isn't fair if you rush in unannounced to their office with little or no work to show and demand the lecturer helps you with your crisis. You need to be planned, deliberate and professional and this includes doing your work *early* and not at the last minute. Of course you may want to have a final check over your work before you hand it in but coming to the lecturer the day before a piece of work is due and showing them very little work is just demonstrating to them that you aren't taking it seriously. In fact one of the things that Pat finds most irritating is marking work which has clearly been done at the last minute and he has to spend time trying to figure out where to find enough marks to enable a pass. If you are in this category, we hope that reading this book will cure you of such bad habits!

Finally, some lecturers for certain assignments will agree to read and comment on a draft before you submit it. If you intend to ask for this, make sure that they agree to it first. And make sure you give them enough time to read it and make comments well ahead of the deadline. There is no point asking for comments the day before the submission date as you won't have enough time to make significant changes anyway. And also remember that whilst your assignment is the most important thing in your world, it is a very, very small part of the lecturer's world!

## 4.6.2 Exams

Lecturers can help you direct your effort when preparing for exams. In Chapter 12 we talk a lot about how to revise and how to take exams. We also mention that the lecturer is an important part of the preparation process. Lecturers really hate it when students constantly ask whether a particular topic is going to be in the exam. A more planned approach is to arrange to meet the lecturer at the start of revision time. As always, do your preparation, so take in previous papers (if available) and show your first notes for revision. Ask the lecturer if you have missed anything. You can also ask about the style of answer that is required. Is it an essay format or perhaps less formal, for example?

### 4.6.3 Module decisions

We know many students have to select streams and modules each year, particularly in the case of general business degrees. This can often be a difficult choice, especially with detailed and academic module guidelines which often make little sense. Lecturers are able to provide in-depth and practical information on what modules entail and which might suit you best.

I personally developed a good working relationship with a lecturer through an office hour appointment, where I asked for his advice regarding the module options within his field. He later became my referee for my job applications and my first point of contact for any academic questions. I was even asked to give a brief presentation during his first year welcome speech, where I shared ideas and advice on how to approach university from a student perspective. I would recommend all students to develop a good relationship with one of their lecturers. The best way to approach them is either after the lecture or during their office hours. By asking them questions related to what they are teaching or researching, students display a genuine interest. Once they know a student they are often more than willing to write references and offer career advice.

Mei Lin Ly, BSc International Business and Management

### 4.6.4 Feedback

Students often say they don't get enough feedback from lecturers and we think one of the reasons is that they don't make the effort to go and see their lecturers for clarification of comments on their work and to ask for specific guidance. This is a good habit to get into as it is well known that people who seek out and act on feedback do better at work than those who don't. It's a habit of learning which you should keep for the rest of your working life. But remember, you might not hear what you want to hear. All feedback is useful even if in the end you decide that it isn't valid. But be very wary of dismissing an uncomfortable message. Ask yourself, 'I don't like this. Is it really because deep down I know it is the truth?' In our view, most of the time you should embrace all feedback and learn from it. Some of the people we have found most frustrating to work with are those who do not seek out feedback – or when they receive it, don't act on it. A key question to ask is, 'What could I have done to gain a better mark?' or 'How should I approach things like this in the future?'. Lecturers will also be very impressed if you show that you have listened to their feedback and acted on it. One way of demonstrating how seriously you take it is by taking notes during your meeting. Pat often notices students aren't writing things down and he finds this difficult because he knows that they are unlikely to act on the advice he is giving and so won't remember it later.

Earlier this year I had been struggling with one of my modules and had received a rather mediocre mark in my coursework. This prompted me to go to see my lecturer to seek advice on how to improve. Going to see my lecturer and asking her to explain what I did wrong and how I could improve, helped me a great deal. It aided me in the subject I was struggling in and she enabled me to understand concepts that I did not before. She also gave me guidance on extra reading which would aid me in my studies. This feedback helped me with my other modules, as it was explained to me how to improve my writing style and referencing, which is important in all aspects of my course. Overall, the experience proved to be very helpful and taught me the importance of asking for help if it is needed.

Sarah Keast, LLB Law with Management

### 4.6.5 Job/networking opportunities

In some cultures potential employers will approach lecturers to recommend their best students. For example, in many universities in Germany the top 10 per cent of students are known as 'The Dean's List' and some recruiters target this list of students exclusively. In other countries it is less formal. In the UK this sort of thing used to happen a lot but these days equal opportunities legislation means it is less likely. However, you never know just what contacts your lecturer has. For example, Pat was recently asked to recommend any former PhD students for a lecturer job. Solely on his recommendation, they interviewed one of his former students. But this is quite rare these days – especially at undergraduate level. However, business lecturers are very often working with businesses and may have knowledge of internships and have contacts who they can meet for informal careers discussions, for example. And most of us are unsure about what career we want to get in to when we graduate so this sort of exposure is always useful.

Back at home when I was in high school, teachers were seen as superior, intellectual entities who were unapproachable and were only standing in front of the classroom to do their jobs, nothing more. Helping pupils outside the designated class hours was definitely not in the job description. That would be private tutoring and if you would want that privilege you would have to pay for it. You can imagine that it came as a surprise to me when I found out about these 'office hours' that lecturers have. An open door policy is what my university encourages when it comes to the lecturer–student relationship and I find that brilliant. The first professor who I went to see in my first year was my second favourite lecturer so far. He helped me choose my streams for the second year. He asked me beforehand the reason why I was going to see him and when I told him I was seeking guidance for my streams in the second year, he was waiting for me prepared with materials, which described all the streams, and schemes where he drew the relationships between certain streams. He was very helpful and after seeing him I had a clear image of what I want to do.

During my second year, I went to see all my lecturers, especially when missing lectures because of interviews or assessment centres. One who helped me most was a lecturer who, at the beginning of the course, said that she was more than happy to help students with any matter – from Consumer Behaviour to placement related issues. Furthermore, she helped me polish my CV, she was there for me with motivational speeches when I was rejected from companies, and she helped me with applications, with presentation skills, with coursework, with revision. I owe her a lot.

Alexandra Cojanu , BSc Business and Management

## 4.7 What is a lecture?

This might sound like another crazy question – just like the one about how to read – but it is important. The key thing is that lectures are not lessons. The basic traditional form is for the lecturer to stand at the front of a large room and dispense their wisdom, which the students write down. Mercifully most lecturers have moved on from this model into something more interactive. But there is a key difference which tends to get in the way of interaction – numbers. Pat's first year lecture has nearly 500 students although, to be honest, once you get over about 100 students the problem is the same. You simply cannot be all that interactive with that number of students in a room. The tendency is for the student to become passive, part of a crowd and not feel involved. Hopefully your lecturer will keep things interesting by using examples and video clips but some subjects don't lend themselves to anything other than a passage of information from the lecturer's mouth and the PowerPoint slide to you.

Perhaps the key difference is that most of the time nobody will check whether or not you turn up. But this should not be taken as meaning you shouldn't go. You *must* go to *all* your lectures. Without fail. All of them. Even if you don't like the lecturer, even if you find the subject less than marvellous. Always, always go. Pat only missed one lecture in his entire university career and he still regrets even missing that one. Chris also never missed a lecture. Some students think they can pick and choose whether they go to lectures but we know from our research and from years of experience that the students who miss lectures *always* do worse than those with a good attendance record. And anyway, a record of attendance is more likely to be kept these days in the UK because of immigration regulations. The best way to approach it is to think of your degree as being like a job – you only get paid if you go to work and you only get the benefit of university by going to all the lectures and tutorials available.

## 4.8 Why do we say you must always go?

The lecture is the place where you will be stimulated into learning about the subjects you have gone to university to study but they are not enough on their own to pass. You need to do lots of follow up work which usually consists of set reading before the lecture, re-reading afterwards, making notes and following up on notes you make in the lecture. Many students make the mistake of thinking that because the lecturer doesn't check whether or not they have done the reading, it isn't important. We discuss this in more detail in Chapter 3, but in the context of the lecture, your pre-lecture reading starts the brain thinking about the topic to be covered. The lecture will put some more meat on these bare bones, and then the post-lecture reading and note taking finishes the job. If you do this all the time, come revision time you will be so far ahead of anyone who is trying to do it at the last minute you can get to the stage where you are learning the sorts of things that will take you from a good pass up to a first.

To put this in more basic terms, the lecture is where you discover about the exam and assessment procedures because lecturers want their students to pass and often give very detailed advice in lectures to help students do so. Commonly you will only get to know this if you actually attend the lectures. Pat regularly does this quite deliberately to encourage students to turn up to lectures. Chris once turned up to a lecture where the lecturer gave hints and tips to students regarding the upcoming coursework and essay. The lecturer did not give any prior warning about this, it was merely done as a reward for those that turned up. And here lies a key lesson, you never know what might happen in a lecture and so it is important to turn up. Taking another example, Chris once turned up to a finance lecture where the lecturer immediately set a random class test that was worth 5 per cent of the module. Anybody who didn't attend automatically lost out on these potential marks. This is quite an extreme example but does go to show how important it is to attend lectures.

Possibly as important, going to lectures is a great way to meet other students on your course. Having social time with your fellow students is an enormous benefit of university and can open your eyes to new cultures, new ideas and often even to lifelong friendships. Again on a more basic level, knowing many other students on your course enables you to cross check on what the lecturer wants you to do in your assessments and gives you access to other people to study with. And it has been shown time and time again that students who find other students to study with do better than those who don't. A recent study (Massingham and Herrington, 2006) showed a direct correlation between attendance at tutorials and grades achieved.

## 4.9 Why sometimes you might not go and how to avoid these situations

In terms of attendance at lectures, students commonly say they can't for various reasons. So here are our suggestions of 'What to do if':

### 4.9.1   You are too busy to attend lectures

We know that most students have to do at least some paid work in order to survive at university. But you need to make sure that you leave enough time for your studies. There is absolutely no point in being able to afford expensive nights out and nice clothes if you aren't going to lectures. You just aren't gaining the benefits of university – but we see this happening a lot. Do the minimum paid work to get by and make sure you find a job with hours that fit your studies. Remember first things first, as we discuss in Chapter 6 on time management. If you are too busy to attend lectures, you are not prioritising the right things.

### 4.9.2 You don't understand the content

Pat clearly remembers his first lecture at university. He didn't understand a single word. In fact, he became so worried about it he nearly left in the first week. However, he persevered and eventually it started to make sense. Many students say that they go to one or two lectures on a module, it doesn't make sense so they stop going. This is a way of making it very difficult for you to pass.

The first thing to mention is don't worry or become stressed if you don't understand the content immediately. Naturally, you are at university to gain a degree and learn new things, and so you won't always understand everything straight away. If you did, you may even be at the wrong university or undertaking the wrong course because you aren't being stretched enough.

If you don't understand the content after you have worked at it, you are probably not doing enough reading and preparation. Remember to complete the reading, listen in lectures and then reflect on the lecture afterwards. Do some more reading and if you still don't understand, book some time with your lecturer. As we discuss in Chapter 5 on fear and stress, everything is in your control. Chris will never forget his econometrics module which never made sense to him. He attended the first few lectures and he simply couldn't understand any of the content. It was the classic lecture, with formulas and long equations on a blackboard. He realised he needed to do a lot more work and so he did extra reading and practised before and after the lectures. Eventually the lectures starting making more sense to him. The lecturer also made more effort to explain things. Remember if you are struggling to understand something, there are probably lots of other students in the class who are also struggling and your lecturer will know this.

### 4.9.3 You are too tired

It may be that you are tired from studying late or working at your job. But we have to say the majority of times students are tired in lectures is because they have been out partying. We do not suggest you stop socialising – in fact Pat and Chris are enthusiastic party goers! (or in Pat's case, he was in the past!). But if for whatever reason you are completely shattered, it's probably best to acknowledge this and don't go. You will probably be better off recovering – and learning not to get into that situation again! Falling asleep in the lecture isn't helping anyone. If you aren't getting enough sleep on a regular basis for any reason, you need to sort this out. And don't forget, if you do fall asleep your lecturer will notice and most likely remember your face when you later ask for help. In these cases, you can guarantee they may be less willing to give you help.

### 4.9.4 Your lecturer is difficult to understand (accent)

One of the difficult side effects of today's multicultural universities is that some of the lecturers will not have English as their first language. Perhaps you will get used to it after a while but if not, you do need to take action. The first port of call (if you can bring yourself to do it) is to raise it with the lecturer directly. Perhaps suggest they speak a little slower. But make sure it isn't just you who thinks they are hard to understand and do tread carefully – it is a sensitive issue. If this doesn't work, then have your course representative discuss it with the course director or bring it up at staff–student committees. Of course if it is a pressing issue the committee might not come at the right time. Either way, stopping attendance at lectures is not a useful solution.

> In first year, I had a Financial Accounting lecturer who spoke very broken English and they often did not explain the material well. To overcome this, I studied the material as best as I could in my own time, using the lecture slides and the recommended reading to try and take control of the situation rather than feel sorry for myself. I found this has often worked best for me as opposed to trying to change the situation which can take a very long time.
>
> Jenna Bonfiglio, BSc Business and Management

### 4.9.5 People talk during the lecture

This can be a difficult problem to deal with since many lecturers take the opinion that students are adults and it is up to them how they conduct themselves. Pat is not of this view and always tries to set out at the start of a module what students should and should not do and talking is not allowed. However, it may be that the lecturer isn't actually aware that people are talking – sound doesn't always travel from the back of the lecture hall to the front. In any case it is worthwhile bringing it to the lecturer's attention. A good way to do this is gather a few like-minded students and either make an appointment or speak to the lecturer after the lecture and ask if they can help. Or you could take control yourself and perhaps sit in a different place from where the noise is. Perhaps it isn't regarded as being 'cool' to sit at the front but maybe this is something you should think about doing. Remember, it is your education that will be suffering and if you upset some other students along the way by insisting on good behaviour in lectures, so be it. If it is your friends who create the noise, then perhaps you should think about sitting separate from them. Whatever you decide to do, make sure you get to a point where you can go to lectures and gain benefit from them.

### 4.9.6 The lecturer's style is to read every single word on slides

This is not acceptable from the lecturer – but all too common. This needs to be taken up with your personal tutor and also through the student representative system. You need to be gaining something from lectures and so hopefully, in addition to the lecture, the lecturer will be available for questions and also have interactive sections in the lecture.

## 4.10 Preparing for a lecture

These days the lecturer will usually provide slides for you to print out for use in the lecture. As an absolute minimum you should do this and bring them to the lecture. More often than not the lecturer will also set reading to be completed before the lecture. In large lectures you probably won't be asked to prove that you have done the reading. However, you *must* do the reading, the reason being that you need to start the process of your brain getting ready to learn something new. The best way of doing this is to do some quick reading on the subject before the intensive lecture. Chapter 3 on reading shows you how to do this. Some lecturers set vast amounts of reading so even if you aren't going to read it all, read as much as you can. Perhaps if you think there is too much, you could ask the lecturer to help you work out what is essential and what is not. But you should do the reading or else you aren't getting the value out of the lecture and therefore you are making things more difficult for yourself come assessment time. You also aren't learning as much which is, after all, why you came to university in the first place (at least it should be!).

You may in some cases not fully understand what you are reading, but don't worry about it. That is the point of the lecture, the lecturer will discuss the topic and it will be a little familiar to you having done the research. Then usually what happens is you have that eureka moment, where you connect what you learned from the reading with what your lecturer says.

Smaller lectures – say less than 50 students in the room – can be quite interactive. Most lecturers want the students to participate and ask questions and make comments. It shows they are interested and have done the pre-lecture reading. For this sort of lecture, it is even more vital to have done the set reading. When he is teaching smaller groups, Pat always starts the session with a 10 minute discussion of the reading. It is a great way for the lecturer to discover how much you have understood and which areas need more explanation. Be prepared to challenge the lecturer on the ideas in the set reading – it shows you are interested. It is a good idea to prepare at least one question for the lecturer every week. In fact you don't actually need to ask this question every time, as just thinking of it will help you do the reading more thoroughly.

My personal technique for prior lecture reading may be inefficient or unconventional in the eyes of others as it can be quite time consuming if done to my ideal level. I actually like to write out the lecture material word for word. So if it is a PowerPoint I write it out into designated lined-paper pads for each subject. Any words I initially don't understand I look up and I get to grips with any details, I only tend to read up if there is a complex diagram

*(Continued)*

*(Continued)*

(especially in economics subjects) or something I really don't understand. For language lectures the same but in more detail. (I study Chinese). I go through the text we will be looking at in the lecture from the work book and make sure I can read every character. I write up lecture slides as well as new vocab. Where I have time I also copy up the 'supplementary' vocab as an extra push for myself.

Lauren Campman, BSc International Business and Management

## 4.11 PowerPoint

We touched on the use of PowerPoint in Chapter 3 but we would like to stress the importance of printing off slides. You might be at a university where they do this for you but in our experience this is happening less and less. By printing off the slides you immediately cut down the amount of note taking you will need to do in the lecture and therefore increase the amount of time and brain power you can devote to the actual lecture. Usually you have the option of what format to use and we recommend three slides to a page. This gives you enough room on the page to make notes and means the type on the slides is large enough to read easily. It's probably better to print them in black and white if possible as big blocks of colour can be difficult to write over – and also uses up your ink cartridges. Remember, you simply cannot write and listen at the same time. All the time you are writing, you aren't listening to the lecturer so having the majority of the basic information in front of you gives you a head start. These days students often look at slides directly on their laptop or tablet in the lecture and make notes from a keyboard. If this suits you, that's fine. However, we can usually write more quickly than we can type, and also, as shown in Chapter 12 on exams, the act of writing helps the information go into your memory far more efficiently and effectively than by typing. Just as importantly, it helps you to avoid distractions. All too often, students with laptops get tempted to surf the internet and go on Facebook. If you do this, you are not getting the maximum value possible from the lecture. Remember you can't do two things at once, if you are on Facebook and trying to listen at the same time, you aren't listening at all! Students sometimes say that they can multitask and do both. It's not true – our brains just can't do it!

## 4.12 Finally, the big secret about lecturers

Lecturers actually *love* the topic they are teaching you. Almost always. Almost everywhere. So if you show interest, do the work and ask questions, they will see that you too are interested in the topic and therefore help you enormously.

## 4.13 Summary

- Always go to lectures.
- Do the reading before and after.
- Do make appointments to go and see your lecturer to ask questions.
- Turn up to your appointments on time and prepared.
- Be nice to your lecturer!

## 4.14 Taking it to work

The closest equivalent to the student–lecturer relationship is that with your boss. There is a lot of material out there on 'managing your boss'. Here's what we think are the important rules:

- Your boss is human – despite evidence to the contrary – so treat them like one. Vital to this is putting yourself into his or her shoes. What are the pressures from their boss?
- Ask for advice – but do your homework first. Never ever go to them with an idea with no working up.
- Be respectful – even in a casual office, even if you don't respect them at all.
- Take any meaningful learning opportunity you can – training, learning from stories the boss tells you, learning from what they do right, and wrong. When you look at the key differential between people who are promoted and those who aren't it's those who learn that win every time. Feedback can be tough to take but always take the feedback, and go out and find genuine feedback. Especially seek it out from people who don't like you. The great thing about feedback is that you don't *have* to take it. But you should take something out of every single piece of feedback you can get. Some of the most important lessons Pat has learned at work have come from people he really didn't like – and in many cases would say he has a very low opinion of. Even they can teach you stuff. Seek feedback. Learn from it. Change. And seek feedback again.

## 4.15 How to get started

### 4.15.1 Professional

- Make an appointment to see a lecturer you haven't seen in office hours before.
- See if you can expand the conversation a little.
- Sit at the front of the lecture room and get as interactive as possible, ask questions if permitted and talk to the lecturer after the lecture has finished.

### 4.15.2 A little more interesting

- Offer to buy your lecturer a coffee and talk to them about something related to the topic you are studying but not asking about the exam or assignment.
- Take time to visit your careers centre and see if you can engage the careers advisors in a conversation about career choice in general rather than just your own interest.
- Try sitting in a different part of the lecture theatre to your usual place – preferably at or near the front.

## 4.16 Our bookshelf

Dufour, G. (2011) *Managing your manager: how to get ahead with any type of boss*. New York: McGraw-Hill.

Jay, R. (2002) *How to manage your boss: developing the perfect working relationship: or colleagues, or anybody else you need to develop a good and profitable relationship with*. London: Prentice Hall.

## 4.17 References

Massingham, P. and Herrington, T. (2006) 'Does attendance matter? An examination of student attitudes, participation, performance and attendance', *Journal of University Teaching & Learning Practice*, 3 (2): 82–103.

# 5

# Fear and stress

### 5.1 Chapter summary

Fear and stress are something that we both feel strongly about. We have seen many students who in our eyes have a very high level of intelligence and potential yet are unable to realise it fully due to fear and stress getting the better of them. This is hardly a surprise, university creates many challenges that students have probably never experienced before so this chapter will cover how to recognise and cope with fear and stress.

## 5.2 Why might you become scared and stressed

The mere fact of starting at university contains features of a stressful situation – mostly due to the novelty of surroundings and all kinds of new experiences. These can – and should – be positive but some can prove challenging. For example, students experience:

- new study techniques that they haven't encountered before
- moving away from home and living independently
- an expensive lifestyle
- sudden inducement of debt and the need to manage finances

The challenge has further increased recently with the increase in tuition fees and a very competitive graduate jobs market. The combination of all these can lead to a great deal of fear and stress, which we personally believe go hand in hand. When people fear something, they begin to do harmful things like procrastinating and questioning their own abilities, which then in turn lead to stress. It can become a vicious circle as seen in Figure 5.1:

FIGURE 5.1   The stress–fear spiral

This is something that is close to us due to what we have seen and what happened with Chris in his final year. Chris was so scared that he was going to fail his exams that he ended up with a high level of anxiety and stress, which ultimately led to him having a severe panic attack that put him in hospital the day before his final exam. In the end, he got the grade he was after but it really brings to life just how fear and stress can affect us. We want to help you develop a proactive approach to fear and stress to ensure it does not get the better of you.

## 5.3 Fear

What scares you? Flying, presenting in public, dancing, exams, driving tests, spiders? All of these represent common fears and we are sure you can identify with one or even a number of them. You may even laugh at the idea of being scared at some of these things but all represent a great fear to many people, the point to take away is – we are all scared of something.

### 5.3.1 What exactly is fear?

To help overcome fear it first makes sense to understand what it is. In short, it is an emotion that produces worry due to the anticipation of a certain event. The key word here is anticipation; in most cases, the event we are scared of has yet to happen. This illustrates that fear is a self-induced emotion, often based on very little if any truth or fact. This ironically is what makes up the majority of our fears, it is referred to as irrational fear. It is perfectly right to be afraid of heights as you might fall but irrational to be afraid of spiders – especially in the UK. It is rational to be afraid (up to a point) that your work might not be good enough and you might not make the grade that you want. However, it is not rational if you have always done well in the subject before. If, on the other hand, you have not put the work in, be afraid because it probably will not end well.

### 5.3.2 Why and how does fear arise?

In terms of how it arises, fear is a natural body process, when somebody feels fear, chemicals are released into the body to deal with it. This is part of the fight or flight response, an ancient response to fear that used to keep us alive. It means that the body is naturally programmed to induce fear instead of rational thought when stimulated in certain ways (Ropeik, 2010). When it comes to the why, the best explanation is that from Susan Jeffers (2007). What she says is that all fears essentially have three different levels and it is the third which explains the why and how of fear. At the first level is the event itself – such as those listed earlier like a driving test. The anticipation of the event can be broken down into two aspects, perceived severity and perceived probability of occurrence. The higher these two things, the more somebody gets scared. At the second level is the deeper underlying fear, these can vary depending on the fear itself but a few of the most common are fear of failure, fear of change or fear of embarrassment. Finally:

> At the bottom of every one of your fears is simply the fear that you cannot handle whatever life may bring you. (Jeffers, 2007: 13)

### 5.3.3 Eradicating fear

The most important point to learn about fear is it cannot be eradicated. It is natural from birth and we will carry it throughout our lives. Fear is also dynamic, once we overcome one fear, our attention will turn to something else. For example, right now you may be afraid of the demands your degree is placing on you. However, upon graduation your fear will disappear and will then turn to the next thing such as finding a new job. You can see this having done your exams at school, how scared you were at the time – looking back it probably seems laughable to think that you were stressed.

The fact that fear cannot be eradicated is not as negative as it may sound. Fear brings with it many benefits that are often overlooked. First, it causes people to make rational decisions. For example, without any fear think of the stupid and somewhat dangerous things people might do! It also forces people to perform: the fear of failure pushes many to work harder by increasing their motivation. Pat has found that academics commonly have a fear of being 'found out' – that someone outs them as actually not being very clever. This fear spurs them on to higher levels of effort and therefore achievement. Similarly, many top sports people say that they are motivated by a fear of losing. Perhaps the most high profile is Ben Ainslie who, after winning Gold at the 2012 Olympics, said that he wasn't elated, just relieved that he had won.

Problems occur when fear reaches a high level as seen in the most common example from students, exams. Fear of exams can leave you prone to floundering from the start by:

- Procrastinating crucial tasks, for example, not revising for a certain exam because you are going to fail it anyway.
- Deterring you away from undertaking things that may be beneficial, for example, not asking a lecturer to clarify the exam format due to the fear of looking stupid.
- Setting weaker goals, for example, aiming for a 2:1 as aiming for a first is perceived to be unrealistic.
- Over exaggerating things and creating an unrealistic reality, for example, exaggerating how difficult an exam may be.
- Hindering your decision making, for example, choosing a harder question in the exam to help you fail. This is something Chris did in one of his final year economics exams, he thought he was going to fail the exam so decided he might as well answer a question he knew little about.

The ultimate consequence that encapsulates all these effects is the fact that fear can make the exact thing somebody is scared of come true. Returning to the example of exams, fear causes students to do many things that are unproductive and detrimental – procrastinating revision, not concentrating, picking harder questions, etc. The combination of these make the fear actually become reality.

## 5.4 Tools to reduce fear

Although fear cannot be eradicated, it can be reduced with the use of some tools and techniques. In fact, most of what we have discussed throughout the book helps to reduce fear, including goal setting, visualising and time management. What we wish to do here is explore more specific techniques that help get to the heart of fear.

### 5.4.1 Redefine the word failure

A common underlying fear is that of failure, something that motivates some students and paralyses others. The key to overcoming this fear is to redefine it. In the eyes of many, failure is viewed as something negative and consequently should be avoided. We want to redefine this, failure is an opportunity to learn and develop. This may sound like an old cliché but it remains true. Each time somebody perceives himself or herself to have failed, they have learned something new about themselves and consequently stand a better chance of success next time round. People often use the example of falling over when you are a baby, if you had given up the first time you fell over, you would never have learned to walk. Taking perhaps a more relevant example, Richard Branson is one of the most successful entrepreneurs but to get to this point he has failed just as many times as he has succeeded. In his autobiography, he repeatedly discusses how much money he has lost (which is far more than most people earn in a lifetime) and admits that he would not have reached the success he has without these great failures (Branson, 2006).

> In my definition, I perceived myself to have failed after I discovered my A-level grades and consequently I decided to stay another year at sixth form. At first, I was very upset that I failed. However, upon reflection, I realised it was a very positive experience. I clarified my immediate goals in life and am now more motivated than ever to achieve them.
>
> Giorgio Orthodoxou, BA Business and Management and Economics

The lesson to take away is not to be scared about failing, instead you must learn to embrace it. Once it does happen, learn from it and ensure you do not repeat it. Linking this to the third level of fear, if you fail then you will be able to handle it and move on. However, you need to be proactive about it, the learning will not happen on its own, this is the power of reflection and feedback. Each time you perceive you have failed, ask yourself:

- What has gone wrong?
- What will I do differently next time round?

In this light, it is evident that risks and the possibility of failure are not something to be afraid of, instead they should be something we chase. Obviously, risks should be calculated, for example, buying an ice cream van in the middle of winter is certain to lead to failure. Take calculated risks and if you fail then learn from these, as we shall discuss later on by evaluating your own performance and seeking feedback from others to develop continuously.

### 5.4.2 Question the fear

We do realise that simply telling you failure is not something to fear is not enough to eliminate it. After reading all this you will still be stating you do not know what will happen if you fail ... your parents will dislike you, you will let down your friends, you will not be able to get a job. However, truly thinking it through, do you really know what might happen if you fail? No matter what you think, you do not know the answer to this question. So ask yourself, what is the worst that could happen should you fail? Linking back to earlier, what would happen if you failed to achieve your goals? This question aims to provide two things:

1. A more objective reality of what could happen instead of the creative and unrealistic scenarios so often created by the mind in times of fear.
2. Help to identify how to overcome the consequences.

Often when we ask this question, we give an unrealistic sense of reality, i.e. exaggerate what could go badly wrong (Ropeik, 2010). For example, many students are scared that they may not secure a graduate job. Granted, there are obvious benefits to this and we understand why students are so keen to achieve this. However, is it so bad if this is not achieved? Absolutely not! You may have to work part time for a while, which will develop your skills and provide you with a better chance of securing a good job in the future that may or may not be on a recognised graduate training scheme. Alternatively, you may secure a job with a smaller business, which frequently provides many more benefits than one of the large firms where your experience might be strictly limited to one area.

### 5.4.3 Change your vocabulary

Change your vocabulary to use more positive words, a technique recommended by Tracy and Stein (2012). A few common phrases, which can be rephrased to place a positive spin, are:

- It is a problem = It is a challenge.
- It isn't my fault = I accept blame.
- I have to = I choose to.

Comparing these phrases reveals the power of this technique. For example, 'it is a problem' implies something very negative and potentially harmful as opposed to something that is a challenge, which implies something positive with great potential. Taking this further, problems and challenges can be represented as opportunities. Moving away from phrases, a few of our favourite words are shown in Figure 5.2:

FIGURE 5.2   Positive fear-busting words

Reading these words alone sends positive energy throughout the body. Try it out yourself by reading them out loud. How does it feel? Taking this further, if something negative does happen try to concentrate on the positive. As human beings, we are experts at seeing the negative yet not so good at seeing the positives. Often there are positive benefits that occur but we cannot see them. Many seem to believe that this technique involves seeking fake benefits, and this is where the technique of positive thinking falls flat on its feet. To truly gain power from this technique, you must seek truly positive benefits that you believe.

> Finding the benefits that have flowed from negative life events may seem like wishful thinking. However, there is some evidence that such benefits may be genuine. (Wiseman, 2009: 185)

To take this even further, write down on paper how you have benefited. 'Do not withhold anything and be as honest as possible' (Wiseman, 2009: 187). Writing benefits down has been proven to help in the most extreme of circumstances including illnesses (King and Miner, 2000), so we are sure it can help you for less severe yet still important events. The benefits stem from writing thoughts down in a structured and objective manner as opposed to listening to the inner voice that often has no logic (Lyubomirsky et al., 2006; Pennebaker, 1993). Amazingly, the benefits are so strong that even writing about an imaginative trauma has benefits (Greenberg et al., 1996).

Another benefit which is often overlooked is that it can prove funny to look back on these writings after a couple of years. For example, Chris recently found a piece of paper where he had written about the night he went to hospital, he read his comments about how many security people came to his room and how his flatmate was trying to make him laugh.

### 5.4.4 Do it

The ultimate stage in overcoming fear is to just do it, as the great Richard Branson puts it, 'Screw it, let's do it' (Branson, 2006). The previous techniques help to reduce fear but only by doing the very thing you are scared of will you ultimately overcome the fear.

Chris remembers when he was scared of his first assessment centre. For weeks, he researched everything he could about assessment centres and did his preparation. However, he was still frightened. However, on the day he just got on with it and he greatly reduced his fear. From there onwards, every assessment centre got a little easier and after eight of them he was no longer frightened.

## 5.5 Stress

The harsh reality remains that many students suffer from a high level of stress that can have similar effects to fear. To get a sense of how severe it is, a recent study found that over 75 per cent of students suffered from stress, the causes in order of severity were found to be:

1. exams
2. exam results
3. studying for exams
4. too much to do
5. the amount to learn. (Abouserie, 1994)

Much like fear, stress is a natural result in times of pressure such as university and it can be beneficial, but too much can be detrimental. This is why it is important to learn about stress. It becomes an issue when it reaches too high or too low a level, known as distress. It may surprise you that distress can occur when stress is even too little, resulting in boredom and the need to overcome this in good or bad ways.

### 5.5.1 What exactly is stress?

In essence, stress is about the perception of not being able to manage something. A more formal definition refers to it as:

When perceived demands exceed the individual's perceived ability to cope, they can be said to be experiencing a negative emotional state that is referred to as stress. (Arnold et al., 2010: 438)

The key learning to take away from this is the idea of perception, often we are in control but we perceive ourselves not to be and hence stress occurs. This also means that everybody has different levels of stress, even when under the same circumstances. For example, two students having to complete the same piece of coursework will feel significantly different levels of stress.

### 5.5.2 How does it work?

How stress works can be seen in the definition, which is split into two key halves, as shown in Figure 5.3:

FIGURE 5.3    The stress formula

The demands tend to come from the environment whereby an individual perceives something of importance to be at stake in terms of harm, threat, loss, challenge or even benefit. This tends to be referred to as the primary appraisal, i.e. the first stage. Second, the ability to cope comes down to individual abilities that, depending on the source of stress, can include skills, knowledge and experience. Boiled down it means stress has an external and an internal element which go through a two-step process. Knowing this, it is easy to figure out why students are so stressed, there are huge new external demands from the university whilst at the same time little direct experience, knowledge and skills, which creates a low perceived ability to cope.

## 5.6 Reducing stress

There are some very interesting and effective methods to help reduce stress that can be broadly placed into three categories (Murphy, 1988):

1.  Primary interventions: aim at changing the sources of stress.
2.  Secondary interventions: aim at changing individuals mindsets.
3.  Tertiary interventions: aim at dealing with the after effects of severe stress.

### 5.6.1 Primary interventions

Primary interventions get to the exact causes of stress and take the necessary action to reduce or even eradicate them. The list of possible sources of stress for students would be too long to go through and there is no need as we have discussed many of them throughout the book. For this reason, we are going to skip over primary interventions which include:

- Redesigning the work environment – we have discussed utilising different places to work.
- Creating goals and planning to achieve them, which we have discussed extensively.
- Working effectively by taking breaks.

You could say that everything we have covered in this book will directly or indirectly help to manage stress through primary interventions. Nonetheless, they do take time to implement and become accustomed to. For example, it is not easy to suddenly start working more effectively by reading differently and taking breaks.

### 5.6.2 Secondary interventions

To make the most of this method is it valuable to learn about something known as the locus of control. Essentially, there are two types of locus, which identify the extent to which somebody feels in control of their own life:

1. External locus: somebody believes most things and events are outside their own control.
2. Internal locus: somebody believes most things and events are under their own control.

These sit along a continuum, as shown in Figure 5.4:

External locus                                    Internal locus

FIGURE 5.4

These two extremes are often discussed in isolation but they lie on a continuum where people are either strongly external based or strongly internal based. The important thing to take away is that people with an internal locus perform higher than those with an external locus (Abouserie, 1994; Rotter, 1966). Thinking it through, it makes perfect sense. Somebody with an external locus does not have any control of their own life as they constantly blame everything and everybody else. With this mindset, there is nothing somebody can do as it is *perceived* to be outside his or her control.

This is opposed to somebody with an internal locus who is in control of their own lives and will maximise opportunities to overcome challenges. Unfortunately, in today's society we generally have a high external locus of control and this is one of the major causes to the great deal of stress we see today. It is easy to see this by looking at the effects of the current recession, society is now full of external people who are suffering, for example, 'It is so hard to get a job because of the recession' or 'There is no way my business can succeed in the current recession'. Many of the most successful people have capitalised upon the opportunities within the recession and this truly reveals the difference between those with an external and internal mindset. Ideally, it would thus be beneficial to develop an internal locus of control as found in many of today's CEOs (Miller et al., 1982). Imagine the CEO of a company blaming everyone and everything else when something went wrong – the whole company would go down. If you are interested in which type of locus you have, try looking at some of the statements below:

- A lot of things in my life are down to luck.
- Success usually comes down to being in the right place at the right time.
- Whenever I do something good, it goes unnoticed.
- Whether I pass at an interview usually depends on whether or not they like me.
- If things are meant to happen, they will.
- Setting goals is pointless.

If you disagree with most of the statements then you are likely to have an internal locus of control. This theory is useful when it comes to reviewing the sources of stress and overcoming them. The key question to ask is, are you worrying about things that are in your control? For example, when it comes to exams a lot of students worry about what questions may arise. We have seen many students obsess over this in case they have a 'nightmare exam' where they cannot answer any questions. Considering the locus theory, does it make sense to worry about this? Of course not, as it is outside one's control.

> Chris taught me a little about the locus of control theory on holiday and it has proved very beneficial since. Often when I am stressed I start to blame other people for things that have gone wrong. I remember the theory and ask myself the question: is it under my own control? Often the answer is actually yes and I am able to do something about it. For example, when recently stressed about a presentation I had to conduct for an interview, I decided the only thing I could do was practise as much as possible, which I did and successfully secured the job.
>
> Costa Pouzouris, BSc Accounting and Financial Management

TABLE 5.1  What is and is not under your control

| Task at hand | Under own control | Out of control |
| --- | --- | --- |
| Exam | • What to revise<br>• Time spent on revision<br>• How to revise<br>• The final mark | • The questions in the exam<br>• How the exam is marked |
| Securing an internship | • Level of effort in completing applications<br>• Quality of application<br>• Preparation for interview | • Number of internships available<br>• Interview questions<br>• Format of the assessment process |

To help makes this theory come to life Table 5.1 provides some examples of common tasks at university and what things are and are not under people's own control. These give an idea of where to concentrate your thoughts, effort and, most importantly, time.

### 5.6.2.1 Maintain a healthy life

Maintaining a healthy life can proactively help to manage stress. Some of the obvious tips include eating well, exercising regularly and getting enough sleep. Spending time on each one of these leads to a healthy lifestyle, neglecting one will negatively impact the other and subsequently your life. Considering the importance of maintaining a healthy lifestyle it may be something you wish to add to your goals. It sounds almost stupid to say but it is surprising how easily somebody's lifestyle can deteriorate in times where there is high potential for stress, as the example from Samuel illustrates.

The weekend before Global Entrepreneurship Week (GEW) in 2012, after weeks of preparation, I discovered that I had a nasty ear infection ... in both ears. This meant that I really struggled to hear anything whatsoever. That week, I had to give an assessed presentation in one of my Spanish modules, as well as run an AE event in partnership with the Aston Alumni Association and be interviewed as part of GEW. I spent the week completely guessing what people were asking me and sounding partially deaf when talking out loud at events. I found out from the doctor that the infection was caused by being run-down and stressed. It taught me that overworking myself at the cost of my health just isn't worth it – from that point on I slowed down and dedicated more time to just relaxing and not trying to do everything at once!

Samuel Wilson, BSc International Business and Modern Languages

We don't want to provide you with a wealth of information about how to live a healthy lifestyle as there are plenty of books, articles and websites that provide this, and we have provided a few recommendations at the end. Nonetheless, there is one key thing that we do want to discuss briefly, which is learning to switch off. Like it or not, you cannot *always* be working on your goals. You should set some time apart in which you can completely switch off, such as half an hour of TV. Chris learned this the hard way, after packing away his computer, TV and leaving his phone at home he literally got to the point where he was dreaming of journals. He laughs about it now and, looking back, he realises how stupid he was. Sleep is another area which we know many students underestimate. There seems to be a great myth that you can do without sleep and that you can make up for it at the weekend. This really is not the case and we must stress that sleep is essential to maintaining a healthy lifestyle. Ideally, you should sleep for about six to eight hours each night and if possible take a 20–30 minute nap in the day. It is important to not nap anymore then this as the body falls into deep sleep which will then make wakening up difficult as well as hinder falling asleep at night.

> This is the single most powerful investment we can ever make in life – investment in ourselves. (Covey, 2004: 289)

### 5.6.2.2 Quiet and noisy time

The two extremes of quiet and noisy time can both help to reduce stress. These really can be whatever you wish, essentially whatever works for you. Feel free to scream out loud, meditate or write everything down, cry or laugh, which we discussed earlier. Levy (1999) even suggests singing or writing a song. The essential point is to do whatever works for you.

> There is some evidence suggesting that crying may be rather bad for one's health status. This is not to say that crying is a useless behaviour. It has strong effects on the environment, promoting comforting and helping behaviour, possibly indirectly resulting in positive mood and health effects. (Vingerhoets et al., 2000)

### 5.6.2.3 Question the stress

A very useful task to realise the extent of stress is reflecting upon previous times in your life when you have suffered from stress. Just think of three times when you were stressed, think what you did to overcome it and what actually happened in the end. Looking back you will probably think that you had little reason to be so stressed. For example, to be in university you will have most probably undertaken A-level exams or something equivalent. There was probably enormous pressure upon you and hence you were stressed. However, upon reflection would you say that you were under control and it was not as bad as you thought? If the answer is yes, this is the next thing to learn about stress, it is often exaggerated and misplaced.

### 5.6.3 Tertiary interventions

Unfortunately, because of stress's psychological nature it can easily occur. Even when managed it does not take much for it to reoccur. Because of this, we want to briefly cover some tertiary interventions that aim to overcome the more serious consequences of stress. Obviously to undertake tertiary interventions one must first be aware that they are suffering from stress, which somebody can only do by knowing the signs. Some of the initial signs of stress include sleep problems, headaches, dizziness and loss of appetite. For a short period, these can prove problematic but not fatal. However, left to get worse these can turn into serious effects like anxiety, pounding heart, sweating, breathing problems and depression.

It can still prove difficult to identify when these are due to stress or for other reasons. As a general rule of thumb if you are suffering from a number of the symptoms then you are likely to be suffering from stress. To be more certain, you could try completing an online survey. Often people do things that are neither healthy nor productive when dealing with some of the more severe effects of stress, including alcohol, drugs, over eating, ignoring/denying the problem. We want to cover some healthier and much more effective methods of dealing with the after effects of stress.

### 5.6.3.1 Escape the madness

Sometimes just getting away from everything can be a fantastic method of reducing stress. When we say get away, we truly do mean get away. Try to escape to a new location that is slightly unusual for you such as a new city or cafe. Alternatively, this can be as simple as going outside. We know a lot of students who lock themselves away and in these circumstances going outside for a walk and some fresh air can work wonders. We have even known of students to get up and go to another county during stressful times at university.

I joined one of the societies at university when I was in first year and have been a member or part of the committee since then. This is the salsa society. After a long day at uni, I like going to salsa and dancing until I drop down! I also like visiting friends that study in other cities in the UK so I can change the scenery, get away from it all and I usually come back rested and more inspired to keep on studying.

Zhenya Urilska, BSc Marketing

## 5.7 Seek professional help

If these techniques don't make a significant impact, then we strongly suggest you seek professional help such as a student counsellor. Many students seem to be embarrassed at the idea of this, maybe because they perceive it as a sign of weakness or simply they might be scared because it is something that they have not tried before. Seeing a professional counsellor can be a great method to overcoming stress, specifically they can help to:

- identify the sources of stress
- give you expert advice
- provide somebody to talk to
- help you come up with a plan and provide personalised tips to help overcome it

The problems of stress are well recognised at universities and each one of them has a bundle of resources and services in place to help. The most useful of these are student counsellors. These are trained professionals who will listen to your challenges in a confidential and non-judgemental manner for free. They will offer you sound advice and provide you with plans and exercises to help overcome problems. We can't emphasise enough how helpful student counsellors are, from both our personal experience with Chris using them to hearing from other students how they have benefited. To see one, the process is very easy and you will normally have to make an appointment a day or two in advance via the phone, an online booking form or email. You will then have a one-to-one, face-to-face meeting, although there are many universities that now offer online and telephone support. Many also run workshop and group sessions where you will have the opportunity to explore your experiences with people who are facing similar challenges, for example, exam stress.

If things are very stressful and you are thinking of applying for extenuating circumstances then student counsellors can provide evidence for you, and many universities are more lenient about grant extenuating circumstances when you have seen a counsellor.

Student counsellors are not the only people on campus who can provide you with help. There are chaplaincy and multi-faith centres where you can talk to somebody who believes in the same religion as you. There are health centres if your stress is leading to serious physical issues. And there are your lecturers who will be very familiar with talking to students who are stressed, particularly if it is regarding their module.

If you don't want to speak to a counsellor, then there are some great websites out there with people wanting to help. These can sometimes prove easier by not having to talk with somebody face-to-face about what many consider to be embarrassing issues. Some of the websites we recommend are:

- Mental wealth – a student led group that helps students to maintain a healthy mind by overcoming such things as stress. www.mentalwealthuk.com/
- Nightline – this is exclusively a listening service that is again run by students. As the name suggests, it is open all night long for when times get tough. www.nightline.ac.uk/

In my final year fear and stress got the better of me and it caused me to become very ill in a number of different ways. For a long period of time, I kept my problems to myself and tried to finish my degree by essentially ignoring the problem. However, it soon became apparent that the only way I was going to overcome the stress was to seek help as it reached an unmanageable level. I spoke about the issue with my friends, flatmates, family and a professional counsellor. This was by no means easy but it was vital to helping me overcome stress and free my mind to eventually allow me to finish me degree and achieve my goal of securing a first class honours classification.

Anonymous , BSc Marketing

To get the benefits of both worlds, we recommend first talking to a friend and then talking to a counsellor. A friend can help to reduce stress but they do not always know the best course of action. A counsellor does and in the long term you can get to know them and so also receive the benefits of friendship. Using friends and counsellors can thus make for a powerful strategy.

## 5.8 Taking it to work

Fear and stress are responses that people experience throughout their lives, new challenges constantly arise that bring with them fear and stress. Learning to manage fear and stress can prove valuable across your life. For example, when you graduate you will get your first taste of true working life which will bring with it things that you have not experienced before such as key performance indicators, bonus objectives, a line manager and a work schedule. We definitely recommend using the tools and methods that we have provided to reduce your fear and stress so you can concentrate on what really matters.

Back in the 1980s, Pat came out of the army and landed a job working in sales. The job was highly competitive and everyone had to justify their job week by week in terms of the sales they made. He gradually increased his working hours to such an extent that he realised all he was doing was working and sleeping. He averaged nearly 90 hours at work a week. This eventually started to affect his health. At this point he took time out and went on holiday to New York for two weeks. He realised (a) he was stressed and (b) the sole cause of his stress was his job. He immediately quit and set up in business with a friend. This breather enabled him to make the major career change – he went to university for the first time aged 29 – and has been there ever since!

## 5.9 How to get started

### 5.9.1 Professional

- Next time you are stressed, try writing it all down instead of bottling it up.
- If you fail to reach a goal, think about what you would do to overcome the consequences.
- See a counsellor to discuss a challenge you are currently facing.

### 5.9.2 A little more interesting

- Complete something small that scares you every day for one week (pot holing, abseiling, singing).
- If you get stressed in the library, go for a walk, and try working in a local cafe or park.
- Make a random speech in a public place like a supermarket or park, often we are scared of presenting so this is a good way to overcome a common fear.

## 5.10 Our bookshelf

Jeffers, S. (2007) *Feel the fear and do it anyway*. London: Random House.
Susan is a highly acclaimed author on fear, having sold her book worldwide. The book provides detailed advice and comes with a number of real life examples to really bring it to life. We definitely recommend her book and if you enjoy it, she has a number of other equally valuable books on related subjects to challenge and develop your mind.

Mckenna, P. (2009) *Control stress: stop worrying and feel good now!* London: Transworld.
Paul is a very famous author and provides a number of self-development books. In this book, he runs through a wealth of research and techniques to help people overcome stress and relax. It even comes with a useful relaxation CD to support the text.

Wiseman, R. (2009) *59 seconds: think a little change a lot*. London: Macmillan.

This book is quirky in nature, with Robert Wiseman describing himself in the field of Quirkology. It is thus quite different and very entertaining, though extremely powerful in providing effective yet quick recommendations to deal with situations of fear and stress as well as a number of other areas of life. All in all, an entertaining and interesting read and we are sure you will enjoy it.

## 5.11 References

Abouserie, R. (1994) 'Sources and levels of stress in relation to locus of control and self esteem in university students', *Educational Psychology: An International Journal of Experimental Educational Psychology*, 14 (3): 323–330.

Arnold, J. and Randall, R. with Patterson, F., Silvester, J., Robertson, I., Cooper, C., Burnes, B., Swailes, S., Harris, D., Axtell, C. and Hartog, D.D. (2010) *Work psychology: understanding human behaviour in the workplace*. Harlow: Pearson Education.

Branson, R. (2006) *Screw it, let's do it: lesson in life*. Virgin Books: London.

Covey, S.R. (2004) *The 7 habits of highly effective people*. London: Simon & Schuster.

Greenberg, M.A., Wortman, C.B and Stone, A.A. (1996) 'Emotional expression and physical heath: revising traumatic memories or fostering self-regulation?', *Journal of Personality and Social Psychology*, 71 (3): 588–602.

Jeffers, S. (2007) *Feel the fear and do it anyway*. London: Random House.

King, A.L. and Miner, N.K. (2000) 'Writing about the perceived benefits of traumatic events: implications for physical health', *Personality and Social Psychology Bulletin*, 26 (2): 220–230.

Levy, L. (1999) *Undress your stress: 30 curiously fun ways to take off tension*. Naperville, IL: Sourcebooks.

Lyubomirsky, S., Sousa, L. and Dickerhoof, R. (2006) 'The costs and benefits of writing, talking, and thinking about life's triumphs and defeats', *Journal of Personality and Social Psychology*, 90 (4): 692–708.

Miller, D., Kets de Vries, M.F.R. and Toulouse, J.-M. (1982) 'Top executive locus of control and its relationship to strategy-making, structure, and environment', *The Academy of Management Journal*, 25 (2): 237–253.

Murphy, L.R. (1988) 'Workplace interventions for stress reduction and prevention', in C.L. Cooper and R.L. Payne (eds), *Causes, coping and consequences of stress at work*. Chichester: Wiley, pp. 301–342.

Pennebaker, J.W. (1993) 'Putting stress into words: health, linguistic and therapeutic implications', *Behavior Research and Therapy*, 31(6): 539–548.

Ropeik, D. (2010) *How risky is it, really? Why our fears don't always match the facts*. London: McGraw-Hill.

Rotter, J.B. (1966) 'Generalized expectancies for internal versus external control of reinforcement', *Psychological Monographs*, 80 (1): 1–28.

Tracy, B. and Stein, T.C (2012) *Kiss that frog! 12 great ways to turn negatives into positives in your life and work*. San Francisco, CA: Berrett-Koehler.

Vingerhoets, A.J.J.M., Cornelius, R.R., Van Heck, G.L. and Becht, M.C. (2000) 'Adult crying: a model and review of the literature', *Review of General Psychology*, 4 (4): 354–377.

Wiseman, R. (2009) *59 seconds: think a little change a lot*. London: Macmillan.

# 6

# Making time work

### 6.1 Chapter summary

Every day there are things that need to be completed, depending on the way time is managed this can be either easy or difficult. This reality is one that will continue throughout your entire life, both in a personal and professional sense, so it is crucial to master the skill of time management, particularly with such a finite amount of it. The fact that time management has been linked to higher performance isn't exactly a major surprise (Britton and Tesser, 1991). Managing time effectively allows you to achieve so much and at the same time live a balanced and healthy lifestyle. You should already be aware from the earlier chapter on goal setting what you want to spend your time on. Now it is about ensuring you spend your time on achieving your goals. This chapter should prove quite thought provoking by teaching you:

- effective methods to write and manage to-do lists
- how to eradicate common time wasters
- how to ensure productivity is maximised each day in an efficient and effective manner

## 6.2 To-do lists

We would immediately like to eradicate the word 'to-do list'. The word brings so much negativity and fear on everything you need to do or have not done that it is not worth using. Instead, we advocate calling it an achieve list. This sounds a lot more positive in two ways: first it is not as mundane as saying this is what I need to do; second, it implies that you have already achieved some things and so it isn't a never-ending list. In actual fact, nobody really aims to get everything done; it's just a matter of completing all the important stuff. For example, if you were to have finished everything at work, you would probably be about to lose your job. However, for the sake of simplicity, we will use the term to-do list in this chapter.

### 6.2.1 Types of to-do lists

There are many different types of to-do list and everybody advocates a different one, so which method should you use? There really is no answer to this question, it comes down to personal preferences and how best you work. However, there is one thing we both fully agree upon which is that having a long list of things to do simply does not work. This method encompasses pretty much everything that is wrong with most to-do lists, including:

- No sense of prioritisation, i.e. which tasks to do first and which to do second.
- Too negative and daunting which results in procrastination.
- Encourages choosing the easier option, i.e. doing the tasks that require the least effort even though these are the least important.

We are briefly going to talk you through some alternative methods that overcome the weaknesses of the type of to-do list highlighted above.

### 6.2.2 The time matrix

The time matrix has become a well popularised method, mainly down to Covey (2004). Essentially it is a two by two grid that splits tasks up depending on importance and urgency. Typically, it looks like the matrix shown in Figure 6.1.

This grid is pretty simple so we do not want to spend ages running through it. In summary, the idea is that you have things to do (we call them tasks) that are either important or not very important and there are tasks which are urgent (need to be done right now) and tasks where there is some time until the deadline. Clearly you should not be spending much time on tasks which are neither important nor urgent (quadrant 4) – you can get round to them if you have time one day. Similarly, you may have things which need to be done right now (if they are to be done at all) but which aren't all that important. So, you might think that it would be a good idea to be in quadrant 1. But you'd be wrong! In fact you should spend most of your time in quadrant 2. This is a proactive way of managing your to-do list as opposed to spending all your time in quadrant 1

high                              **URGENCY**                          low

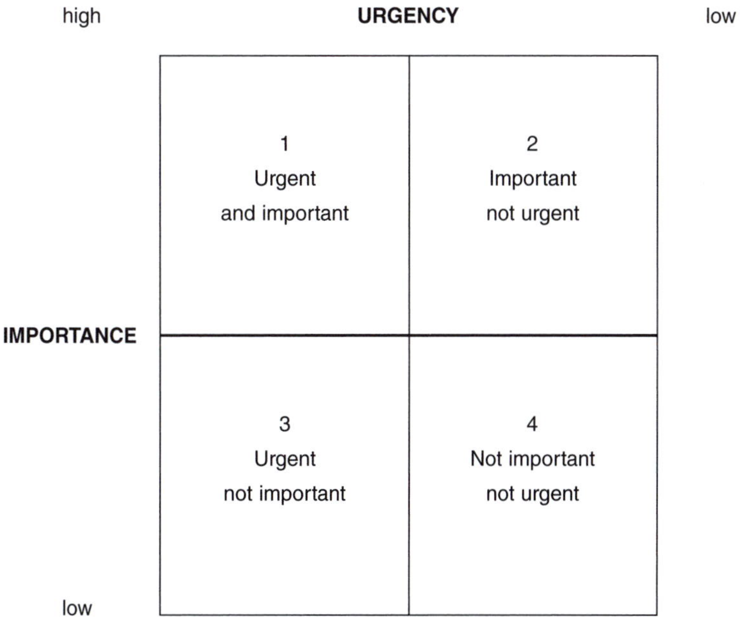

|  | 1<br>Urgent<br>and important | 2<br>Important<br>not urgent |
|---|---|---|
| **IMPORTANCE** |  |  |
|  | 3<br>Urgent<br>not important | 4<br>Not important<br>not urgent |

low

FIGURE 6.1   The time matrix

where you are managing your time reactively. This method is widely promoted though it still embeds a couple of problems with general to-do lists.

### 6.2.3 Using your calendar

Another method is to use your calendar to manage your to-do list. In essence, when a task arises you enter it into your diary. This forces you to schedule your time and set deadlines upon yourself to ensure efficiency. It also provides a good visual image of what you need to complete in a given day or week as opposed to a list which is just a lot of words on a page.

> I manage my to-do list by having a diary. In my diary I write all the lectures for each week, events, birthdays, meetings, interviews, allocate time for certain module work and even allow for hangover time. I generally stick to my plan in my diary each week and it really helps to see it and organise myself fully, especially when I am very busy with numerous deadlines coming up. Just as importantly, I also allocate enough time for fun and even more fun to help ease the stress!
>
> Victoria Saville, BSc Business and Sociology

### 6.2.4 The project style

Not many people use this style but we have seen a couple of students use it. Essentially you have a detailed list of all your projects and for each project you have a list of steps that need to be completed along with a number of deadlines. Your daily to-do list is then just looking at your project list and completing what has been scheduled for that day.

Of course these methods are not mutually exclusive, you can use elements of each of them. For example, Chris is currently using a mix of all three styles to try and create an effective diary. It is certainly weird when you use a new method but you never know until you use it. We are not going to dictate which method you should use, simply try different methods and see what works for you. There is also the decision of whether to complete these online or offline. We personally like to use paper but there are many good computer and phone applications you could use. To help you our suggestions include: Evernote, Remember the Milk and Wunderlist.

Pat remembers a moment quite recently when he suddenly felt overwhelmed by the things he needed to do. He found a whiteboard and drew a large Mind Map of all the things he had to do. He then went through the Mind Map and crossed out things that he didn't need to do and the remainder he put into order of priority. Just by dumping all these tasks and projects onto one visual map really helped him work out the priorities. He remembers feeling stressed beforehand and far, far calmer after he had spent only about half an hour on this activity. Pat's example highlights that it is a case of whatever works best for you, for some, writing on a blackboard really might not help but for Pat it worked wonders.

At university, I seem to always be busy with academic work, society commitments, social commitments, entering competitions or running small projects. I love being involved with so many different things but there has to be strict organisation otherwise it would be very difficult to fulfil the needs of all the commitments. I think my smartphone is crucial to me being able to manage my to-do list. I have all my deadlines in a calendar, reminders/alarms to remind me to do certain tasks and a plan every morning about what I set out to achieve for the day. However, it does get very overwhelming. When my to-do list becomes too hectic, I have to prioritise tasks by their deadline, urgency and time needed. If I find that it is almost impossible to carry out all the tasks to the best of my ability then my academic work always comes above anything else and I would prioritise this against other commitments.

Neil Kumar, BSc Business, Computing and IT

## 6.2.5 Improving the effectiveness of to-do lists

Whichever type of to-do list you prefer, there are common things you can embed which will improve its effectiveness. First of all, which links back to your goals, is to include fun things on your achieve list. It is surprisingly easy to forget to have fun, students can get caught up in a high level of work that can possibly start leading to stress and anxiety. In fact having fun on a list ensures it is not forgotten, adds further positivity and provides a reward for completing work.

Breaking down tasks that need to be completed into manageable actions dramatically improves the effectiveness of a to-do list. For example, stating 'complete essay' is an incorrect method as it is too daunting. Carrying this example forward, breaking down the essay into actionable stages is a lot more manageable as seen below:

- create essay title
- write 100 word essay plan
- write first 500 words
- write second 500 words
- proofread first 500 words

Immediately the difference between 'complete essay' compared to the broken down stages is evident, it is more manageable, less daunting and identifies clear steps. However, we have not listed every single step, this is to ensure that the to-do list is kept up to date and relevant by focusing on the more immediate tasks at hand. Victoria does this perfectly to achieve her rather large task of securing a placement.

> I planned to get a top placement and was conscious of how much time applications would take up. To overcome this, for two weeks straight I ensured I got up an hour earlier than planned and applied for one job every day before I got dressed. It worked and before I knew it, I had lots of interviews in the pipeline. Forming hard tasks into a mini project where I could see the light at the end of the tunnel helped me greatly, especially when I had a lot to do.
>
> Victoria Saville, BSc Business and Sociology

To further develop and support your to-do list, it is essential to have a calendar due to the amount of group meetings that you will have. Within your diary, enter your lectures, meetings and any social commitments you have.

Again, this can be done electronically with programs such as Outlook or using a paper diary which is a surprisingly popular method amongst students considering the digital age we now live in.

A final small technique which is very effective is to tick items off instead of rubbing or crossing them off. You can take this further by ticking them with a great big green highlighter or by using a tick icon if using a digital achieve list. This is something Chris regularly does and adds another element of positivity as opposed to rubbing/crossing things off and remaining with a never ending to-do list

## 6.3 Time wasters

We are both fascinated by the concept of time management and how to maximise it. The key aspect of making a to-do list work is spending time on it. Just think for five minutes, how much time do you actually spend doing what you are supposed to be doing, i.e. working on your goals and subsequently your to-do list?

An easy way to determine this is to keep a time log. For just one day write down everything you do and how long you spent on it, from brushing your

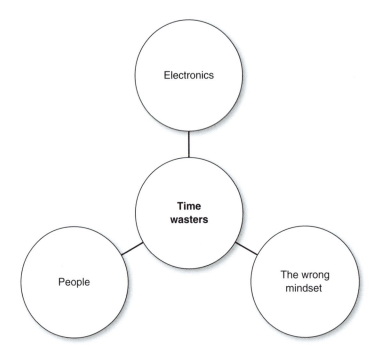

FIGURE 6.2    The main time wasters

94

teeth, watching TV to walking home. From doing this you can immediately realise how much time you waste, i.e. time not spent on achieving your goals. However, this is not a task to put you down. Instead, it is an effective method to highlight areas for development and discover time wasters that can be better managed. Do this for a few days and notice the patterns as recommended by Mackenzie (1997).

We are briefly going to talk through some of the most common time wasters and suggest some tips to overcome these. A lot of activities can waste a significant amount of time yet can be very easily eradicated. Figure 6.2 shows three key categories of time wasters which we are going to discuss.

### 6.3.1 Electronics

With technological advancements forever getting smarter everybody has now found themselves on electronic devices more than ever. Whilst this has resulted in a number of positive changes, it can play havoc with our ability to concentrate and focus.

We believe that one such time waster is TV. A lot of people will say TV is an absolute waste of time. However, it is hard to completely eradicate TV having been part of the generation that has grown up with it. An easy way to reduce the time you spend watching it is to make it as hard as possible to do so. For example, unplug your TV from the socket. The extra five seconds spent connecting your TV can easily help you eradicate it. Alternatively, you may watch internet TV which is becoming increasingly popular within student residences. If this is the case, then delete the application. On-demand TV has made this a lot easier to do. If there any programmes that you truly cannot live without then record them and watch them later as a reward using catch up TV.

Having a mobile phone within immediate reach can be a major distraction. We have so many worries nowadays and are having to constantly be alert, from texting, emailing and talking using our phones that we find it difficult sometimes to concentrate. We are all prone to this distraction and it takes real discipline to eliminate it when needed. We feel inclined to reply immediately to a message or answer a phone call. An easy way to overcome this is to put the phone on silent mode and place it in another room or even leave it at home when going out to study. No matter what you think, we do not accept the excuse that you cannot last without your phone. As we are writing this, there are more people around us using their mobile phone than studying – a quite scary thing to witness but it highlights the extent of the problem. A recent student was shocked that Chris didn't take his phone to work and stated, 'But what if your friend texts you?' The answer here is how likely is it that you will receive a majorly important phone call or text? Very unlikely is what we think, apart from a rare few students who we know that have very ill family members.

The internet is becoming a growing source for wasting time as we become more and more reliant on it. There are so many ways it can prove a distraction: social networking, email, random videos, news, etc. Thankfully, there are many ways to overcome these. To overcome email, you need to think about how often you need to check your email. We personally suggest you could get away with checking it once a day or even every couple of days. We have seen people in offices check their email every five minutes or even sit with their email open all day – this is definitely overkill and is very unhealthy. In addition, read your emails and reply to them in one go. Reading them once and then writing the reply another time means having to reread the email which is technically a waste of time. If a long response is needed, draft a quick response and then refine it the next time you look at your inbox.

What is probably more relevant is social networking as these sites are such an easy medium to waste time on. We have recently discovered that some top students use Facebook a lot. It seems that they are focused in their use of it and it is a means of them getting support from their friends rather than a distraction. Since practically all students use Facebook very frequently, it would be dumb of us to try and prevent you from using it. We just want you to use it smartly and efficiently to ensure it isn't a distraction. We suggest a couple of things to help you to do this. Download a collaboration suite so you can use all your social networks from one platform. For example, you can write a status which will be published on all your social networks and view all your messages using Hootsuite, a free and easy-to-use website. Second, block these websites and others so they cannot distract you, using a program such as Leechblock. This is a great tool which allows you to input websites that are distracting. With a simple click of a button it will block these websites and the only way to gain access it to restart your computer or to type a 64 character random password. This is something that Chris personally uses each day and loves due to its great simplicity and effectiveness.

### 6.3.2 The wrong mindset

It is no surprise that our minds can be a major source for time wasting, though often we don't realise just how severe this issue is. Little things in our mind can waste a significant amount of time, which we are briefly going to run through. You may be surprised at some of the things we point out.

*Aiming for the perfect result.* Perfectionism can consume a huge amount of time for a very small return. For example, when working on an essay, you could spend 20 or 30 extra hours making something perfect and achieve a couple of marks more. However, if you spent those 20 or 30 extra hours on something else, would you gain a greater reward? It is a fine line to know the difference between perfectionism and correction so it is a real one to watch out.

*Multitasking.* This is often carried out incorrectly and hence can waste time. As human beings, we are not as good at multitasking as we think. The misconception is that if we spend time doing multiple things simultaneously then we will get more done. However, what can happen is that less time and brain power is devoted to each task and hence people are in fact less productive. This applies to many aspects of your life which you may not have considered. For example, when in a group meeting don't check your phone to see if you have any messages. If you do, you will read it and immediately your brain will go off in another direction thus taking you away from the task in hand, i.e. the meeting. As we sit in the library, writing about this, we can see so many examples of bad multitasking:

- making notes whilst talking on the phone
- revising whilst talking to a friend
- writing an essay whilst exploring shopping websites

However, there are situations where multitasking can work, which we would like to label as multi-goaling. Obviously, we have just made this word up but we have no intention of getting into the Oxford Dictionary. What we mean by this is working on multiple goals at the same time that are complementary and can be carried out simultaneously. One of the most common examples we have witnessed is going to the gym with a friend. It allows you to work out and simultaneously spend some time with a friend though there is a balance in this case between how much exercise and socialising are achieved.

*Working for a long time without taking a break.* This is another source of the wrong mindset. Generally people significantly over estimate how long they can work for. Whenever you are working on something which requires over an hour, take a break. There really are no ifs or buts. In addition, when taking a break be sure to get away from the task in hand. For example, if you are revising for an exam and you decide to simply stop for 10 minutes then your subconscious is still going to be looking at the papers in front of you and hence thinking about the exam. Ideally, for any given break take a walk to a different room or area for at least 10 minutes. We all seem to know of that person who is able to sit in the library for hours and hours working, reading and revising all day. Let's break this myth right now, there is no such person and if there is they are not working to their full capacity, especially when studying as it takes a lot of brain power to study effectively.

*Leaving things unfinished.* All too often we leave things unfinished due to frustration and boredom – don't do it! Whenever you stop working on something like an essay be sure to leave yourself in a good place so you don't have to waste time figuring out where you got to the next time you come to work on it. For example, when you are working on an essay, finish the paragraph or journal you are on. Don't do the brash thing of just shutting the book or switching off your computer. If you have sufficient breaks and work in the right way you shouldn't get to this point. If you do just want to stop working, take a few minutes out and then quickly finish off to leave you in a healthy place for when you next come to work.

*Thinking.* This can certainly be a waste of time, and this is one thing that Chris will admit to. Self-reflection and some creative thinking are good but when you start daydreaming or thinking for long periods it can prove a big drain on your time. Returning to the example earlier in Chapter 5 on fear, Chris thought about his exam and how he was going to fail it for two hours. After he returned from hospital he realised this was in fact a great waste of time and chose instead just to concentrate on revising.

*Procrastination.* This is closely related to thinking. It is one thing which we are all familiar with. An easy way to get over procrastination is to plan to spend just 15 minutes on something. It is difficult to say you are going to spend a whole day doing something when before you know it you get bored and end up doing something else. In contrast, 15 minutes is nothing, it is a lot easier to commit to and allows you to build momentum. Often when using this technique you will find you spend longer than 15 minutes due to the momentum gained.

*Untidiness and a lack of organisation.* These can be major wasters if you need to constantly look for things. This really is a simple case of maintaining a clean and tidy desk and staying organised. We do not think there is a need to go into more detail on this as we may just end up sounding like a pestering parent. Most probably what is more important is keeping your files tidy on your computer. If you are constantly saving files and essays in multiple places then you have to waste time finding them and trying to remember which one is the latest version. You may wish to think about putting all files into one place using a website such as Dropbox where you can access your files online from anywhere in the world.

*Spending every minute trying to do something.* It may seem strange to state this as the wrong thing to do but you need to have some idle time. This is essentially time to do things that require very little if any brain power. Why is this so crucial? Simple, it gives you the time to come up with the best ideas. This could be for an application you are writing, an essay you are drafting or a business idea you are working on. This is about letting your subconscious come to life. Ways to do this are relaxing in coffee shops, jogging and random walks. Obviously you do not want to be idle all day, that is called being lazy, and it is certainly no excuse to watch TV all day.

*Commuting to university*. If you have a daily commute think how you can better use this time. For example, if you drive to university can you take the train instead and get some work done? Alternatively, can you buy a revision tape and listen to it on the way?

*The time illusion*. Due to the long deadlines imposed upon students there is a common illusion that there is loads of time left. This is a time waster in itself, watching time go by before all of a sudden a deadline draws near. We suggest that whatever deadline you get, you reduce it by at least 10 per cent. For example, if you have an essay to complete in three months' time, commit to completing it in two months. This may prove difficult at first so work your way up by handing assignments in one day early, then two days, then three and so on.

> I usually find it the most challenging bit when it comes to working hard. I always think I shouldn't push it that hard because there is loads of time left, but then, when I realise I'm three days away from the exam, I start to freak out and I'm not able to concentrate. I have worked very hard to change this even though it is not easy.
>
> Denisa Dumitrascu, BSc Human Resource Management

### 6.3.3 People

We all get frustrated with other people and just wish people could be better, smarter, quicker and so on in order not to waste so much of our time. However, often it is the things you do which determine what other people do and so there are a number of ways you can better use other people and at the same time not waste so much of your time.

This is the art of delegation! Delegation is realistically one of the most crucial things anybody can do to reduce the amount of time they waste. In an ideal world, using delegation there would be no such thing as a to-do list and instead you would just get everybody else to do things for you. Although this is somewhat unrealistic, it should be something to envisage and aim towards. This is the thing that allows directors and CEOs to get so much done. However, something that is so beneficial also has its associated costs and a certain skill level is needed to carry it out effectively, otherwise it can prove a major source of wasted time. The questions that need to be asked are:

- What tasks should I delegate?
- Who should I delegate them to?
- How do I monitor the work?

Almost on the opposite side of delegation is the skill of saying no. Having identified where you want to spend your time through your goals, you have to develop the ability to say no to people. Again, this is something people seem to struggle with as it is seen as rude or impolite. However, remember that it is ruder if you choose to take something on and then do not deliver on it. In terms of how to say no, try to explain in full why you cannot undertake something by stating what you need to work on and the possible risks to them, i.e. not completing it properly. Then to be truly helpful, offer some alternative solutions such as somebody else who might be able to help.

Finally, when it comes to people, one thing we can all be guilty of is having pointless conversations. We all like to have a good chat but just be mindful of how long these last. We are helping you to try and avoid situations where you talk and talk and afterwards have that nagging thought – what a waste of time that was.

We have discussed a lot of time wasters hence we have summarised them all in Table 6.1.

TABLE 6.1  Potential time wasters and how to avoid them

| Category | Time waster | How to overcome it |
| --- | --- | --- |
| Electronics | Watching TV | Unplug it and use catch up TV to watch any crucial programmes |
| | Mobile phone | Leave it at home and/or put it on silent |
| | The internet – social networking sites | Block time wasting websites and download a collaboration suite |
| | The internet - email | Check it every couple of days and instantly reply to emails |
| The wrong mindset | Perfectionism | Watch out for it and aim for good enough instead |
| | Multitasking | Question if it is productive and multi-goal instead |
| | Working for long periods | Take sufficient breaks and be sure to get away from the task |
| | Thinking and procrastination | Be mindful of it and try spending just 15 minutes on something |
| | Untidiness | Maintain a tidy desk policy and keep your electronic files tidy |
| | Working all day | Allocate some idle time |
| | Commuting | Ensure you do something productive |
| | Time illusion | Set yourself earlier deadlines |
| People | Delegation | Always delegate effectively when possible |
| | Taking on too much | Learn to say no |
| | Pointless conversations | Be mindful of how long they last |

## 6.4 Each day

Your to-do list will tell you what you need to complete at a given point in time. Obviously, you cannot get it all done in one day and hence there will be different things that you need to complete each day. As part of this, you will need to set a daily amount of work to complete. Having had many conversations with students this is something that is quite difficult to do. Typically, many students set themselves a heavy and unrealistic workload that they are unable to complete. At the end of the day, they feel guilty that they did not complete it all. Hence, the question arises, what exactly do you set each day?

You certainly need to set yourself a challenging workload but the key is to be realistic. For example, assuming you will be able to work every hour of the day is pretty unrealistic yet so many of us seem to have this mindset when planning out a typical day. Instead, be realistic and account for the fact that something may crop up that you did not plan for by setting some slack time in your day, for example, for a friend that may ask you for help or a phone call that may come from home. On top of this, remember that you are human and that you will need to cook, relax and socialise at some point. Sounds rather silly but many seem to forget these important needs when planning out what to do in a given day.

The same change of mindset needs to be made for deadlines as well. Many people are good at creating unrealistic deadlines. For example, today I am going to spend the whole day completing my essay. Instead create short manageable deadlines like: in this next hour I am going to write 300 words. In addition to this, arrange something fun with a friend in order to further increase motivation as well as provide a reward at the end. Rewards are very powerful in helping to get things done, from the small ones such as a coffee at the break, something that we both do, right down to the larger rewards such as some retail therapy.

Complete the most important tasks first when you begin working. Often these are also the most complicated tasks and take the most energy, so these are the ones people procrastinate from most. Get them done first so you can dedicate the maximum amount of energy and productivity to them. The day will only get better from then as well!

At the end of the day, write down or think about the things you have completed. It is so easy to focus on what you have not completed and what still needs to be done. By writing down three things you have done it forces you to be more positive. Chris started doing this six months ago and he found it amazingly difficult at first, but after six months he can list an A4 page of things he has completed each day.

Most people tend to plan their schedule and to-do list on a daily basis. A more effective time frame is a week – plan out what you need to achieve each day across a whole week. It is a more long-term technique to manage yourself.

This can be quite difficult to do, especially when you have never done it before. This is something Chris has personally tried and has struggled to carry out successfully, often just resorting to his old way of working. One way to overcome this is to use a two-day basis, once you become accustomed to this, try stretching yourself to plan a whole week.

So in answer to the earlier question, the workload you should set each day is one that is realistic, challenging, prioritised and positive just like Jenna does:

> Each day, I create a to-do list with all the tasks in priority order, along with a deadline of when each task needs to be completed by. The list even takes into account any events occurring on that particular day and daily living things I need to do such as shopping and cooking. Even if a task is not urgent, I plan to finish all tasks on the list within a few days of them being put on the list to ensure I stay on top of things.
>
> Jenna Bonfiglio, BSc Business and Management

## 6.5 Taking it to work

Once you begin working life there will be a number of things you will need to complete each week and day. If you learn to establish an effective method for managing your to-do list and time you will be able to achieve a lot more in your working life. If you choose to start your own business, it can seem like there are a million things that need to be completed simultaneously. Remember the tips provided here, particularly to prioritise commitments and maintain a healthy balance as it is all too easy to try and dedicate every working minute to your business.

> One thing that is critical to making my company work is ensuring I retain focus and I manage my time effectively. I have been caught out when I have been a 'busy fool', e.g. not strategically networking at events, doing peripheral tasks within core hours, getting distracted by irrelevant phone calls, etc. Time goes by at an incredible rate when you run your own company, and learning how to qualify it and knowing when to slog it out and when to take a break is a skill that only develops with time.
>
> Good task management is also critical. Combining a good diary system integrating Google Calendar with my iPhone and also utilising a task management system (I combine Wunderlist, Insightly and my database) works well for me. Also getting set up on a Sunday for the coming week has worked well for me and shows people that I am committed!
>
> Sanjay Aggarwal, Director, Taylor Lloyd Mason

## 6.6 How to get started

### 6.6.1 Professional

- Plan out your day tomorrow from start to finish (remember to allow for some flexibility).
- Keep a time log for two days and then review it to discover key distractions and where your time is currently spent. When we say log, we mean log absolutely everything to get a true sense of how you spend your time.
- Determine three ways you can multi-goal and try to implement these in the coming week.

### 6.6.2 A little more interesting

- Ask a friend how organised and effective you are at managing your time, you may be somewhat surprised to hear their thoughts.
- Try not to watch TV for a whole week and see what it feels like by the end of the week.
- For one day, go to work in the library or a local cafe and leave your phone at home. Chances are, you will realise you have missed no majorly important texts or phone calls.

## 6.7 Our bookshelf

Allen, D. (2001) *Getting things done.* London: Piatkus.
This is one of the most famous books on time management and we thoroughly recommend it – Pat is a particular fan of this work. David Allen's book revolves around the 'do it, delegate it, defer it, drop it' principle and teaches you how to live by this to achieve more and feel less stressed. He also provides a great deal of information to better use electronic programs like Microsoft Office to help you achieve your goals. We suggest reading this for its detailed information and entertaining nature.

Ferriss, T. (2007) *The 4 hour work week.* London: Random House.
This is a very interesting read on how one person got his business work week down to four hours to give him plenty of money and time to do everything he wanted to. There is a lot to take away from this book in terms of how to manage time and it also makes for an entertaining read so we definitely recommend a lot of the ideas – though we chose not to take his advice on getting an online personal assistant from India!

Bannatyne, D. (2010) *How to be smart with your time: expert advice from the star of Dragons' Den.* London: Orion.
In the entertaining style Duncan uses on *Dragons' Den*, he gives straight-forward advice on how to identify what you wish to do with your time and then how to make the most out of it to ensure you achieve it. It is a very

easy book to read and comes with a number of exercises to really get you thinking.

## 6.8 References

Britton, B.K. and Tesser, A. (1991) 'Effects of time-management practices on college grades', *Journal of Educational Psychology*, 83 (3): 405–410.

Covey, S.R. (2004) *The 7 habits of highly effective people.* London: Simon & Schuster.

MacKenzie, A. (1997) *The time trap: the classic book on time management.* New York: AMACOM.

# 7

# Leading and being led

## 7.1 Chapter summary

Whilst it isn't that controversial to say that leadership is important in the workplace, it isn't perhaps obvious why this should be the subject of a chapter in this book. So let us start off by explaining why it is here and what you can get out of it. In terms of being a leader, you will be asked to work in groups throughout your university career and beyond, so sometimes you will be the leader and other times you will be led. We aim to set in motion ideas in this area which you will be able to develop throughout your career. This chapter will give you the foundations from which your thinking and your practice will develop.

## 7.2 Leadership – facts and myths

The fact is that everybody has potential to become a leader in some way and we will all be called upon to take the lead – albeit some more than others. When Pat lectures on leadership, he often asks students to name a leader they admire. Commonly people will name famous politicians (Gandhi, Churchill and Martin Luther King are often cited) or sports people (Sir Alex Ferguson, Ricky Ponting, Sachin Tendulkar) and sometimes military commanders (von Paulus, Nelson, Montgomery) and sometimes business people (Sir Richard Branson is the most frequently cited). It seems we understand that leadership is important and when nominating these leaders as outstanding, words such as 'inspirational' will often be used. Whilst you are at university, we don't expect you to be one of these charismatic leaders. But you are essentially at university to prepare to become a leader when you start work and we think there are many opportunities to start your learning about the practicalities of leadership.

Can anyone learn to be a leader? To be honest, researchers don't yet agree on the answer to this question – and maybe they never will. It is fair to say that current thinking amongst scholars in the field is that different situations require different leadership styles and what style you are most comfortable with depends a great deal on your personality. In broad terms, style can be considered as how you interact with people. For example, an important part of this is how closely you monitor what other people are doing. A directive style of leadership means you tell people clearly what they have to do and how they should do it. A directive leader is quite likely to check up on what people are doing. A *laissez-faire* leader on the other hand will be more likely to let people get on with their work and might check in from time to time. Somewhere in the middle would be a consultative leader who would try to find out people's views and incorporate these into any plans if possible. It is a matter of personality which sort of style we are most comfortable with. But, the situation determines what style would be best. So, when leading a team of well-motivated professionals, it is unlikely that the individuals in the team would welcome too much interference in their everyday work. However, Pat has worked a lot with the Fire Service and despite the firefighters on the scene of an incident being professional, there are times when the Incident Commander would be very directive to ensure the safety of everyone involved. On the other hand, many other situations at work are best suited to a more consultative approach. The authors of this book are good examples of different styles. Pat's natural inclination is to think of the big picture and long term whereas Chris is much more detail focused. They have had different tasks in producing this book – Chris has often had to chase Pat to keep him to deadlines. Knowing that is his strength, Pat is very happy for him to do this. Pat also knows that not all jobs are suited to this character trait. He was recently approached for a new job that would have required him to work out the timetable for a department and also monitor the workload of all staff. He immediately knew this was not the right job for him.

A useful way of thinking about leadership style is to think about whether you are focused on the people in your team or the task in hand – and as we will show, this changes over time. Think of it in a two by two matrix (adapted from Blake and Mouton, 1966), as illustrated in Figure 7.1.

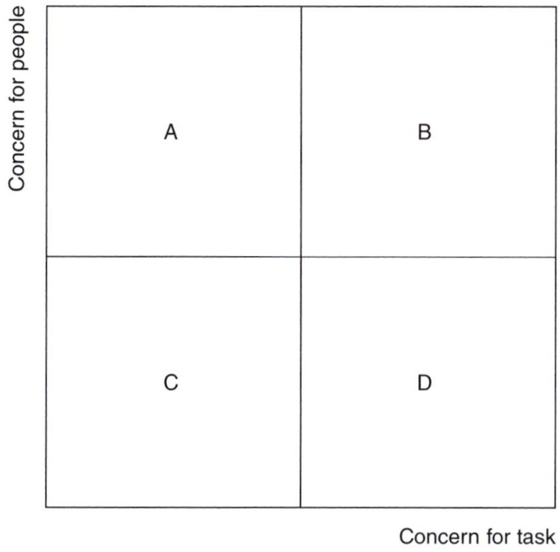

FIGURE 7.1   Blake and Mouton matrix (1966)

If you are in the A quadrant, you have low concern for the task but high concern for the people in the team. Probably this is a good place to be at the start of a project such as group coursework. You need to get to know the people in your team before you start working on the assignment. And do take time to do this so you know what makes everyone tick. What are everyone's interests, motivations, strengths, weaknesses? Once you have established this, you can get to work. The B quadrant is where the task is very important and also the team is as well. This might be when you are at the planning stage of the project where you are still discovering what it is like to work with your team but you now need to do some serious planning about what you are going to do. Quadrant C is where neither the team nor the task are important. We can't really see when this might be the case – perhaps it is when the group isn't really assigned to any task in particular so you can get on with your own work. And quadrant D is where the task is important but the people less so. We think of this as being the sort of time when perhaps the deadline approaches and you still have last minute work to do. In this situation, only the task matters and how people are getting on with each other in the team, for example, isn't all that important – you can deal with disagreements later. There are times when all you need to do is work on the task in hand.

However, a word of caution about using this matrix: in Pat's experience, leaders tend to focus too much on the task and not enough on the team. So, make sure you are working in the right area and giving more attention to your team than you would naturally think is necessary.

Hersey and Blanchard (1977) also have some useful ideas on leadership style and situation which are related to this matrix. They identified four different leadership styles that could be adopted depending on the situation:

*Telling* (high task/low relationship behaviour). This means providing a lot of instructions to people and giving a lot of attention to defining jobs and goals. Sometimes this is recommended for leading new staff, when the work is repetitive or when under time pressure.

*Selling* (high task/high relationship behaviour). The leader still gives quite a lot of direction but also tries to get people to 'buy into' the task. Sometimes called a coaching approach, it works best when people are motivated but still need some guidance.

*Participating* (high relationship/low task behaviour). In this style, decision making is shared between leaders and the team. In fact this is most likely what you will experience in most coursework groups at university. Perhaps you or someone else takes on the role of communicating and coordinating things.

*Delegating* (low relationship/low task behaviour). The leader identifies the tasks that need to be done but then delegates the completion to the team. It is useful when people know what they have to do and are motivated to do it.

Studying my marketing strategy module I had to step up and become a leader. It was a difficult task as with little previous leadership experience I had to develop my style as I went. I tried to be a democratic understanding leader at all times. However, this didn't prove to be effective as after a couple of sessions it was clear some group members were constantly not delivering against their specific objectives. Thus I required a different approach and had to be more autocratic, instructing individuals what was expected of them and setting clear deadlines. This delivered better results from the individuals who had previously not responded well to the democratic approach. However, some group members who had been delivering fed back that they were unhappy with their limited input. This taught me a valuable lesson that in all aspects of life it is important to adapt your leadership style to the situation and the person. Once I had figured this out, the group operated smoothly and we delivered a successful piece of coursework that got a first.

Sunna Van Kampen, BSc Management and Strategy

In broad terms, as a leader you need to think about the following:

- your own personality and strengths
- what the task is
- who the people involved are

# 7.3 Common leadership mistakes by students – and everyone else for that matter!

### 7.3.1 Different types of leaders

Perhaps we have seen someone we admire as a leader and we try to emulate them. There is nothing wrong with noting what leaders do well and seeing how to apply that in our own lives. However, the very best leaders develop their own style rather than try to copy someone else's. So, find the style that is going to suit your personality and play to your strengths. If you are a detail-conscious person, fine. If you are a big picture person that is also fine. But don't adopt a style that goes against who you really are as a person.

### 7.3.2 Being the leader for the sake of it

We see people who try to take over the lead just because they want to be known as the leader. Only ever take on the lead if you really believe that you have something to offer the team by doing so. We know that some people are naturally more bossy than others and so the bossy ones perhaps will take the lead more often than the others. But it doesn't mean to say this is the best thing for the team. Ask yourself this simple question: are you the right person to take on this role? In doing so you have to know beforehand what you are best at. So, you can't really decide whether you are going to take on the lead unless you really understand what your own strengths are.

Sometimes you have to lead – either because you have been nominated as such or because someone has to and it might have to be you. So how can you make yourself become the leader of the group? The key here is that you should be a leader because you make things happen and not by forcing others to say 'you're in charge', just like Shivani did so well in the example below. And don't make the mistake of thinking that you are the 'best' person in the group just because you are the leader. In a well-functioning team, everyone has their role to play and being the leader is just another role.

During my Business Game presentation, individuals within my team became extremely nervous before the presentation. This resulted in these negative feelings spreading within the team and resulted in a feeling of anxiety. As Managing Director, I felt action was required on my behalf and therefore I called a team meeting. I motivated the team and

*(Continued)*

109

*(Continued)*

highlighted that it would only be a short period of time each member would be present-ing. My attempts to fill my team with confidence through the use of positivity worked well and the presentation was a success. I learnt from this experience that negativity can have a bad effect on team performance, however positivity is equally powerful and by using it effectively, it can be extremely beneficial to team performance.

Shivani Sharma, BSc Marketing

## 7.4 Being led

Despite your instincts perhaps pushing you to take charge, there are times when it is better to recognise that someone else is far more suited to be the leader. This is not a sign of weakness in you and you should not always be in the lead. Rather it is a sign of maturity in that you recognise there are circum-stances where the team will benefit more from you taking on a different role. Pat often finds himself in a support role at work when an event is planned, he can be seen sticking up notices, printing things off or even moving chairs around. In those situations, the people who have put the event together are in the lead and his role is to support them in whatever way is necessary to get the project finished. The important thing to remember is that you still have a role to play and you should not sulk because it isn't you calling the shots.

### 7.4.1 Feedback

We describe how to get feedback from lecturers in Chapter 4 but this is such an important topic we are also going to discuss it here in the context of lead-ership skills.

Pat remembers working with a consultancy which had this mantra:

feedback is a gift

At first, he thought this was just consultant waffle – how can it be a gift? Feedback is often difficult and unpleasant. But after a while he realised what this really means. If we want to become better at our job and especially if we want to be able to take on more responsibility (i.e. be promoted), we have to develop new skills. The best way of improving our performance is to seek out feedback constantly and then act on it. The key thinking in this area comes from Donald Schön (1991) and is summarised in Figure 7.2.

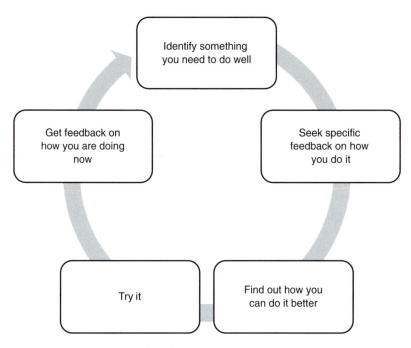

FIGURE 7.2   Learning from feedback

In some ways this is pretty straightforward. The difficulty comes in actually doing it. It is often difficult to admit to yourself that you need to change the way you are working and even more difficult to admit that you are doing something poorly.

As a member of the Professional Mentoring Scheme at my university, listening skills were very important when it came to meetings with my mentor. Sometimes I have a habit of talking for England and not allowing anyone a word in the conversation. My mentor soon noticed this and sat me down whilst forbidding me to talk for five minutes. He explained how when it comes to interviews they have an allocated time frame to get through all of their questions and if I spend too much time talking about one subject and do not finish all the questions it would reflect poorly on myself. As I was forbidden to talk for five minutes, it meant I paid full attention to what he had to say resulting in me changing my ways of talking too much. The knock on effect of this resulted in me securing a placement as I knew exactly when to talk and when to listen.

Lewis Boot, BSc International Business and Management

We love the example from Lewis as he illustrates a great awareness of his weakness, talking too much. Our main advice stems from this and it is important to be specific about what you are looking to change. It isn't useful to say 'I need to do better in team meetings'. First work out what you did well and what you need to work on. For example, did you speak enough? Or did you speak too much? Did you take on too many tasks personally? Or did you hide in the background? Once you know what to work on, then you can set yourself some goals for change. So, if you are someone who talks too much in team meetings, set yourself the goal of not speaking at all for the first 10 minutes of the meeting. Or if you don't speak out enough, set yourself the task of saying something in the first five minutes, for example.

The key is you should always ask for feedback – especially from people who you trust and whose opinion you value. Tell them why you are asking and ask them specifically. So you might say, 'I have a feeling I am speaking too much in team meetings. I'd really like to work on this as it must be annoying for other people and is preventing them from contributing. Tell me honestly, do you think this is the case?' Then you can ask more specifically about instances where you spoke perhaps without adding value. Then you can ask about things you might try differently. But make it specific and something you can work on. And always come back for more feedback after you have worked on it. This shows you have listened and are trying to improve.

### 7.4.2 Seeking advice

Perhaps the best place to receive feedback in a structured way is through mentoring schemes. Most universities have this sort of scheme where more experienced students are paired with newer students so they can learn how to get on at university. We find that very often other students can be a great source of advice about their experience of going through what it is you are going through.

As an EU student, coming from a non-English speaking country, I had a great number of questions about life at university from simple things such as the best mobile phone provider or bank to questions related to my course. My e-mentor managed to answer all my questions via e-mail and she always included more hints and tips and some personal examples about how she managed to overcome the same difficulties. I was extremely privileged to have the mentor that I had, as her help was extremely useful and it helped me to aim for more and be more confident in my skills and knowledge. As the scheme had a great influence on me I decided to become a mentor myself and tried to show a similar attitude and provide the same help to my mentee. She is now part of various societies, does extremely well in her modules and she told me how much my help benefited her throughout this academic year.

Timea Bianca Tyukodi, BSc International Business and Management

Some universities also offer the opportunity to be mentored by external people. At Aston we have experienced managers mentoring second year undergraduates and the students tell us they benefit enormously from the expertise of people who are several years into their careers. With any mentoring scheme, you will only get out of the scheme what you put into it so it is important that you are proactive. Ask questions and push your mentor for all the advice and experience you can (within reason – don't become a nuisance!). Try to open out your conversations beyond the immediate issues of university study and into areas such as leadership. Describe situations you think have gone well or not so well and ask for their advice on how you might have done things differently.

The professional mentoring scheme has been beneficial for me on a number of levels. My mentor has offered a different perspective on challenges that I have faced and on life in general. Decisions are not black and white – the mentoring scheme has encouraged me to generate alternative solutions and to be analytical of everything. I am still in regular contact with my mentor even though the scheme has ended, and self-confidence in my abilities has increased having been able to work on addressing my weaknesses. My mentor also provides constant support to enable me to set and achieve career goals.

Jenna Bonfiglio, BSc Business and Management

Aside from these set schemes, you can seek mentoring advice from people you respect – both inside and outside university. The truth is that people like being asked for their advice and although it can vary in its quality, you can pick and choose which advice you decide to take. But also remember, sometimes if advice makes you feel uncomfortable, it is possibly because you know deep down it is right. Your lecturers can be a great source of mentoring advice and we have more about this in Chapter 4, which focuses on how to get the best out of your lecturers. Family friends can be a great place for mentoring advice. Pat has one family friend who has been a great source of advice about how to get on in academic life. These are people who are on your side and whilst they might not understand the nitty gritty of your course, they might be able to help with your general approach to things like managing team meetings and such like.

Finally, you can reach out to a very large population through LinkedIn. The concept of this professional social network is to link people who already know each other. But these days it is also OK to contact people with whom you have perhaps a very tenuous link. The best approach is to be honest from the outset why you are contacting them – edit the contact notification so it is personal and clearly state what you are seeking from them.

## 7.5 Taking it to work

We have focused on the issue of leadership and being led in the context of student life, but of course these two roles are core features of the workplace. At work the role of manager or leader tends to be set out more clearly than at university and you might think that because you are not the designated leader or manager, this means you have no choice but to remain in the 'follower' category. This is not really true. In order to get ahead at work, you need to be demonstrating your leadership abilities before you are placed into a position where this is formally part of your job description. But trying to take charge all the time can be a risky strategy because it can be inappropriate and can really annoy people. A certain degree of pushiness is a good thing but be sensitive to how your ambition is impinging on others. Our advice is to push your ideas and your contribution when you can genuinely add value. At other times you can show your commitment to team and organisational goals by being a dedicated worker and just getting on with the tasks in hand. A lot of how you play this at work depends on the culture of the business (i.e. how aggressive it is) and also whether you really understand enough about the job to be able to impose your views on the team. How you balance this is crucial and stems from your self-understanding and how you read other people. And this is further underscored by how you go about getting quality feedback from people around you.

## 7.6 How to get started

### 7.6.1 Professional

- Join a professional or peer mentoring scheme as a mentee.
- Find someone outside university who can provide you with some useful feedback.
- If you are not naturally the leader, try leading a group meeting to develop your skills.

### 7.6.2 A little more interesting

- Participate in a mentoring scheme as a mentor.
- Ask for feedback from three of your friends on something you do which you think might be holding you back.
- Lead a new society or apply for a president position.

## 7.7 References

Blake, R.R. and Mouton, J.S. (1966) 'Some effects of managerial grid training on union and management attitudes towards supervision', *Journal of Applied Behavioral Science*, 2 (4): 387–400.

Hersey, P. and Blanchard, K.H. (1977) *The management of organizational behaviour* (3rd edn). Upper Saddle River, NJ: Prentice Hall.

Schön, D.A. (1991) *The reflective practitioner: how professionals think in action.* Cambridge, MA: Basic Books.

# 8

# Working in groups

### 8.1 Chapter summary

Team working is an essential skill which is now sought after by employers and hence universities have sought to develop these skills through group projects. We know that these projects are very unpopular with students but they are not likely to go away so it is really important that you learn how to manage them properly. This chapter serves as a practical and pragmatic introduction to working with others in a team. The lessons learned will serve you well in the future too!

## 8.2 Group assignments

These can prove demanding – talking to many students and from the recent experience of Chris it seems that at some stages group projects are where students dedicate most of their time. As a student, you are part of a number of groups, such as those shown in Figure 8.1.

Because you are working in groups so much of the time, it is easy to see that learning to work effectively within a group is a valuable skill and a key time saver. The fact that many students are required to undertake two, three or even five group projects simultaneously just furthers the importance of this skill. We hope this chapter will allow you to maximise the performance of all the groups you are a part of, particularly coursework groups, which are going to be our real focus here.

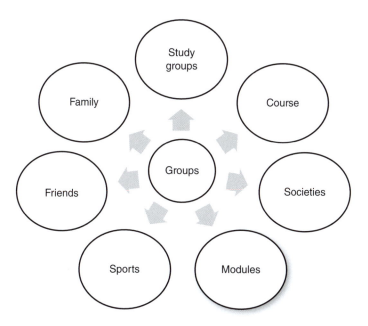

FIGURE 8.1   Some of the groups you are in

## 8.2.1 Benefits of group work

Group projects are a relatively new phenomenon at universities and early advocates shouted loudly about the potential benefits (Gamson, 1994). Already though, we have found a growing number of students growing frustrated with group work, which seems to come down to a few key reasons:

- group members don't get on with each other
- lack of motivation from certain members due to social loafing
- perceived lack of ability within the group

The reasons highlighted can be overcome and consequently group work can prove very rewarding and present many benefits. 'Students break down stereotypes, learn to work together in groups, develop listening skills, learn the art of compromising and negotiating, learn interpersonal skills, and are exposed to a variety of different people' (Cabrera et al., 2002: 31). Another benefit, which is often forgotten, is that you can make some great friends. Chris personally knows this having made one of his closest friends through a final year group project. You must also remember that the core idea of creating a group is that it will be able to perform at a higher level than any of the individuals would be able to achieve on their own, this seems all too easy to forget when thoughts occur such as 'I wish I could do this by myself'. A wealth of research has proved that when students work together they perform at a higher level (Slavin, 1983). Maxwell (2001) identifies this as one of the laws of team working and concludes that every successful individual has had a team behind them. You can apply this in your own life to times when you thought you worked alone, for example, at college there would have been a whole team behind you – family, friends, teachers and partners.

> When we work cooperatively we accomplish infinitely more than if we work individually. (West, 2012: 15)

### 8.2.2 Group processes

It is useful to briefly cover some theory about group work so you can better understand how to get the most out of it. The model by Tuckman (1965) has become well accepted in practice – although some academics grumble about the theoretical basis of it. But Pat's experience is that it is a powerful tool for groups to understand how to work together, so it is the model we have chosen to explain how groups work, it has even been linked to academic groups to find that they go through this process (Kormanski, 1990). In brief, the model is a five step process as shown in Figure 8.2:

FIGURE 8.2    Summary of Tuckman (1965)

### 8.2.2.1 Forming (orientation)

As you haven't met before, you start off being polite and not wanting to make a bad impression on the others. Because of this, group members are quite reserved and don't share very much information about themselves. Ironically this is when members are judging each other and so should be sharing as much about themselves as possible.

### 8.2.2.2 Storming (dissatisfaction/conflict)

Eventually politeness from the forming stage cannot last and conflict occurs. As the name suggests arguments are likely to happen at this stage as you are not yet used to working with each other. It is also possible that sub-groups or cliques might form where like-minded people cluster together in some way. If this happens, it is a real danger sign! Your group must find a way of working together in order to complete the assignment set which often requires that everyone in the group must contribute. Essentially, you (or someone in the group) need to find a way of moving the group to the next stage.

### 8.2.2.3 Norming (resolution/cooperation)

The group should find ways of coming up with rules. Sometimes it is necessary to write these out. When Pat works with teams in the workplace, this process is called 'team chartering' and is essentially a contract that everyone agrees to. Sometimes this is written on a large sheet of paper which is stuck on the wall whenever the team meets. You probably will not need anything quite so formal but you will need to find some rules or 'norms' of behaviour to get the team to work together properly. Once these are in place, conflict begins to disappear and so the team starts to settle. The group begins to scope out roles for each member and set processes that each group member understands. Perhaps this might be something like this: 'We all turn up on time, to do the work we have agreed to do – no excuses! Everyone gets to put their case and we treat each other with respect. No matter what'.

### 8.2.2.4 Performing (productivity)

This is the best stage for a team, where you all feel comfortable within the group and are able to work together in a productive, open and cooperative manner. By reaching this stage, it is pretty much guaranteed that you will be producing good work and as the results start to emerge, such as a section of a report, the group begins to form a picture of how well it will perform. The performing stage is not characterised by a total lack of conflict though. It is vitally important that team members present different ideas – that is the whole point of working in a team! But the high performing team will recognise conflict and know how to deal with it.

### 8.2.2.5 Adjourning (completion)

All university groups eventually complete the project and the group breaks up.

It is important to highlight that groups must go through each stage to effectively perform, by skipping a stage a group is at risk of not performing as highly as it could. It is not easy for a group to go through each stage and it does not happen naturally. It takes a proactive approach and hard work.

All the tips in this chapter are designed to help you take your group through these stages in a natural and productive manner.

## 8.3 Group members

At the heart of any group is a bunch of people who need to get along in order to perform. From this simple logic, many people think it is best to work with friends. However, this is not true. The majority of the time, group members are selected on a random basis by the university but if you do get the opportunity to select members then be sure not to select friends. It may seem a good idea but when times get tough and dysfunctional conflict arises it can be very tough to manage and overcome. The question now arises: who exactly should you pick? In an ideal world, you would select the lecturer but, unfortunately, this is not possible. In order to answer this it makes sense to look at the composition of groups who have been found to perform best.

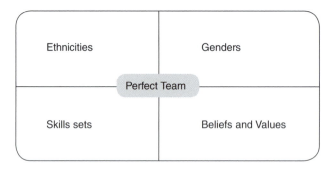

FIGURE 8.3    Team diversity

Figure 8.3 shows how a perfect team will *not* be one ethnicity, one gender, etc. The best teams have the widest diversity of people in them – in any way you care to measure diversity. The difficulty is that this idea seems odd because we tend to like people like ourselves. For example, most people would pick to work with people who have similar beliefs and values. In this case, the group is likely to go through the first two stages quite fast and thus begin performing. However, if group members have the same beliefs and values then there will not be much debate or productive conflict as everybody thinks in the same way. By having members with differing beliefs and values, alternative viewpoints can be generated and subsequently stronger decisions can be made. Unfortunately guys, research also shows that in most situations the more women in a group, the higher the group will perform. At the core of all these recommendations is almost a U-shape where the benefits begin to diminish rapidly at either end of the extreme. For example, two 10 year olds working with two 80 year olds is not likely to work.

There is also the question of how many people to select. The general recommendation is to have no more than eight people as anything over tends be too many – too many cooks spoil the broth. Of course, the size of your coursework group is usually determined by the lecturer so there is little you can do. But be aware that if you are allocated into a group of (say) 12, this will be difficult and you might ask your lecturer if it is acceptable for you to split the task and divide your group accordingly.

Chris had the privilege of choosing his group members in one of his economics modules. He did not know anybody in the class and thus even if he wanted to, could not pick his friends. This forced him to reach out and look at what group he could pick. He immediately spotted the members he wanted to choose, namely down to the fact that the majority of the group members were very clever and it worked out well for Chris as the group got 71 per cent for their presentation. Upon reflection, Chris realised it was the perfect group: there were a mix of genders, different skills sets, three different ethnicities and contrasting beliefs and values.

## 8.3.1 Multicultural members

We briefly want to touch on multicultural groups. Due to the globalising nature of the world and the fact that economic growth is predominantly coming from across the world universities are taking on an increasing number of international students. Because of this, you are very likely, almost guaranteed to be working with international students. This presents a particular challenge and can prove difficult, for example, some things that are 'normal' to you may be different around the world, for example:

- time is not respected by some cultures
- some cultures appear more aggressive than others
- some cultures hide their feelings more than others

Of all the problems most common in multicultural teams, trouble with accents and the directness of communication are most evident, and these have been found to produce negative effects within groups (Brett et al., 2006). This can cause working relationships to suffer as members perceive each other in the wrong manner and cause some members to be unable to present their knowledge and thus lead others to question their capabilities.

> Cultural differences can create substantial obstacles to effective teamwork – but these may be subtle and difficult to recognise until significant damage has already been done. (Brett et al., 2006: 90)

We know this is a common problem through our research. However, there is not the option of getting a new team member or leaving the group and nor should you wish to. Instead, you have to learn to adapt in order to get the most out of each member.

Now here is a really valuable quote for you to remember:

> Nonfluent team members may well be the most expert on the team, but their difficulty communicating knowledge makes it hard for the team to recognise and utilize their expertise. (Brett et al., 2006: 91)

I had to produce a strategy report for the BBC and I was allocated a group that consisted of all international students. I remained un-phased by the situation where many other students got frustrated and angry. Instead, I wondered how I was going to get the most out of each member. To allow this, I really treated them on an equal basis by allowing them to openly express their opinions and trusting them to complete the delegated work. In the end, we did really well and achieved a first class mark.

Alex Howorth, BSc International Business and Economics

## 8.4 Group meetings

Group meetings can end up taking more time than producing the work. They are absolutely critical in business but they are often carried out poorly which costs businesses a significant amount of money and time (Green and Lazarus, 1991). The great news is that it does not have to be this way; meetings can be made effective and efficient and we want to show you how. In fact, the issue of how to conduct meetings should be perhaps the very first thing you decide on. The key to success is to answer the five key questions in Figure 8.4.

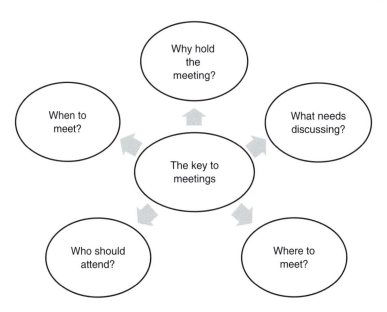

FIGURE 8.4   The five key questions for team meetings

## 8.4.1 Why hold the meeting?

This is the most important of them all, meetings should only be held if there are clear reasons to do so, and it comes back to the idea of working with the end in mind. Without determining the why, people question why they need to turn up and nobody will know if the meeting has been a success. Some key goals for holding a group meeting are:

- establish an understanding of the project
- decide upon a topic for an essay
- generate new ideas for a section of a report or for a product/business to focus on
- proofread the final work
- review progress and determine what needs to be completed

## 8.4.2 What to discuss?

This part is simply expanding upon the goals by providing a brief list of three to five points that need to be discussed. Ideally, you would have three to five sub-points for each goal – a Mind Map works perfectly in this instance. Once you sit down as a group, it is a good idea to write these down on a flipchart or whiteboard so everybody knows the agenda. At the start of every meeting, a brief review of what was discussed at the last meeting should be included and at the end you should give members the opportunity to discuss any other business, i.e. anything else people wish to discuss.

### 8.4.3 Where to meet?

Most often, groups will meet in one place but meeting up in different places can work wonders for generating fresh ideas. This does imply you need to physically meet up which is not actually the case. Advances in technology have meant many groups and teams can meet virtually. This is very easy to do nowadays with a range of free websites including Skype and Facebook which we are sure you are aware of. This may be a viable option if group members live a long distance from each other or if somebody goes away for a long period. If you are going to meet virtually treat it just like a physical meeting and follow everything we have discussed. Do ensure that wherever you meet you have the necessary equipment. For example, do you need a projector, flipchart or even some Post-it notes? The decision of where to meet comes down to the goals of the meeting, Figure 8.5 gives some options.

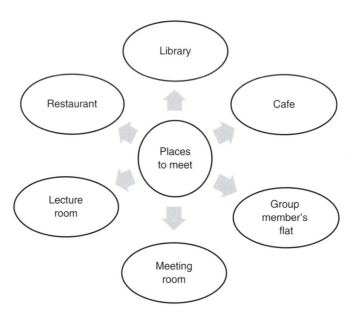

FIGURE 8.5   Places groups might meet

### 8.4.4 Who should attend?

The automatic default when it comes to student meetings is to invite every-body. Whilst this may suit many of the meetings, have a think beforehand about whether this has to be the case. For example, do two people need to get together to work on a certain section of the report? As you are starting to learn, the answer to this question depends on the goals of the meeting.

### 8.4.5 When to meet?

Taking into account individual preferences, does the time of the meeting need to be adjusted? For example, we know many students are happy to sleep in during the morning and work late into the night. Does this mean that the group may need to meet later in the evening? It may well do if it suits everybody.

### 8.4.6 The agenda and running the meeting

The answers to all these questions will fit together to create an agenda for the meeting, a one page document that will outline the objectives of the meeting, what is going to be discussed, where the meeting will take place, who is needed and when it will take place. The agenda should be sent to group members in advance of the meeting so everybody is clear of what to expect. It is then important to run through the agenda at the start of the meeting to ensure everybody is aware of it in case anybody forgot to read it. It also helps to keep the meeting on topic when it goes off on a tangent.

Whilst running the meeting be sure that one member make notes using a standard template and reads the notes back at the end of meeting to ensure everybody is clear. In addition, share these minutes amongst the group after the meeting to act as a reminder, they also provide great references if any disputes occur. Ideally, meetings should last no longer than an hour. Meetings that go on for hours are not an efficient way of working as group members begin to lose concentration and productivity decreases. Nonetheless, we do understand that long meetings are sometimes required, especially for students where last minute working is a popular option! If so, ensure frequent breaks are taken and try to have a change of location to keep things fresh. For example, a group Chris was in had a very long meeting (the day before the deadline, that's right, it happens to the best of us). After working for a few hours in the library, they decided to get something to eat at the pub and enjoyed a few practical jokes with each other. Once they finished eating, they then had a change by working in another building. The meeting lasted 15 hours but the work was completed and they achieved a first class mark. The changing of locations, getting a bite to eat and carrying out some practical jokes helped to keep the group laughing and working in what could have been a very stressful session.

## 8.5 The first meeting

The first meeting is a special case mainly due to the probability that group members have not met before. It will take slightly more time as well but this is fine, it will play a crucial role in the forming stage. Following the approach from above with the five key questions, we want to provide some guidelines, particularly on why hold the meeting and what topics to discuss.

### 8.5.1 Decide upon the target grade

Determining the target grade is fundamental in order to create a common purpose. If one person is seeking a first and yet another group member is seeking a 2:1 then conflict will inevitably arise. Establishing a common goal ensures this is avoided and helps members to form as a group.

### 8.5.2 Decide upon a role for each group member

It is important to determine a role for each group member and that each member voluntarily buys in to it. Doing so eradicates the issue of social loafing as it makes people feel important and valuable to the group and it overcomes the risk of losing out on valuable skills. To avoid falling into this trap, set effective roles by:

- Remembering that whoever is in your group, they are at the same university hence they have just as high a skill set and level of knowledge as you. Subsequently, they are able to produce many things that will be of value and, importantly, just as well as you could.
- Creating SMART roles just like goals (see Chapter 1 for more detail on goals). For example, telling a group member to proofread the work and make it good does not mean much. Exactly what is meant by 'good'? Defining these questions can ensure group members are more motivated, understand more clearly what they need to achieve and help to align expectations.
- Ensuring each group member buys in to their role, forcing a role upon somebody simply is not going to work in the long term. Ideally let each member select a role for him or herself.

In terms of actual roles, selecting a certain section for each group member seems to be the most popular method used by students as it ensures an equal workload. An alternative approach to consider is giving each member a certain focus, for example, one member writing, another editing and one proofreading. The most important role is that of leader but we do realise that this occurs quite informally within groups – most usually a case of who takes control of the group/who shouts the loudest. At the same time, leading a group is not the responsibility of just one person. Each person has the responsibility to lead a group whenever necessary, for example, if they do not agree with where the team or leader is heading then that person needs to speak up about it.

> Within our degree programme, we are required to undertake a working with language data module that includes group work. I always believed that the best way to complete group work is to set deadlines and goals as a way of keeping track of what stage of the project everyone is up to and how we can come together at the end to improve the whole of the work. We had divided the workload between us and given sections to each member to complete in our own time: this was then given a time limit of three weeks so that we could all return as a group and discuss what we had completed. The result was that each group member completed the work and we received the mark that we were after.
>
> Charlotte Voss, BSc English Language

### 8.5.3 Decide upon methods of working and communicating

In the first meeting, it is crucial to establish how the team will communicate and when it will meet up to save time further down the line and to begin creating an open environment. This should be relatively easy to do – before you leave, organise the next meeting and suggest having it at a set time each week, every two weeks or every month depending on the scale of the project. Alternatively, if there is no one set date create two or three times which are good for the whole group. Then when arranging meetings you can have the set times to choose from. As part of this, establish where you are going to meet up to save more time. Be sure to share phone numbers, email addresses and Facebook contact details depending on what methods you have chosen. This all contributes to gelling as a team in those crucial early stages.

To help work collaboratively we suggest that you set up an online working group where you will be able to review work together, have a group conversation, post meeting documents and set up meeting times. There are many programs out there and our favourites are Facebook, Dropbox and Google Docs. We personally prefer Dropbox as it is so easy to use. Nonetheless, the programs can be used in conjunction with each other to great effect. For example, you can use Facebook to have an online discussion and use Dropbox to store documents.

In my Business Game module, communication was key to ensuring we knew exactly what individual members had to do to achieve the superordinate goals we had set. From this we decided that social media such as Facebook would be the easiest form of communication as the majority of our generation has it. This proved an extremely efficient way of communicating, as we were able to place all of our ideas on the group and keep a detailed record of our minutes. The fact that we could upload the different development stages of our assignment was extremely beneficial as it meant we were able to download and continue working on them no matter where we were. Another aspect of the Facebook group which came in very useful was monitoring exactly who was contributing to the group and who was slacking, this was because of Facebook's 'seen' status. All in all, it worked very well for us in many different ways and allowed us to successfully complete the project.

Lewis Boot, BSc International Business and Management

### 8.5.4 Ensure that each member fully understands the task

It is often assumed that each member understands the task but this may not be the case, in fact, it is more likely that everybody has a differing view. It is thus important to talk through the project.

The rest of the questions in reference to the first meeting are simple to answer:

- Where to meet? To provide a relaxed environment meet in an informal place like a cafe.
- Who should attend? Every member should attend.
- When to meet? Meet up as soon as possible so you can begin getting on with the work.

Before turning up to your first group meeting ensure you are fully prepared. This is particularly important in the first meeting where you will each be establishing your opinion and expectations of each other – make sure they are positive. Read the module and assignment guidelines, determine what tasks need to be completed and what needs to be discussed. Finally, be sure to be on time.

## 8.6 Group decision making

At the core of any work produced by a group is a collection of decisions. Groups have to make a number of decisions, from the start to the end of a piece of work. Some of these are small and many can be large, nonetheless, all decisions are important and collectively have an impact on the final mark. Group decision making is a thing that happens naturally and the general view is that a number of people together is better than one. However, without employing some helpful techniques, decision making can fall short of expectations.

> While teams tend to make decisions that are better than the average of decisions made by individual members, they may consistently fall short of the quality of the decisions made by the best individual member. (West, 2012: 126)

The quote from Mike West really hits home how prone group decision making is to falling short of its potential. The problem is much worse in student coursework groups due to groupthink, essentially meaning that group members do not want to upset/disagree with each other. There are three conditions that make this apparent which are all strongly seen in student coursework groups.

Table 8.1 demonstrates how tough it is for academic groups to make good decisions. Either the group is quite fierce and there is constant conflict and debate, or the group is too nice and members just agree on the first decision. The best type of group is what Miller (2010) refers to as 'bold' groups, the healthy middle of both these types. To help become a bold group, we recommend:

- Generating win-win solutions – if two people are in disagreement, generate a way of combining both viewpoints to benefit the whole group.
- Ask for the opinions of quiet members, otherwise you could easily omit a valuable opinion.
- Speak through alternative viewpoints in detail. Groups are prone to social conformity whereby they will go with the majority, this does ensure fairness but not performance. For example, the one person who disagrees most could be the one who is right.

TABLE 8.1   Shortfall in student coursework groups

| Condition | Academic groups |
| --- | --- |
| Group leader has a position | In many groups, one prominent leader emerges who shouts the loudest and gets his or her viewpoint across |
| No procedures/ techniques for decisions | Students generally disregard any procedure to facilitate group discussion |
| Difficult conditions upon the group | Tight deadlines, high workloads and general stress make the conditions for academic groups very tough |

- Value everybody's opinion. A good way to do so is to get every member to write down their views on a subject and then present them in one go. This ensures everybody gets their viewpoint across, the group is not dominated by one member and ensures no social loafing as everybody has to work.
- Always develop alternative options, even when decisions prove tough. It is all too easy for somebody to come up with one idea and then just run with it for ease and convenience.

At the bottom of all these are different ways to ensure each member of the group is given the chance to fully express their viewpoint and in turn give the best chance of making the right decision.

> For my international marketing module we had to pick a product and a country to send it to. Instead of going with the first we could generate, we each went away with the task of thinking of a product. We did this and chose Original Source shower gel, we then tasked each other to come up with a country to send it to along with a few reasons. This ensured that everybody in the group got a chance to contribute in order to come up with the best idea which was Original Source to Brazil.
>
> Paul Alexander, BSc Business and Psychology

## 8.7 The work

Most group projects come down to having to produce either a form of written work (an essay or report), a presentation and/or a personal reflection diary/journal. We have discussed each of these in the other chapters but specific points need to be highlighted when completing them in a group.

### 8.7.1 Written work

This is the most common form of group work and the one that also takes the most time. The writing of the group report can be one of the most difficult aspects as everybody has a different writing style. It is crucial to agree upon a common style for how each group member is going to write. At first, each write part of your section and then review each other's work in your next meeting. Try to analyse the strengths and weaknesses of each member's style and combine these to create a common style. Somebody also needs to combine the different sections and put the final document together.

An absolutely fundamental stage that is often overlooked is proofreading the final report, which we cannot emphasise enough. We recommend that each individual member proofreads the report and generates their own suggestions.

Once done, the whole group should come together to feed back their suggestions and agree collectively what should be changed and how. The fact that this stage is so important means that it should not be left to the last minute, it truly can make the difference between a good and a great piece of work. So always allow enough time. Whilst proofreading the final work ensure that it is consistent, specifically check the following:

- writing style (tense/voice/person)
- each individual section
- use of references, abbreviations and units

Chris learned this the hard way in his final year – after completing the group project 24 hours before the deadline there was no time left to proofread it. After receiving the report and reading it back, the group realised how easy it would have been to score more marks if they had left enough time.

## 8.7.2 Presentation

The key to success of a presentation is to make sure it is a group presentation. This sounds rather stupid at first but it is an easy thing to fail. All too often, one person can end up doing too much of the presentation or each presenter's style can differ resulting in it not being a group presentation. To overcome this, ensure the script is written, practised and presented as a group. To help, use clear linking statements that illustrate you have worked as a group. For example, 'I shall now hand you over to ...' or 'Sarah will discuss this in more detail later on'.

Whilst ensuring each person presents, do not share one section between two people. It is much easier for the audience to follow if one person presents each section and it illustrates to the examiner a clear structure. You may end up with somebody who is too scared to present. In this case, try to reassure them that they will be fine and maybe offer them a smaller part. If they really do not want to present, find them another valuable role, for example, controlling the slides, drawing supporting visuals on a flipchart or answering questions.

When deciding upon the method for delivering the presentation, take into account the relevant skills and knowledge of each group member. For example, do you have a group member who is an expert on Prezi? If so, then make the most out of it. Finally, anticipate things in advance to help the presentation run more smoothly. For example, determine who will answer questions. It is good to decide this in advance so the group is not left standing figuring this out during a presentation. Think about who will control the slide show although we recommend each member clicks their own to avoid the situation where somebody clicks too early or late.

The Business Game module was the first module where I was placed into a group with completely random people, all from different countries around the world. The module involved creating a car manufacturing company from scratch and then pitching our business model to a panel of real life car company employees. We were all really nervous about the pitch but we devised a system that led to our eventual success. I think the key part of this module is that we played to every one's strengths, all members were honest about what they were comfortable with talking about and then we built a presentation around that. The strongest presenters led the pitch but also gave room for others to present and develop their own skills. This worked very well as people who didn't think they could present well actually grew confident and described their topic passionately.

Neil Kumar, BSc Business, Computing and IT

### 8.7.3 Personal reflection diary

Your lecturer may also require you to produce a reflection diary or a journal, essentially an evaluation of how you performed as a group. Again, all the rules from Chapter 10 on essay writing will apply. On top of this, try to write the reflection diary as a group. Get together and discuss:

- Did you have any conflict? How did you resolve this? If you did not resolve the conflict, how could you have solved it?
- What were the key strengths and weaknesses of your group?
- What role did each group member have? How did you come about deciding the roles and, upon reflection, would you keep them the same?
- Did you work efficiently as a group?
- If you were to work as a group again, what would you do differently?

Asking these questions as a group may seem a little weird but it will provide the whole group with valuable material for the reflection diary. Using the agenda and minutes from all the group meetings will certainly help. It is also useful to get an outside perspective. For example, did your lecturer witness how you worked as a group who can give his or her opinion? When possible, try to include academic journals to support what happened in your group. At the end of the day, it is an academic piece of work so it will help. If unsure whether this will be of value, speak to the lecturer and tell them what you plan to do. Finally, when writing the document be sure to write it as an individual in order to avoid the risk of plagiarism.

# 8.8 Possible situations

As Barner (2001) identifies, no teams are perfect and there always things that can be done to improve team effectiveness. Importantly, this is best done by team members, i.e. you and the rest of the team. Often when things go wrong, team members are quick to turn to others such as friends or lecturers without trying to resolve it within the team first. A number of things can go wrong within teams and the most crucial step is to identify the issue. This sounds a rather obvious stage but it is more complicated than it first seems. For example, somebody might not be contributing to the group – this may seem really annoying but if it was later discovered that the group member was suffering from bereavement then everything changes. There are thus two levels to any issue, as shown in Figure 8.6:

FIGURE 8.6    Route to conflict resolution

First you must identify the issue and then, most importantly, the cause in order to generate the solution. Once an issue has been identified, think it through and talk it over with the group. Guttman (2008) summarises this as creating an open environment where the whole group can deal with the issue.

## 8.8.1 Conflict

With such a diverse composition of people and the pressures placed upon students, conflict is inevitable. The traditional view is that it is unproductive and destructive but this depends on the type of conflict – dysfunctional or functional. Dysfunctional conflict is unrelated conflict such as personal disagreements which result in arguments and long-term issues. If dysfunctional conflict arises, take a few minutes out to allow people to think straight or completely move on. Assess why the conflict arose in the first place and remedy the situation. Functional conflict is task related which is beneficial and should be encouraged. It stimulates debate, generates new ideas and ultimately improves performance. There are some great techniques to encourage functional conflict:

133

- use open messages or questions to spark a debate
- bring in an outsider, for example, somebody from another group to challenge your work
- change group members' roles to stimulate debate and motivation

### 8.8.2 'Weak' group members

It is quite possible that you will end up with members that are relatively weaker than you. However, do remember, everybody is good at something as we discussed earlier so be careful not to dismiss people. In quite extreme situations, there is the possibility of ending up in a very weak group, essentially where nobody is of any value – either a member with a very poor level of English, a lack of ability or students that just do not care. In this situation, we suggest you think very hard about their capabilities and how they could be of value. If you are finding it difficult to do, discuss it with the lecturer or your school office.

Ultimately, if you do find yourself in the situation of a very weak group then you must accept it. It comes back to the idea of maintaining an internal locus of control, essentially, you are in control of what happens. We have witnessed many students who have felt sorry for themselves because they ended up with a weak group and subsequently have given up. It is vital to avoid this. In Pat's experience there are very differing views within groups as to who has put in the most effort. It can be galling to see someone apparently not trying but it is the job of everyone in the group to make sure everyone contributes. Ask yourself why is this person not contributing? Do they feel intimidated by the other group members? Have they been overlooked in the meetings? Is there a cultural clash in the group? We tend to jump to the easy conclusion that they are just plain lazy.

We recommend that you do whatever it takes to get the grade that you want. This may mean facing up to conflict in the group, it may mean extra effort on your part either bringing the group together or doing more than your fair share. In the end, it matters less whether everyone has really pulled their weight on a project and more that you achieve the grade you want. The key is to tackle the issue as early as possible, do not leave it until it is too late.

The main issue I have come across during group work at university is that there is always one group member who is unwilling to contribute to the group effort. No matter how much you try to encourage that group member to participate, the work they produce just never seems to be up to the required standard agreed by the rest of the group. In this case, my group has been left with two choices: either continue to use the university system in place designed to punish group members who do not participate (in the hope that they will eventually participate and produce the work to the required level), or divide the work up amongst the rest of the group so that it is completed to the required standard. As has often been the case, the latter is usually the better option. It is a lot quicker and has better results.

Devon Parker, BSc International Business and French

### 8.8.3 Group member becoming ill

If this is for a short period of time, i.e. a day, then just leave that person to recover and carry on any scheduled meetings without them. If the ill member wishes to work, discourage them, allow them to fully recover so they can return to full productivity as soon as possible instead of prolonging the illness. If any meetings are scheduled to take place, reschedule them for a later date. If he or she becomes ill for longer than a week then assess how the work needs to be reallocated and talk it over with the exam office and/or lecturer. Be sure to keep the member in the loop by providing them with regular updates.

### 8.8.4 Change

The fact is change does happen and as a group you must accept it. This could be anything from a change of lecturer to a change on the format of the work, i.e. a report instead of a presentation. You need to create a group internal locus of control. Recognise how the change affects the group and adapt as quickly as possible. The time spent feeling sorry for yourselves could be used for the better.

### 8.8.5 Not getting on as a group

With such a diverse range of people, you may simply sometimes not get on with each other. There are some cheap and even free ways to help you bond. Linking it back to the earlier model on the process of teams, gelling methods help to progress from storming to norming and performing. Even if you are getting on well, the following methods are great in helping you to develop further.

- Go out for an informal session such as a trip to the pub or a dinner.
- Work together on the project for a couple of hours – this may not prove very productive but if this is the case then you can rest assured that you are bonding as a group.
- Work at each other's houses or apartments – this seems to be popular and it helps members get an insight into each other's lives.
- Compete or work with another group.

It can be valuable to undertake these whenever possible. For example, one dinner out together is unlikely to have any lasting changes as opposed to a group meeting over dinner every two weeks, and by dinner we do not mean anything fancy or formal – if everybody is happy with McDonalds then great, money saved.

## 8.9 Monitoring success

We discussed the idea of a scorecard when it came to goal setting and this may or may not have seemed useful. However, it is critical when it comes to group projects, as Lencioni (2005) points out. It helps to define the criteria of what success looks like, it monitors the progress of the plan and it holds members accountable for their actions. Businesses use these all the time in what has become known as the 'balanced scorecard', a powerful tool for summarising a wealth of information:

> The balanced scorecard is like the dials in an airplane cockpit: it gives managers complex information at a glance. (Kaplan and Norton, 1992: 71)

The beauty with this is that it can be as simple or complicated as you wish. Table 8.2 is a quick scorecard we put together to show how one could potentially monitor a group essay.

Simply looking at this, you can see its potential. As each group member is writing their section, they can constantly refer back to the scorecard to identify where they need to improve. When in group meetings, it can be used to monitor the project as a whole and identify areas for improvements. For example, there is a clear need to look at the structure as everybody perceives it to be quite poor, whilst at the same time the group is doing fantastic in terms of number of examples.

There are two potential watch outs with a scorecard. First is to make sure that it is not imposed on the group. The best way to ensure this is by coming up with the scorecard as a team, simply by asking: what do we believe makes a great piece of work? Doing so will generate the criteria to use on the scorecard.

TABLE 8.2   Example scorecard

| Section | Section owner | Word count | Quality of structure | No. of journals | No. of examples | Quality of writing | Quality of referencing |
|---------|---------------|------------|----------------------|-----------------|-----------------|--------------------|-----------------------|
| Start | Sarah | 2000 | 3 | 5 | 4 | 4 | 5 |
| Middle | Tom | 4600 | 2 | 7 | 5 | 3 | 2 |
| End | Jess | 3100 | 3 | 8 | 5 | 5 | 5 |
| Total |  | 9700 |  |  |  |  |  |

Once it is completed, clearly define each criterion. For example, do you believe 2 or 20 journals to be a good number? The second watch out is cheating the scores – it is clearly easy for one person to mark themselves higher. However, further down the line a group will need to proofread the report or presentation and it will be evident whether the score is a true reflection, it is thus easier and better for everybody to be honest – make this clear when creating the scorecard.

## 8.10 Taking it to work

Throughout your working life, you will work within groups and teams. The constant changes that are occurring in today's business environment – including home working, the increasing role of computers and internationalism – are all increasing the challenge of working effectively in a team. The principles and techniques we have provided above will allow you to work effectively in any team in the face of these changes. Whatever role or company you work for, you will be working as part of a team so it is important to start learning and practising how to do this best. Almost everything we have stated in this chapter will be of value to your career.

## 8.11 How to get started

### 8.11.1 Professional

- Create an agenda for your group meeting and send it to everybody in the group.
- Establish three things you are going to do to help your next group gel as a team.
- Set up a Dropbox or Facebook group for your group.

### 8.11.2 A little more interesting

- Create a vision and three goals across a three month time period as a group for any team you are involved in and work towards them.
- Set up a brand new society and put together a group of people to run it.
- Make friends with somebody from a new culture and learn all about how they work.

## 8.12 Our bookshelf

Yeung, R. (2000) *Leading teams: creating a team, resolving conflicts, delivering results through teamworking*. Oxford: How To Books.
This is a pocket-size book which provides advice on leading and working with a team for those who do not have much experience. As students you may not

have much formal experience of working in a group which is why we believe it to be a great read.

West, M.A. (2012) *Effective teamwork: practical lessons from organizational research.* London: Wiley-Blackwell.

Mike West has written several very accessible guides on teams and team working and this latest one we used a lot in designing this chapter.

Maxwell, C.J. (2001) *The 17 indisputable laws of teamwork: embrace them and empower your team.* Nashville, TN: Thomas Nelson Inc.

This book is great at capturing the raw basics of what makes a great team. It is so easy to forget these rules, particularly when times get tough and Maxwell's book helps to ensure these rules are not forgotten.

## 8.13 References

Barner, W.R. (2001) *Team troubleshooter: how to find and fix team problems.* London: Davies-Black.

Brett, J., Behfar, K. and Kern, M.C. (2006) 'Managing multicultural teams', *Harvard Business Review*, 84 (11): 85–91.

Cabrera, A.F., Crissman, J.L., Bernal, E.M., Nora, A.P.T. and Pascarella, E.T. (2002) 'Collaborative learning: its impact on college students' development', *Journal of College Student Development*, 43 (1): 20–34.

Gamson, F.Z. (1994) 'Collaborative learning comes of age', *Change*, 26 (5): 44–49.

Green, A.G. and Lazarus, H. (1991) 'Are today's executives meeting with success?', *Journal of Management Development*, 10 (1): 14–25.

Guttman, M.H. (2008) *Great business teams: cracking the code for standout performance.* London: John Wiley.

Kaplan, S.R. and Norton, P.D. (1992) 'The balanced scorecard – measures that drive performance', *Harvard Business Review*, 70 (1): 71–79.

Kormanski, C. (1990) 'Team building patterns of academic groups', *The Journal for Specialists in Group Work*, 15 (4): 206–214.

Lencioni, M.P. (2005) *Overcoming the five dysfunctions of a team: a field guide for leaders, managers, and facilitators.* London: Jossey-Bass.

Maxwell, C.J. (2001) *The 17 indisputable laws of teamwork: embrace them and empower your team.* Nashville, TN: Thomas Nelson Inc.

Miller, C.B. (2010) *Nice teams finish last: the secret to unleashing your team's maximum potential.* New York: AMACOM.

Slavin, R.E. (1983) 'When does co-operative learning improve student achievement?', *Psychological Bulletin*, 94 (3): 429–445.

Tuckman, B. (1965) 'Developmental sequence in small groups', *Psychological Bulletin*, 63 (6): 384–399.

West, M.A. (2012) *Effective teamwork: practical lessons from organizational research.* London: Wiley-Blackwell.

# 9

# Coursework

## 9.1 Chapter summary

Business schools are using an ever-increasing variety of assessments in addition to the traditional essay (which is covered in Chapter 10). Coursework has been a major contributor to this and there are generally three different types of coursework business schools are now using:

1. Business plans – with a number of students wanting to start their own businesses, modules where you have to generate a business idea and a plan are becoming increasingly popular.
2. Business reports – these are similar to business plans but focus more on a certain aspect of a business such as its strategy, HR or marketing. They will often also be based on real organisations rather than fictional ones.
3. Simulation games – these often involve being in a group to generate and implement a real business strategy using a piece of software. For example, at Aston Business School there is a module entitled Business Game where students have to manufacture and sell a car.

All these require different approaches in terms of researching, writing and formatting which you need to learn. There are similarities to an essay and you will need to follow the rules we discuss in Chapter 10 on essay writing, for example, writing a well-structured and planned piece of work. Always remember this is an academic piece of work and no matter how applied and practical the brief is, the lecturer usually expects to see academic rigour unless told specifically otherwise. However, there are key differences that change some of the rules and so you will need to slightly adapt your approach.

## 9.2 The brief

The most essential part of the brief is discovering what exactly you have to do. This is the most commonly cited mistake that students make and Pat is always having to mark students down simply because they have not answered the question or provided the correct report in the required format. We want to really press you to read the question, make sure you completely understand what is being asked and then answer it. This sounds really obvious but again and again, students make the mistake of working on the wrong answer and presenting their work in the wrong format. This is especially true with the very large variations in the format of coursework. From a tactical point of view, it is also vital that you check how much the coursework contributes to your final mark as this informs you how much time you should devote to the work. We are well aware that this might appear rather cynical but the percentage of marks awarded to a piece of work is the lecturer's way of telling you how much time and effort to put into it. For example, on one module that Pat teaches, there is a short piece of reflection to be done every week which is worth 30 per cent overall – or 3 per cent per week. Clearly each week you should not be spending a huge amount of time on this whereas a journal on the same module was worth 30 per cent. So, understand exactly what you need to do and plan your effort according to how the marks are allocated.

You then need to think about your audience. Who exactly are they and what do they need? Unfortunately, it is not as simple as an essay where the audience will simply be a lecturer along with a second marker. The audience might even be hypothetical, where, for example, you will write a business plan for a fictitious investor. Alternatively, you may be presenting or writing for real business professionals, this is becoming increasingly popular as universities seek to link modules with organisations to make them more realistic. A popular example we have witnessed is conducting a marketing presentation to agencies where students have to generate a marketing campaign for a real product.

Chapter 11 on presentations gives you the advice you need on presentations but you really need to get into the mind of your audience in these sorts of assignments too.

## 9.3 The content

Different modules will require different things but we have provided a detailed list as to the most common things that could be included. By doing this, we hope that whatever you need to write about we have provided some useful tips and processes to help you. The exact structure of your assignment though is specified by your lecturer and if you can't understand precisely what they want you to do, use the advice in Chapter 4 and get to know the lecturer a little and find out from them. But don't ever just guess what they want! Find out and make sure you are presenting exactly what you have been asked to.

### 9.3.1 Generating the idea

Students seem to find this one of the most difficult steps and it is certainly by no means easy. As such, it is crucial to begin as soon as possible. We know of many students who have spent more time trying to come up with the idea than actually working on it which we want to help you avoid. Remember your lecturer will be more interested in how you plan to execute your idea. In most cases, the idea is either to come up with a new business idea or to choose an already existing product and organisation.

The best piece of advice we can give you is not to look for the *perfect* idea. There seems to be a notion that you need to generate an idea that is awesome and unique. However, no idea is ever perfect. The way good ideas are generated is by conceiving a basic idea and then refining it multiple times to improve it. This is what you should aim to do. For example, you may have an idea to generate a new kids' drink. At first sight, you would say this is a poor idea as there are loads of kids' drinks currently available in the UK market. However, by thinking it through you may be able to generate a way to differentiate it and create something different; your bottle could, for example, double up as a football. The way to refine an idea is to research the market and really understand where the trends are and potential gaps lie. Then build momentum on it, keep talking it through and building on it. You will soon discover that your idea will develop into something more tangible and credible. For some inspiration, we suggest you take a look at Springwise.com which lists the coolest business ideas from around the world.

Whilst you're generating ideas, try to create a couple of alternatives. It can be so easy to run with the first idea in the desperation to get it done but be sure to create an alternative even if it is something basic. Try to generate an idea in an area that interests you and the group. This will make it a lot more fun to work on and you will most probably already have knowledge in that area. For example, you may all love shopping, clubbing or a certain sport and even have experience in the area. It may even end up being an idea you seek to develop once you graduate or provide useful knowledge if you choose to apply for a job within the sector.

Studying an entrepreneurial management module, a group coursework brief was, 'Think of an idea and write a business plan to demonstrate your idea's viability'. I approached the idea generation with a methodical approach by initially brainstorming ideas alone. This allowed me to come to my group's first meeting prepared and ready with constructive suggestions to feed into our ideation session. The ideation session consisted of 15 minutes of silent thinking time to just write down all ideas that popped into your head. Once this was done each group member had to share their ideas with the group. Once each member's ideas had been discussed as a group we tried to eliminate ideas that didn't work based on our previous business experience. After a short while of group discussion we had reduced it to just three potential ideas. At this point we decided to adjourn the meeting and go our separate ways, allowing each group member to take an idea and do more research into it. This way we evaluated all ideas fairly and eventually came to a good group decision.

Sunna Van Kampen, BSc Management and Strategy

### 9.3.2 Competition

A key part of any business plan or report is researching the competition. Your audience will want to see that you are aware of your competition and their capabilities. This will come down to undertaking thorough research to really understand your industry and the key players within it. The crucial mistake often made here is assuming there is no competition – there is always competition for any organisation. In this case, you need to consider the indirect as well as direct competitors. For example, if you were to develop a soft drink, competition would include major manufactures like Coca Cola and Pepsi but it would also extend wider to other drinks like coffee and tea. You don't need to concentrate as much on these but you do need to demonstrate a good awareness of them and what the implications are.

Most students will simply look at competitors' websites to research competitors, which are a great source of information. However, this is just one source of many. In addition to this, we suggest:

- ringing competitors to see what they offer and how they treat customers
- visiting a trade conference – this may seem a little excessive but it will provide vital information and even a valuable opportunity to develop your network

TABLE 9.1    Example competitor analysis table

| Name of competitor | Information | Reference |
|---|---|---|
| Website | | |
| Description of company | | |
| Mission, vision and values | | |
| Strategy and key goals and objectives | | |
| Products and services offered | | |
| Strengths and weaknesses | | |
| Market share | | |

- following the competition on social networks
- reading the current and previous annual report
- discovering industry organisations and see what reports they have to offer

Before you do this, develop a framework on what exactly it is you want to know otherwise you will just get lost in a wealth of information. We suggest developing a template with the headings such as those in Table 9.1, including a reference section so you can refer to and properly reference any information if you decide to include it within your coursework.

> As part of our coursework, we had to conduct our own market research to find the best possible market for our company to produce and sell our cars. Not only did we have to find where to sell but we also had to find many statistics of the leading car brands, such as their market share and how many cars they sold each year, to allow us to produce reliable and realistic data to present to people in industry. As this was a group task, we split the responsibility between us to benefit from synergy. Once the data was collected we then had to organise it into tables and charts to allow us to analyse it more easily and choose the best options. Market research and understanding the competition was key to allowing us to complete this section of the coursework.
>
> Lewis Boot, BSc International Business and Management

## 9.3.3 Customers

Any lecturer will want to see that you know who your customers are so be sure to develop an in-depth understanding of your customers:

- demographics – age, gender?
- geographics – where do they live, what type of house do they have?

- attitudes – why do they buy certain products and services?
- psychometrics – what sort of personality are they?

Be specific when researching your customers and try to use as much secondary research as possible. If possible, primary research would be even better although it would involve a lot of work. If you are planning to sell b2b, i.e. business to business, then your customer will be slightly more complicated. For example, one department may use the product but another, such as procurement, may make the purchasing decision.

## 9.3.4 Marketing plan

Marketing can refer to a whole host of things and the 7Ps generally provide the best framework (Chartered Institute of Marketing, 2009):

1. *Price* – price is all about selling something profitably. However, it is about a lot more than this and going for the cheapest price is certainly not the only option, it is often not even the best option. Think about what price you can charge and how that reflects upon the company and value offered.
2. *Promotion* – promotion is about communicating your products and services and making people want to buy them. Too many students get too caught up on social media, it is a great platform but how are you going to use it and what else are you going to do? Remember the other platforms such as TV, radio and newspapers aren't dead and can have many uses.
3. *Place* – this is where your product or service is actually sold. There usually isn't one magic answer here and you will have a blend of places where your products or services are sold.
4. *Product* – think about the product you are planning to offer and how it meets your target customers' needs. Think about every element and whether it is needed. Go beyond the core product and think about everything your product offers. For example, a mobile phone allows people to ring others but also allows people to manage their time, socialise and look cool. This is what is known as the augmented product (Levitt, 1980).

When using services there are three more Ps which are useful to consider:

1. *Process* – look at the process of delivering a service to your customers. Could it be made more efficient or improved? Remember customers' time is key. If they do have to wait for long periods of time, what could be done to support them or keep them happy?
2. *People* – who you are going to hire to deliver your services? The people you use will represent your brand and everything it stands for. Once you have hired them, how are you going to manage them and incentivise them?
3. *Physical evidence* – a service in intangible but physical evidence can provide tangible elements to help bring it to life. For example, a hairdresser often gives people who are waiting a magazine to read, a drink, a comfortable place to sit.

When writing your marketing plan, it can be very useful to include some sample material in your coursework to bring it to life and make it more interesting for the reader. For example, could you include a mock poster or a storyboard of a TV advert? Do not spend too much time doing this, though if it's for a marketing module then you may wish to do so.

We know that nowadays the internet affects many of these and we greatly encourage you to read the paper by Porter (2001) on how the internet affects companies.

### 9.3.5 Forecasting finances

The numbers are a key part of any plan. Lecturers may want to see any combination of a cash flow, financial ratios, profit and loss, balance sheet, etc. Explaining how to go about doing these would be a book in itself so we are not going to. Instead, we would like to give you a key piece of advice which is this: be realistic. All too often students go crazy with numbers and think that a new business could sell millions of products. Remember to achieve this takes a great deal of time and resources, particularly money.

### 9.3.6 Goals and objectives

Goals and objectives are an important part of nearly every piece of coursework, it is safe to say every lecturer wants to see clear business goals and that they are explained in detail. The main tip is to be concise, give three to five key goals and objectives and describe them in detail. Then ensure that they are SMART as we discussed in Chapter 1 on goal setting. As a quick reminder, remember to make them specific, measurable, attainable, realistic and timed.

An absolute must is to justify each one of your goals and objectives. For example, due to the acceptance of the SMART approach you may wish to explain how each goal is SMART and why you believe it to be such an important goal. Also be sure to create a range of short-, medium- and long-term goals and ensure that your long-term goals are connected to your short-term goals.

### 9.3.7 Culture

The mission, vision and values combine to describe your company culture. These things can really help bring a piece of coursework to life and really help your lecturer to imagine what the company would be like if it existed.

### 9.3.8 Mission

A mission statement describes what a company does and what its goals are. Google is often referred to as a good example, with a mission 'to organize the world's information and make it universally accessible and useful' (Google, 1998).

### 9.3.9 Vision

A vision statement provides an outline of where a company sees itself in the future. You may have to create a vision statement for your organisation or rewrite the vision statement of a real organisation. For both tasks, we recommend that you read the paper by Lipton (1996). He gives seven reasons why visions fail which provides a great checklist for creating an effective vision.

### 9.3.10 Values

Values are becoming increasingly important and they describe how a company behaves. Typically a lot of organisations create blend values that are the same as a million other companies, exceptional customer service being one of the most common values, so try to make yours different. A great tip on how to create values is to run through hypothetical scenarios and see how you would deal with them or/and generate words you want to be associated with your company (Spiro, 2010).

To summarise, when it comes to content remember to think about the points illustrated in Figure 9.1.

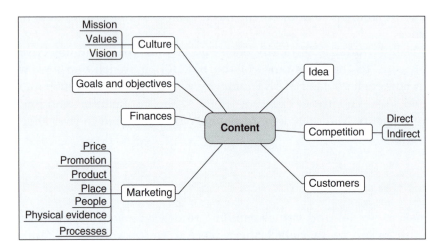

FIGURE 9.1   Example Mind Map planning your assignment

But remember this is a very generic plan and your lecturer and audience will have certain things they do and do not wish to see. Always, always, always ensure you familiarise yourself with this, if you are ever in doubt, go and talk to them.

## 9.4 Academic tools

Being an academic piece of work, you can bet that your lecturer will want to see the use of academic tools. There are hundreds of tools and models in the academic literature but there are some common ones which we often see lecturers request. We want to take you through a few of these tools and share some quick tips with you to ensure that you get the most out of the tools.

### 9.4.1 PEST analysis

PEST stands for Political, Economic, Sociological and Technological. It is a tool that helps a business analyse its external environment. To provide you with a more thorough guide, Table 9.2 lists some of the things you may wish to look into.

When using a PEST analysis, be sure not to list too many points and make it specific to the organisation, for example, instead of looking at the whole population you may wish to study only your target audience. It is crucial that all your points are also fully referenced, even when making well-known assumptions. To learn how to go about conducting a thorough PEST analysis, look online for examples where organisations have carried out this sort of

TABLE 9.2   Example PEST analysis

| Political | Economic |
|---|---|
| • Election dates<br>• Type of government<br>• Levels of corruption<br>• Regulatory bodies and regulations<br>• Funding, grants and initiatives<br>• Political stability<br>• Trade tariffs | • Economic growth<br>• Inflation rates<br>• Exchange rates and foreign trade<br>• Wages, income and employment levels<br>• Tax policy<br>• Interest rates |
| **Social** | **Technological** |
| • Population health<br>• Education levels<br>• Age distribution and demographics<br>• Consumer attitudes and lifestyle<br>• Major events<br>• Ethnic/religion importance | • Rate of technological change<br>• Maturity of technology<br>• Consumer buying mechanisms<br>• Communication platforms |

analysis to see how they have done it. In particular, public sector bodies often publish these on their websites so they can be a valuable source of ideas.

### 9.4.2 SWOT analysis

SWOT has been around for a long time and is one of the most widely used tools and one which we are sure will be useful to you, you have most probably even used it already. It can essentially be split into two parts, Strengths and Weaknesses are internal and Opportunities and Threats are part of the external environment (see Figure 9.2). SWOT analysis helps to draw a picture of an organisation's internal and external environment.

Due to its popularity it can very easily be misused, which lowers its value (Hill and Westbrook, 1997). One of the main problems is that a SWOT analysis can end up as a long list (Dyson, 2004). We recommend that you limit the length of your SWOT analysis to no more than one page of A4. If you do find yourself with a very long list, consider putting it into the appendix and just selecting the top points. This leads nicely to the next recommendation which is to rank points. When ranking points, be sure to use specific criteria and clearly explain what these mean. For example, if you were to rank opportunities then you may wish to consider the size of the opportunity in terms of revenue against cost.

Just like a PEST analysis, make the SWOT specific to the organisation in question, for example, a common threat now placed on SWOTs is the recession

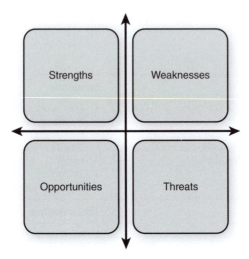

FIGURE 9.2   The SWOT analysis

but what element of the recession is a threat and how it is a threat? In the case of a TV company, for example, you would say the recession has led to lower incomes and subsequently consumers are seeking cheaper alternatives such as internet TV or streaming TV from abroad. The final and most crucial step is to discuss what you are going to do with the findings. Continuing the same example, you could overcome the threat of the recession by developing an online TV channel or investing in an internet company. As with PEST, you should be able to find many examples of SWOT online as it is used very commonly indeed.

## 9.4.3 SBU analysis – GE-McKinsey matrix

This is a visual tool that shows, at a glance, which parts of the business are performing well and which are in growth sectors. The different parts of the business are often referred to as Strategic Business Units (SBU) and are parts of the business that face different external markets. For example, a car company may have one part that sells lorries to businesses and another that sells cars to families. To use this tool, it is important to follow a systematic process (see also Table 9.3).

TABLE 9.3   Business Unit Strength table

| | | Business unit strength | | |
|---|---|---|---|---|
| | | *High* | *Medium* | *Low* |
| **Industry attractiveness** | *High* | | | |
| | *Medium* | | | |
| | *Low* | | | |

1. Identify clear criteria for each axes: business unit strength and industry attractiveness.
2. Identify the SBUs of the business.
3. Set a weighting for each criterion used. For example, you may use market size and industry competitiveness to determine the industry attractiveness, so determine which is more important by setting a weighting.
4. Place each SBU on the diagram using a circle, the size of the circle represents the market size and it is portrayed as a pie chart which illustrates the market share.
5. Similar to the SWOT analysis, use it to recommend strategic actions. Most commonly, the tool is used to decide whether to grow, hold or harvest an SBU.

### 9.4.4 Scenario planning

Scenario planning is used to try and predict the future and then determine how the business will operate in this new future world. Schoemaker (1995) argued scenario planning is most beneficial where uncertainty is high and an industry has experienced significant change, for example, the TV industry which is constantly moving with new technology and platforms. Some advocates even suggest that we operate in such an uncertain world that every business should utilise scenario planning.

Scenario planning also helps to overcome the static nature of PESTEL, helps to overcome narrow mindsets – i.e. we have a tendency to concentrate on what we see now – and helps to take advantage of possible new opportunities. For an in-depth process of how to carry out scenario planning, we recommend that you read the paper by Schoemaker (1995) who outlines a clear and systematic process. We strongly recommend that you perform the process as a group to benefit from a wide range of opinions, remember you are trying to create a world which doesn't yet exist.

When using academic tools be aware that they are not mutually exclusive: the results from one will guide you with answers to the other. For example, the SWOT analysis is often derived from a combination of all the other tools, particularly the PEST analysis when it comes to analysing the threats and opportunities. Again this is a very generic list and we have raced through it in a fairly limited amount of time. We do this as we only want to open up your eyes and mind, not give you all the answers. If you decide to use any of the academic tools we have mentioned, conduct extra reading on them and thoroughly understand their strengths and weaknesses.

## 9.5 Tips for all types of coursework

Let's move on to some more practical tips. The first tip to give you is that a piece of coursework is not always a strictly formatted academic essay, so find out from your lecturer whether or not to include journals and theory. It can be easy to assume that you have to include theory but don't make this mistake. Chris made this mistake in a group project when writing a strategy report about the BBC. He spent a lot of effort in making a theoretical essay but didn't gain marks for the theoretical element because this was not required. Similarly, talk to your lecturer to determine their preference on what tools and models should be used. Business academia is full of models and tools and we have discussed some of the most common ones. However, make sure you talk to your lecturer as they will have a preference for certain tools and for using them in a certain way.

As coursework tends to be quite practical, it can be very beneficial to get an external viewpoint like a business professional to discuss your coursework. Business professionals are busy and will not want to read your whole coursework or read your whole presentation. However, more often than not they will be happy to talk through your basic idea and your plan. For example, if writing a business plan, you could get an entrepreneur to check it.

Make sure every aspect of your coursework is realistic. Some of the most common mistakes and assumptions include:

- Making a profit in the first year: very few companies are immediately profitable so be sure you are being realistic. If you really do believe you can make a profit, clearly explain how you are going to do so.
- Related to this is a lack of cash: remember to make money, you will need to spend money.
- Assuming there is no competition: remember there is always competition, whether it is direct or indirect.
- Generating an idea that is too expensive or requires a huge amount of money: remember that no investor would give somebody millions of pounds for just an idea. So if you were planning to build a hotel on Mars to compete with Richard Branson and Virgin you may wish to consider another idea.

Finally, do not copy from the internet, we have discussed plagiarism elsewhere but it can be even more tempting for coursework. For example, things like PEST analyses on companies will already exist on the internet. The marker will be aware of these and you will get caught out. By all means use them to learn how the process might look in practice but do not copy them.

## 9.6 Working with tables, data and graphs

We either love or hate numbers and graphs but when it comes to business coursework they are crucial, particularly within simulation games as there is a magnitude of data available. There is never usually anything advanced that has to be completed, it is normally just about including some tables and graphs to make the coursework easier to understand. As such, mistakes made are only ever minor but they can make a huge difference.

One of the most common mistakes it not clearly labelling everything, sometimes what you think is a given may not be clear to somebody else, for example, when it comes to time you may be discussing minutes, hours or days. For example, Figure 9.3 could be interpreted in a number of ways.

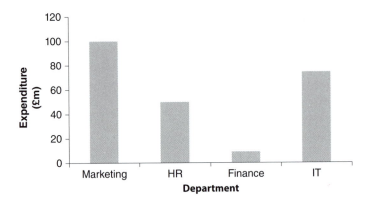

FIGURE 9.3   Expenditure graph

In this sort of graph it would be sensible to use simple colours, one in this case, which makes it easier to understand. It can be very easy to go crazy with colour which can make a graph very difficult to understand. Chris recently found some of his coursework and cringed when he realised he tried to be too fancy and in fact made the graphs rather hard to read. Similar to colour, are the use of effects. We strongly suggest that you do not use 3D graphs, they may look good, but can make it difficult to understand. The same advice goes for shadows, multiple gridlines and pictures behind graphs.

Whatever graph or table you include make sure that you analyse it, it can be very easy to include a table or graph but then not discuss it. Consider what its significance is and what impact it has. If you are struggling to make a case for its inclusion, then you may question its value and delete it.

As part of my coursework in the making managerial decisions module, I was required to analyse a case study for a pre-press company. Within the coursework, there was a spread sheet element with which I was held as the responsible group member to complete. I linked up cells from different sheets of Excel as the sensitivity analysis was required to show how key input variables would affect certain output factors. Finally, I drew two sets of tables relating to these output factors. One table had the output factors changing according to changes in input and another table had the same output factors that do not change due to changes in inputs. These two different tables were drawn as a means of comparison between each other and added a lot of value to the coursework, as the lecturer was able to use them to compare two different situations.

Sagar Pau, BSc Accounting and Management

## 9.7 Designing the coursework

Unlike an essay, there is plenty of scope to add some creativity in your coursework. For some inspiration, we suggest that you look at the annual reports of top companies. They convey a great deal of information but spend a great deal of money and time making them interesting and visually pleasing. Some of our favourites include Diageo (makers of Smirnoff) and Coca Cola.

If you are writing about a fictional company or discussing a new business then we recommend that you brand it to make your coursework come to life. Specifically, we suggest that you create a logo, name and colour theme. The name is notably the most difficult step here and it is easy to just sit there within a group trying to think of a name – a great waste of time. To help you, we suggest the following process:

1. Get the group together.
2. State a time limit on creating a certain number of names, to get you started we suggest that you create 10 names in 5 minutes.
3. Swap papers with the person to your left and generate 10 new names.
4. Do the same again.
5. Write all the names down on a whiteboard or large piece of paper.
6. Ask each person to decide upon three names.
7. Ask each person to pick one.
8. Decide upon the best name.

Once you have your name, use online logo creators to bring it to life. Generating a logo along with a theme can really enhance a piece of coursework. But be careful not to spend too much time on this.

## 9.8 Proofreading

Proofreading coursework can provide its own challenges, especially when you are used to writing formal academic essays. The key to success is to make sure that it follows a set structure and it is easy to read. If you planned your coursework effectively then this should come through and structure shouldn't be an issue. However, you will always need to proofread your work to make sure that you haven't made any minor mistakes that could impact your mark. As a quick checklist, we suggest you check:

- Redundancy: have all unnecessary things been removed? Does every graph and table need to be included? Conversely, is there anything that could be added?
- Front cover: does it include all the essentials – module code, organisation name, team name and any specific requests from lecturers?

- Headings: include clear headings throughout the report to guide the reader, along with a contents page and clear page numbers (all too often, students have included a contents page but then omitted to number the pages).
- References: have these been included and are they all accurate?
- Jargon: is it jargon free? If you have used any overcomplicated words or sentences see if there is a way to simplify them.
- Appendices: if you have used one and is everything referred to correctly?
- Presentation: is it easy on the eye? In aiming to be creative, you can risk going overboard and making it difficult to read. Make sure your eyes don't wonder round the report.
- Legibility: print off a colour copy and check that everything is clearly legible.

Make sure you leave enough time to proofread your coursework, it really can make all the difference to your final mark. We suggest that you leave at least three days before the deadline to give you enough time to proofread it as a group and individually and have enough time to make any larger changes should you deem it necessary. It also allows for any unforeseen circumstances. Chris remembers a time when, due to deadlines across multiple courses, hundreds of students were using the printers and there were queues in every room. Colour ink soon ran out and a group member had to run home to print a 100 page report in black and white. The work was handed in literally one minute before the deadline and was in black and white making it difficult to read the graphs.

## 9.9 Taking it to work

When you begin work, you will undoubtedly have reports to write for either your team or managers. The tips we have discussed here will be very useful, particularly when it comes to keeping it to a minimum and presenting it in an easy and understandable manner. You may even wish to start your own business and many of the tips will certainly apply when creating a business plan.

There are two key things I try to remember when writing a report. Firstly, understand who you are writing for, i.e. who will read it, and tailor the report so that it suits your audience in respect of their level of background knowledge and assumed understanding. I have a range of different clients and I'll write different letters depending on whether I'm addressing a little old lady or a company CEO. Secondly, say what you need to say but keep it short. There are no prizes for the longest reports and the greatest way of demonstrating your own intelligence is to write in the most succinct way possible. Your audience will appreciate it and are more likely to pay attention to what you have written. I often save a document and reread it a little while later to check for clarity and whether I really need every word I've included.

Ian Burrows, Investment Manager at Brewin Dolphin

## 9.10 How to get started

### 9.10.1 Professional

- Review whether everything you have included is actually needed. Could you delete things from a report that would make it easier to read and understand?
- Brush up on your Excel skills, it is used very widely in organisations so it's well worth learning and it will help you to quickly develop professional tables, data and graphs.
- Try to finish your next piece of coursework three days early so you can thoroughly proofread it.

### 9.10.2 A little more interesting

- Use the academic tools for one of your favourite businesses to help you practise and even develop knowledge which you can use for exams.
- Create a rough business plan for a random idea you may once have had.
- Get creative with the next piece of coursework you have to write.

## 9.11 Our bookshelf

Osterwalder, A. and Pigneur, Y. (2010) *Business model generation: a handbook for visionaries, game changers, and challengers.* Hoboken, NJ: Wiley.
This is a rather entertaining book on how to develop a basic idea into a viable business model. It is packed with illustrations, visuals and examples to really bring it to life. It is a great read and will help you with any business plan or coursework to guide you through some key stages and help you develop ideas.

Saunders, J., Armstrong, G., Kotler, P., Wong, V. and Wood, B.M. (2010) *Principles of marketing* (5th edn). London: Financial Times/Prentice Hall.
This is the bible of marketing and it will help you develop every aspect of your marketing plan.

## 9.12 References

Chartered Institute of Marketing (2009) *Marketing and the 7Ps: a brief summary of marketing and how it works*. Available online at: www.cim.co.uk/files/7ps.pdf (accessed 20 December 2012).

Dyson, G.R. (2004) 'Strategic development and SWOT analysis at the University of Warwick', *European Journal of Operational Research*, 152 (5): 631–640.

Google (1998) Company overview. Available online at: www.google.com/about/company/ (accessed 31 January 2013).

Hill, T. and Westbrook, R. (1997) 'SWOT analysis: it's time for a product recall', *Long Range Planning*, 30 (1): 46–52.

Levitt, T. (1980) 'Marketing success through differentiation – of anything', *Harvard Business Review*, 58 (1): 83–91.

Lipton, M. (1996) 'Demystifying the development of an organizational vision', *Sloan Management Review*, 37 (4): 83–92.

Porter, M.E. (2001) 'Strategy and the internet', *Harvard Business Review*, 79 (3): 62–79.

Schoemaker, H.J.P. (1995) 'Scenario planning: a tool for strategic thinking', *Sloan Management Review*, 36 (2): 25–40.

Spiro, J. (2010) *How to create a company philosophy*. Available online at: www.inc.com/guides/create-a-company-philosophy_pagen_2.html (accessed 31 January 2013).

# 10

# Essay writing

## 10.1 Chapter summary

The origins of this chapter lie in Pat's accumulated experience of many years tutoring students from first year undergraduates to experienced managers on Masters degrees and Chris's recent experience of suddenly having to learn what on earth an essay was. We don't pretend that business life involves the formal, stylised exercise of essay writing but in fact the whole process is designed to make the student think logically, defend their arguments with evidence and write with clarity and succinctness. These are massively important skills in all walks of life as anyone who has waded through a badly thought out, poorly written report will testify.

The chapter presents some pretty hard and fast rules. These are rules that aren't usually written down but they are definitely expected to be understood. So it is one of those times where we are breaking open the locker that contains the secrets of success at university. But first we have two health warnings. These rules usually apply to essays but some lecturers have their own variants on this. Make sure you use the advice in Chapter 4 on how to use your lecturers and find out whether yours have any particular idiosyncrasies you need to know about – and follow. Also, the advice here is for *essays*. There are many types of assignment, which we cover in Chapter 9 for different types of coursework and Chapter 12 on exams. If your lecturer has a particular form of written assignment which is not an essay, many of these rules will still apply, but you need to make sure which ones first. The concepts of planning and how to make a point, which are central to the advice in this chapter, apply pretty universally. The majority of this

*(Continued)*

*(Continued)*

chapter is about coursework essays but there is also a section on how to write essays in exams in Chapter 12.

There are four parts to this advice which can be summarised as: how to get started, how to read, how to plan, how to write. The most important advice is this: *do not start writing immediately*. You will know that any project that starts without a plan is doomed to failure. The same is true of essays. So how do you get a plan? Let us start at the beginning …

## 10.2 How to get started

A journey of a thousand miles begins with a single step. (Confucius)

Sometimes the most difficult thing is knowing where to start and many students spend a lot of time thinking about which question to choose (if there is a choice) or what sort of approach to take. Perhaps the essay question requires you to pick two theories to compare and contrast and so often students find themselves trapped, unable to decide which ones to pick. Most of the time, the best thing to do is quickly pick a topic or the theories, run the idea past your tutor or fellow students, and then get on with it! It might not end up as being the absolute best example you could have chosen, but the time spent debating which example to use is generally not well spent. But do be careful of selecting very specific/niche topics where there is little research available. Sometimes students have a keen interest in a particular field or theory but there is little research available. Then when it comes to researching and writing the essay they find it very difficult to find supporting evidence and journals. To avoid this type of situation, spend a couple of hours doing some brief research when you have selected your topic. How rich is the area in journal articles? How many books are available on the topic? This brief research could help you avoid wasting loads of time later on.

But there are different sorts of essay question and each require their own approach.

## 10.3 Types of question

Essay questions vary considerably between topics and between lecturers but in broad terms there are four types of essay questions. Each of these are asking you to produce different answers.

## 10.3.1 'Discuss'

In this type of essay, you are frequently given a statement (often contentious) followed by the word 'discuss'. For example:

Taylorism is still a relevant model to leverage performance gains in the workplace. Discuss.

To answer this question you would start out by describing what Taylorism is then perhaps evaluate the features against literature or studies which contradict the idea that it does lead to gains. You then might return to the theory and extract any points which still have relevance.

## 10.3.2 'Describe'

The question asks you to provide information about a particular topic but does not ask you to evaluate this. It is very unlikely you will be asked only to describe something although this might be just part of a question – many essay questions have multiple parts and it is vital you make sure you note how many parts there are to a question and ensure you answer all of the parts. So a question might be:

Describe the Taylorist approach to productivity.

In answering any of these question types, you should always use the SED format, discussed in more detail on p. 164.

## 10.3.3 'Compare and contrast'

This format is very popular and you need to find the similarities and differences between two things. You should look to find equal numbers of similarity and difference and come to some sort of conclusion. If no conclusion is specifically asked for, just bring the essay to a close with a summary of the similarities and differences. For example:

Compare and contrast two theories of motivation.

## 10.3.4 'Evaluate'

This is rather like the 'compare and contrast' question but the examiner has given you some more latitude in how you go about answering the question. You don't particularly need to give equal numbers of points for and against but the custom is that you give both sides of the argument regardless of what you feel the evidence shows. So, you need to find at least something to say on each side. You are usually asked to come to some sort of conclusion and justify this through an evaluation of the evidence. Another favourite version of this question type is *critically evaluate* which essentially means the same thing. For example:

> Critically evaluate to what extent the Consumer Protection from Unfair Trading Regulations 2008 have reduced the instances of customers being taken advantage of by unscrupulous traders.

Note that some essays require you to do more than one thing. For example:

> Outline the main organisational theories underpinning modern management and *discuss* their relevance to your professional area.

Clearly you need to describe the theories and then evaluate their relevance to your profession. If you only describe the theories, you are unlikely to pass. If you do not describe the theories sufficiently (perhaps you just name them), similarly you are very unlikely to pass.

The most frequently written comment on essays by markers is something to the effect of 'you have not answered the question set'. Figure 10.1 contains probably the most important advice in this whole book.

So, quickly decide on your general approach. Sketch out the idea – a few sentences/bullets are enough at this point. Do some quick research and now go to your in-depth reading.

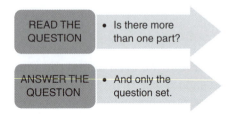

FIGURE 10.1   The two things you must remember about essay writing

## 10.4 How to read

Chapter 3 covers our generic advice on reading at university. If you haven't read this chapter yet, we suggest you do this now as we will be building on those ideas here. This is the general rule:

> Before you do any writing, you need to read.

This seems obvious – but students frequently misunderstand the task of essay writing. They often think it is only about writing and they obsessively count the number of words they are writing and focus on how many more they need to write before the essay is finished. Actually an essay is set as an exercise in critical thinking – being able to pull out the important pieces from a theory, then pulling it apart in a critique. The actual written essay is really only the record of this activity having happened already. We do really mean it when we say that you need to read a lot, significantly more than almost any student imagines they should. In fact, diving in to the writing stage without enough reading is perhaps the most common mistake made by students. We quite understand that you want to get going – and dare we say you might have left the starting of your essay pretty late so you are a little rushed for time. No matter how rushed you are, do more reading than you think you need to. There is only one exception to this rule. Those of you who find that spending more time reading is a way of putting off the actual start of writing the essay. Or putting off deciding which theories. Or just putting things off. If you are in that category, have a look at Chapter 5 on fear and stress and Chapter 6 on to-do lists. But for essay writing, you need to assemble a deep understanding of the relevant theories before you structure your work. And you will struggle if you start to write without a structure.

Read any follow up papers and chapters suggested by the lecturer and go over your lecture notes on the topic. If the essay has not been covered in a lecture, usually the best starting point is to find a key chapter or paper on a particular topic followed by a recent review paper or a critique of the theory. Using a mixture of text books to start off with and then following up with academic papers is the best way of going about your reading. By the way, academic papers are the ones you can find usually through your library's web page. The best ones are 'peer reviewed' and are given the highest level of checks before they are allowed to be published. Not all journals are well regarded though and you might like to look at the list of the better ones on the website of the Association of Business Schools in the UK. It means you probably need to be in the library for a reasonable amount of time because this is where the books are. Of course, you can usually access all the academic papers you need online remotely but there still is a very valuable role for books in essay writing. Make sure that at least some of the books you are reading are recent (i.e. published in the last three years) so you can be reasonably sure they contain the latest thinking.

By starting with the broad ideas first, you can get the key facts about a theory and the current controversies. The critical thing is to do this before you dive into the theory you are going to analyse for your essay.

## 10.5 How to plan

So you should now have a set of notes about theory relevant to the issue you are going to analyse. Now you need to create a plan – and again, do not start to write *anything* until you have one! There is an old saying in scuba diving:

plan the dive and dive the plan.

In other words, make a plan and then stick to it. So, you need to be sure that your plan is a good one. Make sure you really, really do have a proper plan and that it is based on the reading. This sounds like we are making the same points again and again – and we are! It is just that I know how busy students are these days and many of you have part-time jobs – and there are lots of non-academic things to enjoy at university too! But simply being pressed for time is no reason to scrimp on the reading and planning of your essay. The idea of a university degree is that it teaches you to think and going through the process of writing an essay is a massively important part of that learning. So try to enjoy it – it is doing you good!

What you need at the end of your reading and planning is a set of headings and bullet points describing exactly what you are going to write. The key thing is to sketch out exactly what you are going to say. This is how you work on the flow of the argument before even starting to write. It means you can hold the main ideas of the essay in your head rather than being bogged down by all the detail (the detail is going to come next).

Take time to hone your plan, take more time than you think you have. But resist the urge to start writing sentences even now. The idea is that you get completely clear in your head exactly what you are going to write before you start. Then when you do start writing, you will know what you are trying to say and where the argument is going. Do the reading and the planning well, and the writing will be extremely easy. If you don't do the preparation work, writing will be difficult, time consuming and probably not all that good. This sounds rather easy to do but it isn't. You have to be strict on yourself, keep reading more and more and constantly update your plan before you even begin writing. Chris remembers doing one essay that was worth 10 per cent of his degree. With such a weighting he thought it was critical to develop a solid plan. He read absolutely everything on the topic he was writing, cross-departmental team working. He started off with broad topics to get an understanding of the subject. He then looked up the references from the books and read the journals. And then looked up the references in the journals and read those. He kept going until he got to the core of all the theories and where they began along with all the critiques and reviews of them. Once he did this, he was in a great position to analyse all his notes and build his arguments to create a solid plan.

## 10.6 Writing (at last!)

So you have done the reading, made notes and formed a plan. Now it is time to write. There are two things to remember at this stage:

Don't start writing until you have a plan.

And ...

Follow the plan.

TABLE 10.1   The parts of an essay

| Section | Description | Tips |
|---|---|---|
| Introduction | A general short opening statement (one or two sentences). An overview of what is going to be in the essay. How the question will be answered. One (short) paragraph. | Make sure it isn't too long or you spend too much time thinking about it and re-writing it. The introduction only needs to describe how you have decided to answer the question set and you could almost write it last. Often students get hung up on trying to get this right. If you are struggling to write the introduction, you probably haven't planned the essay properly. Make sure that you tell the reader what to expect in the main body of the essay. Check that what you say you are going to do will answer the question. |
| Main body | Several paragraphs. Each paragraph will have self-contained arguments. Each paragraph will answer part of the question. | This is where you really earn your marks. Follow the outline made in the introduction. Each section should follow the format: statement of claim evidence discussion/evaluation. Justify *everything* you write using references to published material (i.e. journal articles or text books). |
| Conclusion | A short summary bringing together the arguments. Possibly assessing the limitations of the arguments. Showing how the question has been answered in parts and as a whole. One or two paragraphs. | Summarise the points made in the order you have made them. Your conclusion must answer the question set – no more and no less. Make sure it matches what you set out in the introduction. |

Overall you will need an introduction, body of the essay and a conclusion/ recommendation part. Table 10.1 provides more information about these.

The introduction should be short – usually a single paragraph is enough on a two or three thousand word essay. You need to include a description of what you are setting out to achieve in the essay – what you want to illustrate, prove, disprove. As for how to write the assignment, I recommend the SED format for each section:

*Statement of claim* – write what you are going to prove. For example, 'money does not of itself motivate employees to work harder'. On its own, a statement of claim has no value (i.e. will not provide you with marks) because without evidence it is only a view. Perhaps somebody might actually believe that money is the only way of motivating people, for example. But, if you provide evidence for it and then discuss and evaluate what it means, you are earning marks.

*Evidence* – for your assignments relevant evidence is a combination of scientific papers and some other objective evidence such as from case studies. But mostly it should be papers.

*Discussion* – this is where you evaluate the evidence for and against your claim especially in the light of the application of the theory to your workplace example. You might also include a critique of the origins of the theory in order to give your argument more power.

The conclusions part will re-state what you set out to achieve in the first paragraphs and reflect on how you have achieved this. It is best not to introduce any new ideas in this section as it should all be there in the main body of the assignment. It is usual for this section to include recommendations.

## 10.6.1 How to write your essay

We quickly want to touch on this subject to help you avoid another common mistake, trying to write the perfect essay. All too often, when students write an essay they constantly debate how to write it using the perfect language and ensuring it fits within the word count. However, unlike an exam you have time to go back and edit your writing. So when writing out your essay use the following approach. Get it all on paper. Use your plan and get all your thoughts out of your head. Don't worry about the word count, don't worry about how it sounds and don't worry if it doesn't fully make sense at first. Once you have got it all out of your head, go back over your answer and reread it. Make it sound smarter and stronger and make it more concise. We suggest doing this for each paragraph that you write: write it, re-read it and edit it. Once you have completed your essay, go back over the whole thing. Read it, edit it and make it more concise to ensure it fits within the word count.

Chris remembers one of his essays where he had to write 5000 words. He had so much to say that he wrote 11,000 words. Through the process above he condensed it down to 3500 words and then managed to write some additional analysis. The trick is not to worry, we naturally write more than we need to at first and you shouldn't try to stop this.

Once you have finished writing and editing your essay, ensure it fits within the word count. Most of the time you will have a 10 per cent lee way, where you can write 10 per cent under or over the word count but never presume this and always check first.

## 10.7 Referencing

Once you have written your essay, take a break and have some fun. But unfortunately it isn't the end yet, there is still the rather important and time consuming task of referencing. What is referencing? It is the means through which you acknowledge other writers' work. Referencing is important as it demonstrates the range of reading you have done and is the means by which you give authority to your conclusions. It also enables readers of your work to follow up your sources. It is vital that you acknowledge *all* sources with references to avoid being accused of plagiarism. Students sometimes struggle to get used to referencing and it does take some practise. But most of it is very straightforward and you can see how it is done by looking at your set text book or by reading academic articles. There are two main things to remember about referencing: (a) do it and (b) do it exactly in the precise format you are supposed to be using.

And this is where it gets a little difficult. Referencing comes in specific styles although far and away the most common is called the Harvard system. But there are many slight variants on this and, if in doubt, you should refer to your library which will have guidance on this or to your lecturer. But remember, the format needs to be *exactly* what is laid down. Not approximately. Exactly! Every dot, comma, space/not a space needs to be as the rules state. But don't worry, as we said, the most common tasks are easy to learn. We will focus on the Harvard system – there is another system called the Chicago System which uses numbers and end notes and you can find more information about this in Tissington et al. (2009).

## 10.8 Harvard referencing – the basics

There are two parts to the Harvard system – a note in the text and a list of references at the end of the essay.

## 10.8.1 In the text

When you have summarised the key points from a theory, for example, after the summary you state where you got the reference by quoting the names of the researchers who wrote it and the year. This is placed in parentheses at the end of the sentence. For example, this is a quote from a paper Pat wrote:

> Formally speaking, social identity salience is produced interactively by the cognitive accessibility of the category and how much it fits the situation (Oakes, 1987).

A key skill to learn in essay writing which is related to the issue of referencing is paraphrasing. In the example above, Pat and his co-authors have summarised a particular point and then shown the reader where it comes from. This means the reader can, if they want to, now go to the list of references at the end of the paper and look it up. Sometimes it is better to quote a short extract verbatim (word for word). In this case, you not only give the name of the author and the year of publication but also the page number where the quote is from. A word of warning though: most lecturers do not like to see very large extracts quoted directly – even if it is referenced correctly. Only use direct quotations for things like definitions or for a technical term. The rest of the time you need to put the ideas expressed in the paper or book into your own words – and then reference where you are summarising from.

## 10.8.2 The reference list

At the end of your essay, you need to add a list of the references you have used in the text. This is a list of references and not to be confused with a bibliography which is a more general set of work which is related in some way to the text. These are presented in alphabetical order by the surname of the first author. You need a list of references and this is where the style comes in. There is a very precise way in which every element of the reference needs to be written. The reasons for doing it this way are largely lost in the mists of time but essentially everyone expects it to be done this way.

It is made up of a list of authors with each entry presented in this format:

> surname – comma – capital letter initials separated by points – comma between authors – and or & sign before last author – year in parentheses – title – journal name in italics – volume (and issue) number – page span – full stop.

It looks complicated but when you see how it is done in practice, it makes more sense. Here is an example reference illustrating the style outlined above.

van Dick, R., Ullrich, J. and Tissington, P.A. (2006) 'Working under a black cloud: how to sustain organizational identification after a merger', *British Journal of Management*, 17 (1): 69–79.

This is the format for a journal article, whereas a book is slightly different:

Surname – comma – capital letter initials separated by points – comma between authors – and or & sign before last author – year in parentheses – title in italics – city of publication – colon – publisher name – full stop.

Another example:

Tissington, P.A., Hasel, M. and Matthiesen, J.K. (2009) *How to write successful business and management essays*. London: Sage.

We are yet to find a sensible reason why you need to record the city where the book was published, but you just have to put it in!

Of course there are lots of variations – different numbers of authors, different publication types, etc. but these two are the main ones. We suggest you go to your library's online resources to discover what support your institution has for referencing. In our experience, all libraries have something like this but in case yours isn't helpful, we have included some links at the end of the chapter which might help you.

A word of caution: there is a format for referencing websites but our advice is *never* refer to material on a website. That doesn't mean academic journals you happen to have accessed online but websites run by consultancies, for example. You can never be sure that they have interpreted the concepts correctly and lecturers very rarely count these as credible sources. It is very poor practice to cite them – don't do it!

When you have finished your essay, it is a very good idea to check just before you hand it in that (a) all the references in the text are in the reference list (b) that all the references in your reference list are actually used in the text and (c) that they are in the right order and format.

## 10.9 Common errors

### 10.9.1 Not answering the question set

To be honest, this is the *big essay mistake*. If you only learn one thing about essay writing this should be it. Time and time again, markers have to write comments on essays to the effect 'this was interesting but has not really answered the question'. The golden rule is to read back the sentence you have just written and ask yourself:

Does this sentence answer the question?

If you are thinking it is background, or introduction or something else, then by all means leave it in your essay. But you will not be gaining any marks whatever for it. You only get marks for answering the question. Very often, the introduction is too rambling and is in fact you getting your head around the topic. Go back to it and see if the essay actually looks better without it. If it does, regardless of how long you took to write it, delete it. It was gaining you nothing and wasting space – and incidentally annoying the marker.

### 10.9.2 Starting to write too soon

This usually stems from students wanting to get the assignment under way and they have limited time to devote to the course. Pat has found students to be motivated and hard working but they do tend to jump in unprepared – or at least not prepared enough. By too soon, we mean the following.

### 10.9.3 Not reading enough literature

Reading can appear to be a rather open ended exercise – and indeed in some ways it is. At work we will get used to having issues summarised on a single sheet of paper (or less!) but in learning at university level, reading around a topic is needed. This may appear to involve dead ends – reading things that do not appear in the assignment. But this is also a very important part of the learning. My advice is to spend far more time than you think is necessary on reading. Don't just use the set text, follow up the key references and read the original papers. Frequently you will find information there which isn't reported in the text books. Also you may well find them easier to understand than you first thought. When Pat was researching his dissertation he found there was one key paper that everyone in the field referred to. He eventually tracked this paper down – an unpublished thesis. He could see that almost none of the key researchers had actually read the paper and that over the years the study had been mis-reported.

### 10.9.4 Forgetting to proofread

You really do need to proofread your essay, no ifs or buts. You will be amazed at some of the mistakes you can find, and these can so easily be eradicated through sound proofreading. If you want to be extra prudent, get a friend to proofread it for you and return the favour by doing it for them. Chris used to have a close friend who was not afraid to say his opinion and so he was perfect for proofreading Chris's essays. He would often say what he did like and just as importantly what he didn't like and what didn't make sense. This honest approach always gave Chris the insight he needed to perfect the essay and he returned the favour by doing it for his friend as well.

However, this can lead to another mistake made by students – getting the wrong person to proofread your essay. Chris's friend let her boyfriend proofread her essay once and he deleted one of the text references and put his name instead. She only found out after she handed it in and as you can imagine she gave her boyfriend the silent treatment for quite a while. So be careful when it comes to who you select to proofread your essay, ensure they are doing well in their modules, are confident to give their opinion and who you know will be deadly serious.

## 10.9.5 Falling into the 'Google trap'

This is ignoring all the scientific literature presented and typing the key words into Google. This is a sure fire way of wasting time and/or presenting dubious material. A simple rule for this is – don't do it! Always start with general text books and then go from there to journals. There are very few exceptions to this rule – perhaps research published on learned societies' web pages (for example, CBI, CIPD) or perhaps government sites such as the National Audit Office. But don't think that any old website you come across is a suitable source. If in doubt, don't use it. There are so many great resources your library will have in terms of peer reviewed journals and text books, these are the ones you should concentrate on.

## 10.9.6 Writing without a clear plan

We recommend having a complete plan of the essay before even starting to write. Your lecturer can tell when students have just started out with some ideas in their head but no plan on paper. You must have this in place before doing any writing. (This advice is mentioned elsewhere but is so important, we have restated it.)

## 10.9.7 Doing the referencing once you have finished the essay

Referencing is far easier to do and less time consuming when you do it as you go along. All too often, students wait until they have finished the essay and then go back to do all the referencing. They then have to waste time trying to remember where they found everything and editing the essay, which can adjust the word count.

### 10.9.8 A brief word on plagiarism

Pat sees basically two forms of plagiarism. The first is when a student has quoted a passage and forgotten to attribute it properly. When you quote, you need to show it is a quote using quotation marks and by giving the proper reference. This is a mistake but might be regarded as cheating in some cases. The basic rule is to reference everything that doesn't come straight out of your own head. Make sure you do your referencing properly and this will never be a problem for you.

The second sort is deliberate cheating by passing off other people's work as your own. This is a pointless activity because by doing so you aren't learning – surely what university is about. And you are very likely to be caught. Lecturers can tell from the style if it is your work or not and also most essays are scanned through a system which checks your work for this. These systems are now very sophisticated and in common use. If you get caught, it could be the end of your university career – and indeed the end of your career! The simple rule is – don't do it!

## 10.10 Finally

Keep copies of your work – you should make sure that you have at least one separate copy of your essay and beware of leaving memory sticks in university computers – our lost property office has literally dozens of them. Put your name and contact details on yours to be safe and think about keeping it on a lanyard. One option is to email yourself copies of your work in progress so it is stored on a server as well as on your computer. We have found that using a cloud based storage system such as Dropbox means that you never have to worry about losing your work – as long as you back up regularly. Pat uses Dropbox to do this so his two laptops and his desktop all have completely up to date exact copies of all of his files. He also backs up to a USB hard drive too from time to time. You simply cannot be too careful when it comes to making sure you never lose your stuff!

Make sure you finish the essay *before* the deadline. If you want some final comments from your lecturer before submitting, remember you will need to make sure that if he/she has some suggestions for you, there will be enough time for you to work on it. Pat has frequently had to say that he could give comments but since there would be almost no time for the student to work on any suggestions there is little point. In fact the best way of working is to finish even earlier than this, put the assignment to one side for a few days and come back to it fresh before submitting it for comment. This requires quite substantial discipline but is well worth it. Essays are not best handed in with the ink still wet!

In conclusion, it is worth stating that writing essays is a critical part of the learning experience at university. By working in depth on a particular topic, you will really get to grips first with the theory and then with how to be critical about it. This is such a valuable skill to take through your life and comes from working hard at the essay. The form can appear rather arcane at first, but the outcome is so beneficial and lasts a lifetime.

## 10.11 Taking it to work

Clearly essay writing is a skill pretty much exclusively for university. It is there as a means to make you think critically and present a cogent argument. As such, the 'rules' of essay writing don't translate directly to the workplace. But you would be wrong to think there isn't anything you should learn and apply at work even from this rather arcane set of rules. All managers have to write reports and whilst the format and length will vary hugely, common threads are:

- write in a clear structure so the reader knows where they are being taken
- have a beginning, middle and end
- provide evidence to support your claims
- work from the literature *always*

When I write any marketing materials, it is important that I am clear about the purpose of the material, who it is aimed at and what I want the reader to take away from it. For example, is the piece intended to inform? Build desire? Or for the reader to immediately pick up the phone and to buy? Every piece needs to have a clear call to action so the reader is clearly signposted as to what they should do next. With any new product we communicate, there are clear guidelines about its positioning, the key selling points we should mention and who the target audience is. It is important that the body copy follows these guidelines staying true to the products positioning and that the tone of the copy is appropriate for the target audience.

James Morrison, Corporate Marketing Manager at BMW

## 10.12 How to get started

### 10.12.1 Professional

- Review a recent essay and using the principles in this chapter, determine what you would do differently.
- For your next essay, produce a 100 word plan that contains just a summary and the key headings.
- Read three books before starting an upcoming essay.

### 10.12.2 A little more interesting

- Submit your next essay a week earlier than the deadline.
- Proofread your friend's essay and give them in-depth feedback on what they should change based on what we have discussed.
- Do all the reading and research for your next essay without the use of Google.

## 10.13 Our bookshelf

Ó Dochartaigh, N. (2012) *Internet research skills*. London: Sage.
Be really careful about how you research on the internet – see the section on the 'Google trap' in this chapter. But this book will help you track down academic papers and use a number of online databases.

Tissington, P.A. and Hasel, M. and Matthiesen, J.K. (2009) *How to write successful business and management essays*. London: Sage.
Look we know what you're thinking – Pat's cross selling his other book. But students tell us that the sections on referencing and the actual essays which are pulled apart in the book are really helpful. If you have no clue how to write an essay, then this book will take you there step by step.

## 10.14 Online

www.learnhigher.ac.uk – vast amount of online resources available free of charge! See www.learnhigher.ac.uk/Students/Referencing.html for particularly useful advice on referencing.

www.harvardgenerator.com – online tool which helps you format your references. You would be better off learning how to do it yourself and it won't do all the various forms you need, but it really helps.

http://libweb.anglia.ac.uk/referencing/harvard.htm – well thought out website from Anglia Ruskin University. In fact most universities have this sort of resource. Some are only available to registered students but this one is free (at least it was at the time of writing).

www.associationofbusinessschools.org/node/1000257 – Academic Journal Quality Guide which lists the journals by quality. If a journal you are reading isn't on this list, it probably isn't very well regarded and you would be better off finding another source.

## 10.15 References

Tissington, P.A., Hasel, M. and Matthiesen, J.K. (2009) *How to write successful business and management essays*. London: Sage.

# 11

# Presentations

## 11.1 Chapter summary

Presentations are becoming an increasingly popular form of assessment because so many employers are now seeking graduates with effective presentation skills. This is why universities in general and business schools in particular require students to learn this skill set. Some people seem more confident to present than others – although in our experience sometimes that confidence is misplaced! This chapter assumes that you have no knowledge or confidence as a presenter and takes you through the process. Of course you will eventually develop your own personal style but we are presenting tried and tested techniques that will make your presentations work – and stand out.

## 11.2 Presentations – why and how

As a result, learning to deliver a presentation that stands out has become a very important skill, both for personal and professional reasons because:

*Life is a series of presentations.* (Jeary et al., 2004)

We love this book title because it highlights the importance of learning to present, each day people conduct presentations and the better you can become the more success you will enjoy. A great number of students and even business professionals believe that presentations are easy as the slide in Figure 11.1 shows.

---
**Slide 1 – Creating a Presentation**

1. Put some PowerPoint slides together
2. Read them aloud and maybe include a joke
3. Thank the audience for listening and ask them if they have any questions

---

FIGURE 11.1    Presentations – not as simple as this!

However, presentations encompass a lot more than this, like most things, a good presentation takes time, planning and preparation. One of the key aims in delivering a presentation is to deliver one that stands out, we see and hear so many presentations nowadays that it would seem this would be a hard task. However, it is actually very achievable due to the amount of bad presentations that we see. This chapter will provide the tools, techniques and knowledge to make this happen.

## 11.3 Planning

As we have said before, planning is vital and this most certainly applies to putting a presentation together. Specifically, you must be able to answer three questions:

1. What is the purpose of your presentation?
2. What is the audience expecting?
3. What are the key points of your presentation?

### 11.3.1 What is the purpose of your presentation?

Most will say the aim of any presentation is to influence; however, this is not always the case, particularly at university. There are in fact three purposes to any given presentation (Jeary et al., 2004):

1. to influence
2. to inspire
3. to inform

Why does this matter? Deciding this simple question will determine how you are going to present and what you choose to include within your script. Most of the time, a combination of these will be needed, in fact, probably all three for a successful presentation.

### 11.3.2 What are the lecturer and the audience expecting?

The first step is to determine what the lecturer is seeking. Without knowing this, there is the risk of creating something that does not meet the lecturer's requirements and hence not score marks. There will be several clues about this usually from what the lecturer has said in class and more specific guidance from the module outline as well as any supporting material such as a brief. Be sure to read these inside out before progressing as it is very easy to omit something important. If you are unsure about anything then make time with your lecturer. Specifically, you need to be able to answer:

- How is the presentation going to be marked? This will be broken down into different elements and will greatly determine the structure and content of your presentation.
- What is the choice of topics available to present on? Depending on the module, there may be some choice in the purpose of the presentation.

Usually the audience will just consist of the lecturer but increasingly the audience for academic presentations is increasing and it is important to consider these people, be it business people, fellow students or additional lecturers. We cannot emphasise enough how important it is to understand your audience. At a recent student business conference Chris attended, one speaker was very passionate and engaging. However, at one point she began to speak about how students should quit their degree as they are useless and instead use their time to start a business. As you can imagine this did not go down well with the hundreds of students in the room.

Below are some questions to help you think about your target audience and help avoid situations like the one above:

- What does the audience already know?
- What are the essential points that you need to tell them?
- What do they expect from you?
- What will interest them?
- What will keep them focused throughout the presentation?

It is really is important to get into the shoes of your audience and answer these questions, doing so will ensure you write the script with the eyes of the audience, those who are ultimately going to listen and determine the quality of your presentation.

### 11.3.3 What are the key points of your presentation?

After thinking about the purpose and audience, the key theme for a presentation can be generated. This is the key point that you want the audience to take away and remember. Whatever your idea, it should be concise enough to summarise in one sentence. For example:

Social media has changed the world of marketing.

The theme will be the key driving force of your presentation and will determine everything you are going to say so it is vital to get it right. It will also form the bedrock of your title, which needs to be catchy and engaging. For example, Chris used the title in Figure 11.2 at the start of his placement year and it is fair to say he is rather embarrassed about it in hindsight. All it says is that Chris is going to discuss himself for 20 minutes, if he was a celebrity this might have worked but he is not. He would have been better with titles such as: 'How you can help me', 'Where Chris is going' or 'How I am going to help you'. If the key theme has been developed thoroughly enough, it can in most situations be used as the title.

Even if the topic of the presentation has been decided by the lecturer, you can still decide upon a theme. The theme, which you are going to present, is different from the topic. A topic is the general subject which you are going to discuss such as digital marketing whereas the theme is the exact aspect you are going to focus on such as marketing with social media.

Within the main theme, there should be three sub-points. No matter how complicated the theme of a presentation, it can be boiled down to three key points. Why is this so important? Simple, people remember things in threes (this is a great tip for revision when condensing notes, which we shall come

FIGURE 11.2   Slide Christos created about himself

TABLE 11.1   Outline for a presentation

| Title | Points | Three key messages | Sub points |
|---|---|---|---|
| 'Social media has changed the world of marketing' | Facebook is very powerful and is gaining popularity | 1. Aims of marketing and social media | 1.1. Generate brand awareness<br>1.2. Build relationships with customers<br>1.3. Develop the brand image |
| | Twitter is also gaining popularity | | |
| | What are the aims of marketing and how does social media fit in? | | |
| | | 2. Types of social media | 2.1. Video sites<br>2.2. Social networks<br>2.3. Image sites |
| | What has the success of social media been so far in marketing? | | |
| | | 3. Good examples of companies using social media | 3.1. Nike<br>3.2. Coca Cola<br>3.3. Smirnoff |
| | Good examples of companies using social media | | |

to later in the book). Any more than three and people tend to find it difficult. This rule also applies at any point in a presentation – bullet points, agendas, etc. – to ensure the audience remembers what you want them to.

Sometimes it is difficult to do this but it is essential. Returning to a couple of the titles from earlier, there could be a million things to say but each could be boiled down to three key things.

Table 11.1 shows how far you can take the rule of three, if you wanted to you could even take it further by developing point 2.1 to identify the three most well-known video sharing sites. A good method to help reveal the three main points of a presentation is to ask yourself: 'If I had just one minute, what would I say?'. This question helps to get to the core of a theme and its messages by forcing you to eliminate any unnecessary material.

Once you have a theme, it is then important to ask, why does it matter? If people were asked this when putting together a presentation, many would struggle. Chris's manager often does this by asking him, 'So what?'. It is a great question to ask and if it cannot be answered then the theme may need reconsidering.

## 11.4 The script

The theme and three key points will begin to develop what you are going to say in your presentation but more detail is needed. This is the role of a script, the most important ingredient of any presentation and hence where the focus should lie. Developing a script really helps to organise your thoughts and plan what you are going to say.

There are two options when scripting a presentation: write it word for word or create a broad outline. The method that you choose is going to depend on your abilities and preferences. For example, both of us personally like to create broad points in order not to be too rigid and ensure we do not read off a page. However, writing a word for word script can ensure an effective well-written speech and ensure you never forget what to say. Even if you do prefer to write rough bullet points, we recommend you write it word for word and then turn in into broad bullet points as this helps to create a more polished script.

If you do not know which you prefer, the best recommendation we can offer is to try both methods and determine for yourself what you prefer. Whichever method you choose, it is crucial to write the script or a rough outline before working on the method of delivery. If this is not done, then you end up trying to write a script using PowerPoint, which is ineffective as it is unstructured and creates the risk of concentrating on the slides rather than the content. A good analogy to illustrate the importance of this is that of *The Simpsons*. Before anything is animated, 20 writers produce and repeatedly review the script to ensure it is perfect. Imagine trying to create the scenes before the script has been created, it is an impossible task – the same goes for presentations.

> The single most important thing you can do to dramatically improve your presentations is to have a story to tell before you work on your PowerPoint file. (Atkinson, 2005: 14)

When writing the script it is vital to constantly bear in mind the structure where the old saying still applies just as much as ever before:

1. Tell them what you are going to say.
2. Tell them.
3. Tell them what you have told them.

What this essentially means is to create a clear introduction, middle and end.

## 11.4.1 Tell them what you are going to say (start)

Ironically, the start and end are often overlooked but they are the most important sections due to the primacy and recency effect, which basically mean that people tend to remember what they hear at the start and end of a presentation. Because of this, all the key points need to be included at the start and end. Also, the way you begin sets the tone for the whole presentation and will have a significant impact on the impression given to the assessors. If you start off with a polished, well thought out, interesting introduction, you are well on the way to a great mark. As Weissman (2003) puts it, a presentation is like a game of chess and the opening is the most important move, where the game can be lost or won.

Often the advice here is to simply give an agenda or list of what is going to be discussed, however, there are so many more options out there. First, let's start by discussing what not to do. We personally believe one of the worst ways to begin a presentation is to introduce yourself or the group and then say, 'In this presentation I am going to talk about this, this and that'. This is crucial information but it is not engaging enough to make the audience want to listen. You really have to think about what is going to grab your audience and make this your opening, which should be related to your theme.

For example, Nancy Duarte, a famous expert on presentation skills, uses this to perfection in one of her videos on Ted entitled 'The secret structure of Great Talks'. She begins her speech by saying 'You have the power to change the world', followed by, 'Deep inside of you every single one of you has the most powerful device known to man'. I doubt anybody can say this is not engaging, as soon as we heard it we were captivated. Its power comes from the fact that it creates anticipation and suspense: what is she going to talk about? What is this great power and how can I get my hands on this power?

In light of this, there are many ways to start a presentation and some examples are given in Table 11.2.

TABLE 11.2  Example opening lines for presentations

| Options | Example |
| --- | --- |
| A comparison of two worlds | 'Imagine a world where all businesses are ethical as opposed to the current state of play where banks and businesses alike are unethical' |
| Shock Silence | Loud music or switching off the lights to make a shock entry |
| A question | 'What do you believe to be the most important aspect of HR?' |
| Piece of news | 'One in five businesses are now failing' |
| A task | 'Please can I ask everybody to stand up' |
| A fact | 'The world population will double in 10 years. What does that mean for governments?' |
| A quotation | 'Work hard, play hard. This is the essence of how to create the perfect workplace office' |
| A short story | 'In my life, I have learned two lessons. First, you must lead your own life and second, you must learn to respect those around you. These lessons are nowhere more important than in the world of business and this is what I would like to discuss today' |

These different options illustrate the amount of possibilities in beginning a presentation. A combination of these can also be used to create an ever stronger effect. For example, stating a fact as a question – did you know that 95 per cent of students do not know what they want in life? At this point, we would advise you to visit www.ted.com. This is simply a collection of the world's most inspiring and engaging speakers on every topic you could possibly imagine. It is a fantastic website for learning how to present, especially how to start a presentation, as the example by Nancy Duarte illustrates.

We do acknowledge that in academic presentations it is often expected that you introduce yourself and give an indication of what you are going to discuss. Hence, what we advise is a two phase start. First, the more interesting and captivating start followed by the formal dignitaries, i.e. name and agenda.

### 11.4.2 Tell them (middle)

This is the main part of the script and hence it needs to be good. Returning to our point earlier, there should be three main points that you wish people to remember. Each point is like its own little script, each should almost represent a story. At the same time, don't assume the audience will remember the agenda, be helpful by reminding them each time you move to a new point.

### 11.4.3 Tell them what you have told them (end)

The end can be where it all comes together or where it all goes wrong. It is where everything from the presentation needs to be pulled together. Like the start, a two phase process is best. For example, 'Thank you for listening today and before taking questions, I want to leave you with one final point ...' An effective technique here is to link to the start, i.e. 'Let me answer that question that I posed at the start'.

If executed properly, an audience should be able to tell the start, middle and end without being told. For example, returning to our earlier example of *The Simpsons*, there is no commentary that states this is the start, this is the middle and this is the end – great execution ensures that it can be implicitly understood, without being explicitly told.

### 11.4.4 Ingredients of a good script

No matter what the topic or method there are some key ingredients to include in every script. The first, which we personally believe to be the most crucial, is to include stories. No matter how formal/academic a presentation may be, including a story will always add value. There does seem to be a notion that stories are something that a proper business/academic person should not use. However, this is entirely wrong. Pat is a good example of this, he uses stories in every one of his lectures and year on year he receives positive feedback. You can see this for yourself, next time you are in a lecture, monitor how you and the audience changes in terms of interest and engagement once a story has been initiated.

It is important to make clear what we mean by a story as we do not want to be held responsible for students presenting their weekends out although it could be relevant in the right circumstances. A friend of Chris's once said that the best stories were 'tangent trains' and we agree. These stories have a point that add value yet go slightly off topic to keep the audience engaged.

> A well-told story conveys great quantities of information in relatively few words in a format that is easily assimilated by the listener or viewer. (Gershon and Page, 2001: 31)

A great example that has made the history books is the Steve Jobs commencement speech where he presented about his personal life and what students could learn from it. He did this by discussing just three stories from his personal life. The speech has been widely recognised as one of the best ever and really illustrates just how powerful the use of stories can be. If you have not seen it, we recommend you do, which is why we have included the link in the reference list.

Whilst presenting in final year on the subject of ethics, I had to present on sustainability, a dry subject to many. To overcome this, I looked to head off in a slight tangent to keep people's attention, which was already fading half way through this group presentation on a cold Wednesday morning. By linking topics from my own personal life such as sustainability in cars and in food through to the HR topic, I was able to engage on areas of wider interest, aided by some amusing and eye-grabbing images.

Craig Lodzinski, BSc Human Resource Management

Ask questions of the audience, a presentation should not simply be one person speaking for 20 minutes. We personally love the use of questions as they engage the audience and they work very well right throughout a presentation so long as you do not ask too many. They can be used at the beginning to engage the audience, in the middle to stimulate the audience, particularly useful in a long presentation, and at the end to leave the audience thinking. When using questions try to make them as easy as possible for the audience to answer, for example, 'Please can I have a quick show of hands' or 'Have you ever wondered about ...'. There is nothing worse than asking a question in a presentation and nobody answers. Alternatively, a rhetorical question can be asked. For example, in a recent presentation Chris attended, the lecturer spoke about the power of positivity and asked the question, 'When was the last time you were happy?'. This forced attendees to think about the question in their head due to its simplicity and directness. There are also many options as to who to ask which will depend on the size of the audience:

- everybody, as a rhetorical question
- specific individuals, a great way to personalise a presentation
- the whole group, through a show of hands
- two different halves of an audience

Create rapport with the audience. People in general love to hear and talk about themselves as it provides reassurance and enhances self-esteem. Hence, if you can involve your audience in your presentation then it will help to engage them. An easy way to do this is to use group language, for example, 'What can we learn?' or 'What do we need to do?'.

Add some passion to your presentation, it is a lot more enjoyable for you to deliver and for the audience to watch. Obviously, this is going to be easier if the topic is a personal interest or passion of yours. If not, then try to look for ways to add passion such as a relevant tangent story. If you watch Gary Vaynerchuk (a social media expert), you will see just how powerful passion can be in a presentation, just Google his name and watch one of his conferences.

Comedy is a very effective method for adding interest. Nonetheless, it can be disastrous when it is not funny. For an academic presentation, we generally recommend steering away from it. If you use the tips and tools given throughout this chapter then you will not need comedy to make your presentation stand out. However, if you believe you can add something funny then do so.

Quotes are very powerful in adding credibility to a presentation. When using a quote be sure not to make the mistake of simply reading it off, ask the audience to read it or say it yourself with no supporting slide.

Flexibility is also important. Any script must allow for contingencies in case something does not go according to plan. As part of this, allow some flexibility with possible things that could be dropped. Whenever possible, try to keep a presentation to a minimum. Just like essays, it is a case of quality and not quantity. Try to keep the presentation to a maximum of 20 minutes.

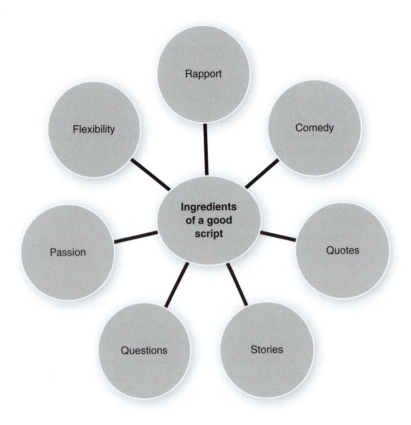

FIGURE 11.3   Ingredients of a good presentation script

After this, human beings take a real dip in concentration. However, where you must go on for longer, which is so often the case in academic presentations, then the principles we have discussed are of even greater importance. For example, stories and questions will help to maintain the audience's attention.

As a summary, in Figure 11.3 we recommend some techniques for a great script.

## 11.5 Delivery methods

Most people have come to accept that PowerPoint is the only method for delivering a presentation but this is not the case, it is just one option. We shall briefly cover three of these and explain best practise techniques for each and when we believe they are most suitable.

1. PowerPoint
2. Prezi
3. Speech alone

## 11.5.1 PowerPoint

PowerPoint has now become ubiquitous with the word presentation. However, it is fair to say that it has been used ineffectively. For example, as a student, we are sure you have sat through lectures where the lecturer simply reads the slides. And this is dull for everyone concerned! To give an idea of just how severe the issue has become, a political party has been conjured in Sweden entitled the Anti PowerPoint Party. Their one aim is to ban the use of PowerPoint as they have calculated that it costs Europe €110 billion per year from people having to sit through boring presentations.

So why is there so much hatred towards PowerPoint? PowerPoint was originally created to display images, no more, no less. This is one reason for its failure, it has been overused and overstretched. Second, the way many people use PowerPoint requires the audience to read text and listen to their voice at the same time. However, human beings are incapable of doing so. The third reason is that it has simply become dull to watch, too many bad presentations have made it a rather boring affair. Nonetheless, PowerPoint still remains very useful when used properly.

It is particularly useful when:

- Somebody has a low level of confidence as it can provide a useful guide as to what to say.
- The delivery of visual material is needed such as financial accounts.
- Marks are allocated to the quality of PowerPoint slides, in this case there is no other choice!

One of the ironic things about PowerPoint is that many people moan about having to sit through so many boring PowerPoint presentations yet do not do anything different themselves, thus just reinforcing the problem. Knowing how boring it can be, do not do the same thing. There are a number of techniques to create interesting slides which come down to three rules:

1. Minimise the content.
2. Make the content entertaining.
3. Be consistent with the content.

It is really important to follow all three of these otherwise it will not work. For example, we could write 200 words on a slide and make them look amazing by following the second rule, but the fact is there are still 200 words

| Learning how to write slides effectively | The how of slides |
|---|---|
| 1. It is crucial not to write anything you plan to say on a slide<br><br>2. Your aim is to keep slides as brief as possible to force the audience to listen<br><br>3. It is recommended to write no more than three points on any | 1. Crucial?<br><br>2. Aim?<br><br>3. Rule of thumb? |

FIGURE 11.4   Two slides used to make the same points

on a slide and it will scare the living daylights out of any audience. Pat has worked for organisations which ban people from using more than 30 words on each slide. This is not a bad guide as the slide should be there to prompt and guide rather than provide the whole content.

*Minimise the content.* Foremost, and absolutely key, is do not write everything you are going to say on the slides. If you do this, then you are inviting people to just read and not listen to you.

> When presented with a slide full of text, we are faced with a dilemma: either read the text or listen to the speaker. We cannot do both unless the speaker reads the text with us, in which case we might question the added value of either speaker or slide. (Doumont, 2002: 65)

The quote from Doumont is just fantastic in highlighting why it is so crucial to minimise the text on a slide, we cannot do two things at once. To overcome this, you should keep your slides as brief as possible and aim to give the listener an indication of what you are going to say. A general rule of thumb is that you should write no more than three points on a slide. For example, look at the slides in Figure 11.4 and have a think about what each slide invites the audience to do.

The slide on the left invites the audience to read whilst the other gives an indication of what the presenter is going to say and hence forces the audience to listen, the aim of a slide.

Be efficient with the number of slides, generally speaking we would say do not go over 40 slides although this will depend on the length of the presentation. In the case of a particularly lengthy presentation, we would actually argue that it is more important to be efficient because too many slides can become very boring and daunting for an audience. In this case, think about employing other techniques such as flipcharts and just speaking without slides. At the same time, we do acknowledge the view of Reynolds (2008: 60):

> As for how many slides, that really is the wrong question. There are too many variables involved to make a concrete rule to be followed by all the

same way. If your presentation is successful, the audience will have no idea how many slides you used, nor will they care.

Overall, when putting slides together just be conscious of how many slides you have by asking yourself whether they are all crucial and, if there are too many, what alternative methods could be used. Pat once needed a colleague to stand in for him and so sent the colleague the slides he was going to use for the session. Despite being extremely experienced and a superb lecturer, the colleague was simply not able to follow them. Indeed, he said he could not understand how Pat only needed four slides for a two hour lecture. Other times, he has used a great many slides for short presentations. It all depends on the points you are trying to get across.

A final tip in minimising content is to include a couple of blank slides, this really is taking the word minimal to the extreme but it is a very powerful method in forcing the audience to listen. When doing this, just state, 'I would like to briefly say something/draw attention upon/highlight a key point so it is clear that you have not made a mistake'. If you decide not to use blank slides, a tip with PowerPoint is to press the B key on the keyboard and the screen will go black. Press it again and the slide comes back. (Incidentally, pressing the W key turns the screen white.)

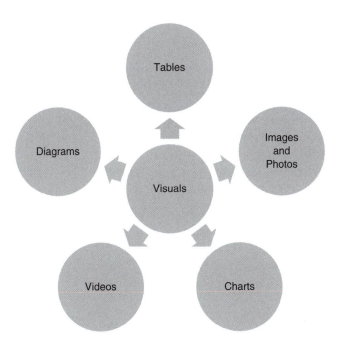

FIGURE 11.5   Suggestions for additional content for your slides

*Make the content visual.* All too often only words are used on slides but as human beings we can understand far more than this and actually find it easier in most circumstances. Bullet points particularly have become overused, many seem to believe that they have to be included in a presentation but this is simply not the case, which leads nicely on to the visuals available, with some suggestions in Figure 11.5.

One of our particular favourite visual methods is the inclusion of a You-Tube video, as it can prove refreshing and entertaining. Just ensure these are not too long and have them ready to play before you begin your presentation. For any visual content, ensure it is relevant to the presentation, this is particularly easy to forget when using pictures, all too often random pictures are thrown into slides that do not really mean much.

> some words may convey concepts better than a thousand pictures. (Doumont, 2002: 219)

The quote from Doumont highlights that pictures and more generally visuals are not always relevant or useful. When you do decide visuals are useful, be sure to make them of high quality as they can easily become distorted on large projectors. In terms of photos, there are some great websites out there to get professional high quality images:

- www.stockfreeimages.com
- www.pixelperfectdigital.com
- www.flickr.com
- www.freeimages.co.uk

There are really no excuses for using poor quality images and there definitely is no reason for using Clipart as it has been used far too much as well as the fact it looks awful.

During an assessment day at Marks & Spencer I was asked to create a presentation on 'Why consumers prefer to shop for childrenswear in-store than online?'. There were many ways to approach this question; however, I thought the best way would be to use good quality visual content that would not only answer the question, but also give the assessors something memorable. I started by making a mood board which was on A3 paper and included information about Marks & Spencer and my thought processes when thinking of ways to answer the question. I then decided to go to a few M&S stores and ask the consumers and staff directly whilst videoing them. I used the footage within my presentation and also gave the mood board to the assessors. They seemed to be impressed and even asked if they could keep the mood board. I received very good feedback and used this to help me secure a placement.

Henna Mehta, BSc Business and Psychology

A final warning is not to overcomplicate things, for example, trying to represent the whole world on one chart. With charts particularly and all visuals only include what needs to be included, for example, things like grid lines and background images on the chart can be removed. Remember less is more and by trying to include everything you can end up including nothing.

*Be consistent with the content.* The best way to do this is to create a theme and use it throughout your presentation. As part of this, use very clear fonts such as Arial or Calibri and do not use the templates provided on PowerPoint, like Clipart these have all been overused. Finally and most simply, make sure the audience can read the content:

Printing PowerPoint slides as a six-per-page handout (bringing slide width to about three inches) is a straightforward test of viewing comfort: whatever strains the eyes of handout readers is likely to strain the eyes of slide viewers. (Doumont, 2005: 67)

There is one slide which you can almost get away with not being consistent which is the opening slide, in fact, not being consistent often works better here. More often than not the opening slide will be ready on the screen and as soon as the audience see this they are going to pass an opinion on your presentation, be sure to make it a good one.

### 11.5.2 Prezi

An alternative method to PowerPoint is Prezi. This is a form of online presentation software that allows you to create interesting presentations through the use of dynamic features, notably a customised theme and dynamic zoom. This does not sound impressive at first but it is most certainly is. It actually encompasses many features of Mind Mapping combined with all the features of PowerPoint so it can make for very powerful uses. Before reading on, we suggest you quickly visit www.prezi.com and view one of the example presentations to get an idea of what it is all about, a particular favourite of ours is the one by Coca Cola.

We personally really like the use of Prezi as it simply provides something different. For example, the first time Chris saw a presentation delivered through the use of Prezi he was immediately captivated. In fact, the whole audience that attended the presentation clapped afterward and enquired about the software, which truly illustrates how powerful it can be. Preliminary studies in higher education even highlight that it has the potential when used properly to help overcome many of the issues of PowerPoint, the main one being boredom. Just as students have become bored of viewing PowerPoint presentations so too have lecturers (Gabriel, 2008). In terms of when to use Prezi, we recommend it when:

- Marks are not allocated to PowerPoint slides.
- You are presenting something quite creative such as a business plan, as it provides a great platform to convey creativity and innovation.
- Conversely, when you have something relatively dry to present as it can help to make it a little more interesting.

Before deciding to use Prezi there are two things which you must know. First is that all Prezi presentations are made public unless a private account is purchased and hence is not useful if confidential information is being presented. Second, a live internet connection is needed otherwise it cannot be used. Pat's experience of giving presentations in many different venues is that this is quite often a problem – never assume that the internet connection will be working. Always test it yourself first.

In terms of how to use it Prezi is surprisingly easy but like any IT tool it takes time to learn. We suggest that you first play around with it before undertaking an academic presentation. For example, if you are a part of a society then create a Prezi based presentation for your next meeting. We strongly suggest that you immediately begin using Prezi to become accustomed with how to use it, the earlier you begin the easier it will become.

Best practice methods in using Prezi are very similar to those of PowerPoint, hence we shall not repeat them. Very briefly though, be mindful not to go crazy with effects. You can create truly amazing presentations that zoom here, there and everywhere but the danger is that you can make your audience motion sick and keep them more focused on your graphics rather than on you.

One useful feature to point out is 'Prezifying PowerPoint slides'. Essentially, PowerPoint slides can be imported into Prezi to use its dynamic path and zoom functionality. This also allows you to design slides using the familiar PowerPoint functionality and then use Prezi to add the final touches. This is actually rather simple to do and instead of going through the detail it is easier to point you towards the two minute video created by Prezi which can be found at www.prezi.com/learn. You will then see a video entitled 'Prezify Your PowerPoint or Keynote Slides'. Also on this page are plenty of two minute videos that teach the full functionality of Prezi.

Whilst competing in the final of an Enterprise Pitching Competition my business partner and I used Prezi to present our business plan. Prezi not only allowed us to present information, but also gave us a unique and marvellous approach to the visualization of this information, which allowed our pitch to stand out amongst our competition who used basic and rather boring Power Point presentations. Prezi really allows you to express an idea beyond words and allows every presentation to be truly unique and bespoke to what you're trying to get across to your audience.

Anthony William Catt, BSc Management and Strategy

### 11.5.3 Speech

A third option is to use no computer material and instead deliver a speech. This takes a lot more work but when delivered properly can make a refreshing change and thus can generate a higher mark. Times that we suggest it is appropriate are when:

- Advanced visual aids are not necessary.
- The length of the presentation is relatively short as it takes a lot of work compared to using a computer.
- You are very confident with your presentation abilities, as there is only you and your words to rely on.

If you are going to use this method then it is even more crucial to spend time on the script as there is no reliance on anything else apart from it. Nonetheless, you may wish to include a PowerPoint slide with this method to support the script. Alternatively, the use of a flipchart works really well in conjunction with a speech. For example, a diagram could be drawn or a rough chart outlining some numbers.

## 11.6 Supporting materials

Whichever delivery method is chosen, supporting materials can be created to enhance the presentation, the main one being a printed handout. They can provide a tangible aspect and leave the audience with something to remember the presentation by. Handouts are also incredibly useful when there is too much information to fit into a presentation. With a handout comes the responsibility of deciding when to pass it round – at the beginning, middle or end. If handed out too early then it may distract the audience, too late and there is the risk that the audience may not read it. When to hand it out depends on the aim of the handout, if it is something to remember a presentation by, then at the end may be best. Alternatively, if it is to support the content of the presentation then it would be better to hand it out at the beginning. The great thing about creating handouts is that some fun can be had, should it be appropriate, as the example below highlights.

Each year I teach a module entitled Advanced Marketing Communications. The project that comes with this is students must create a full marketing campaign for a product I have chosen. A part of the assessment process is that students must present their campaign to me and business professionals. For example, last year students had to create and present a marketing campaign for Horlicks in front of me, a representative from GlaxoSmithKline and Cogent Elliott. The students demonstrated the usual creativity in terms of the variety of supporting materials, some of the best examples include:

A mock advert with a full storyboard

Demonstration point of sale material

A full product range

Biscuits and chocolates.

Keith Glanfield, Marketing Lecturer

As a general rule of thumb, we would suggest never to hand out a copy of your slides. The point of slides is to support the presenter and thus if done properly slides as a handout would be useless. Going back even further to the purpose of PowerPoint, it is a tool for displaying material not creating reports. Thus, the fundamentals of building handouts using PowerPoint are flawed.

## 11.7 Practise, practise, practise

After compiling a script, selecting the delivery method and editing the script there is only one thing left to do, practise. We really can't stress just how important it is to practise, a well-practised presentation ensures risks are mitigated, e.g. slides do work and the script sounds as it good as it can do. It also provides the opportunity to create notes for the presentation.

We know of very few students who do not use supporting notes to present. Even when somebody is confident enough we recommend creating notes to help omit the risk of losing your place and forgetting what to say. When creating notes, some useful tips are:

- Use colour to highlight distinct sections.
- Number each page in case you drop your notes.
- Use a large typeface/writing to ensure it is easy to read.

Linking back to Chapter 2, Mind Maps can prove very useful in developing notes as they clearly highlight distinct sections and everything can be fitted onto one page to ensure you are not scrambling round your notes.

Once you have created a set of notes, keep practising with them. It sounds simple but the more you practise the easier it will become. The best way to do this is to practise with people in the room and importantly not just your friends. The fact is you are probably very comfortable around your friends and they may be hesitant to give you constructive feedback. For these reasons, they are obviously not the best people to practise with. Instead, try to practise with people who you don't know so well, for example, somebody on your module or a lecturer. Ideally, try also to practise in the examination room or somewhere similar in order to get familiar with it. Finally, try to practise some Q and A. Ask whoever watches you in your practise session to play devil's advocate so that nothing will surprise you on the day.

## 11.8 On the day

There are a number of things that need to be completed on the day, before, during and after the presentation. Some of these are basic but are nonetheless crucial whilst some of these will help make your presentation stand out even further.

### 11.8.1 Before the presentation

- Dress appropriately, if you are unsure of how to dress than ask your lecturer.
- Get familiar with the room you will be presenting in and if possible practise within it one final time. But be aware not to practise too much on the day, if you have practised adequately enough then a couple of run throughs should be enough.
- When you are familiarising yourself with the room, check that you can be heard at the back. Remember an empty room does not absorb as much sound as one full of people. If in doubt, see if there is a built in microphone/amplifier system. However, only use this if you have tried it first as it can be difficult to get it to work properly.
- Buy a bottle of water as it is all too easy to get nervous and develop a dry mouth.
- Make sure you get something that will provide you with indication of the time to ensure you stick to your time limit, such as a timer, watch or clock at the back of the room.
- Create a positive mindset just before presenting, for example, think of three things that recently made you happy as it will put a smile on your face.
- Ensure you can be seen by getting your hands on a clicker, it will give you the freedom to move around the room instead of being tied to a computer.

### 11.8.2 During the presentation

During the presentation there is a lot to concentrate on, in addition to the script and the audience you need to concentrate on your language, both oral and body. To help create positive body language, be sure to stand up, even when you are able to sit as it will help to project your voice and become more confident. If you are also able to walk around the room then do so as it will further project your voice and help to maintain the audience's attention. Be careful not to fidget or pace up and down though – some movement is great but the best rule is that 'less is more'. It is very common for people to adopt some form of nervous tick when presenting and you won't be aware of this. Make sure that when you practise, you get feedback on this. Or you could video yourself. It's difficult to do but definitely worth it.

Make contact with your audience as much as possible, especially eye contact, although it is easier said than done. If you find this difficult to do then try looking just underneath their eyes, it is not as intimidating yet it still creates the same effect. If you are presenting to a large group, try to make eye contact with as many attendees around the room as possible, walking around will help to do this.

Use your hands to make further contact with your audience. Obviously, do not go crazy and wave your hands around everywhere otherwise the examiner may get a little scared. An easy way to do this is to point to certain things on the screen (assuming you are using slides). A tip is to make sure that you don't make your presentation facing the screen – believe it or not this is very common! Only refer to the slide on the screen, your main attention is on your audience.

Vary the volume, pace and pitch of your voice. If there are certain points you wish to emphasise, increase your volume and slow down your pace. In terms of pace, speaking too slow or too fast is as bad as one another. Ideally, you should aim for somewhere in the middle. If you have a natural tendency to speak too slow or too fast then the best way to overcome this is to pause throughout the presentation as it allows you to catch a breath and ensure a consistent speed. Chris has a tendency to speak too fast and to help he writes a reminder to pause on his notes. When Pat started out, he used to rush consistently so he used to write 'slow down' in large letters on the top of his notes.

### 11.8.3 After the presentation

Ask the audience if they have any questions. If a question is asked, repeat it to make sure that you have correctly understood it and so too has the rest of the room to ensure nobody is left out. Keep your answers as brief as possible, it is far easier for the audience to comprehend and helps to clarify the answer in your own head. Also, do not be afraid to take a second or two to think of an answer first, nobody would expect you to have an immediate answer. It is usually better to get questions at the end of the presentation as it can be disrupting. Also, questions are often answered in the presentation if people wait. You could think about saying this at the start of the presentation – for example, 'There will be plenty of time for questions at the end'. If you truly do not know the answer, simply acknowledge it, at the end

TABLE 11.3   Summary of presentation advice

| Before the presentation | During the presentation | After the presentation |
|---|---|---|
| Dress appropriately | Stand up and walk around (a little) | See if the audience have any questions |
| Buy a bottle of water | Make eye contact | *Chill out* |
| Get familiar with the room | Use your hands | Gather feedback |
| Create a positive mindset | Vary the volume, pace and pitch of your voice | |
| Get a timer/clock/watch | Pause and take a breath | |

TABLE 11.4   Troubleshooting your presentation

| Possible issue | Reactive method | Proactive and our recommended method |
| --- | --- | --- |
| Nerves | Acknowledge it and tell people how you feel, more often than not, you will get some sympathy | Practise, practise, practise |
| | | Look at speakers/presenters who you believe to be good, study them and ascertain why you believe them to be so good. Then use some of their methods |
| | | Make yourself feel confident through positive associations – clothes, jewellery |
| Drying up on stage/losing your place | Acknowledge it and move on, the worst thing to do is to say nothing as it just looks unprofessional and that you are trying to pretend it never happened | Practise, practise, practise |
| Projector or computer breaks | Depending on your lecturer's preferences, complete the presentation without your slides or delay it for a future date | Practise without PowerPoint by developing a thorough script and comprehensive notes |
| | | Take a spare laptop and test the equipment beforehand |
| | | Remain flexible, things can go wrong and you must be prepared to change things if necessary |
| Lack of time to prepare the presentation | 'Presenters under time pressure would be better off forgetting about slides altogether and focusing on defining their key messages instead' (Doumont, 2005: 69). | Effective planning and time management should ensure there is not a lack of time |
| Audience looking bored/distracted | Acknowledge it and ask if everything is ok | Make sure you get into the minds of your audience and create an engaging presentation in which you know they will not get bored |

of the day it is not the end of the world to say you do not know, though do offer to get back to the audience about it should they wish, this shows that you are not looking for an easy way to escape the question. As a more proactive method, try to anticipate any possible questions so you can think about possible answers in advance.

Table 11.3 provides a summary of this advice.

## 11.9 Troubleshooting

So far we have assumed a pretty perfect world: prepare, turn up, do your stuff and then leave happily to gather feedback. However, we know things can go wrong, no matter how much planning has been undertaken. Table 11.4 lists some of the most common things that can go wrong and what we believe can be done about them. What you will hopefully realise is that everything can be pretty much dealt with in advance to ensure you are in full control.

Going through this, we hope you realise just how important thorough preparation and practise is – with it, virtually nothing can go wrong. Pat makes many presentations in a very wide range of places. The week of writing this chapter was reasonably typical: he presented at a Fire Station, in a conference room and (memorably) in a cocktail bar. There were problems with all of these – no password to log in to the PC provided, no projector and loud background noise. The common theme was that because he had prepared and arrived early at all the venues, he was able to sort out the problems before the presentations. His experience has taught him to check the equipment and allow enough time for glitches to be sorted out. He even runs through all the slides he is going to use on the equipment in the room to make sure nothing changes in the move from his memory stick to the computer in the room. He always checks that there really is the internet connection that people promise and that he has a backup plan if the connection can't be made (this happens frequently!).

## 11.10 Taking it to work

As part of your career you will be required to present at some point, whether it will be presenting a new marketing campaign, the strategy of a company or financial accounts. If you choose to start your own business you may even be required to present to an investor, Dragons' Den style, as well as pitching your products and services to potential clients. There will not be any formal requirements like you get at university but you will certainly require the tools, techniques and skills developed in this chapter to deliver what will be implicitly expected of you. Delivering a great presentation is also a sure fire way of building strong relationships with team members, making a good impression to wider employees and ultimately taking you closer to realising your goals.

One thing I was surprised about when I started in my first job after university was how true many of the office stereotypes were. Certain types of personalities really do gravitate towards certain roles – and this phenomenon becomes exaggerated the bigger the company you are in. As such, coordinating cross departmental projects is a real skill. You have to acknowledge and understand all of the pressures and concerns that are facing other departments. Persuading, cajoling, peace-making and patience are all key skills – many of which you might have to implement at the same time! The key is to get the objectives agreed upfront and set a clear and realistic time plan for completion. Get the key contributors to suggest the time frames for delivery, so they've got no excuse for missing the deadlines! Finally, be flexible in your expectations, things rarely go exactly as planned, but as long as you've achieved your objective you can be proud of your achievement.

Harriette Luscombe, Marketing Manager at Brantano

## 11.11 How to get started

### 11.11.1 Professional

- Have a go at using Prezi at the earliest possible opportunity.
- Summarise your most recent presentation in just one sentence and three key points.
- Get into the mindset of one of your lecturers and think about what they would expect, like and appreciate from a presentation on a topic within their field.

### 11.11.2 A little more interesting

- Find two videos on TED in a subject you are interested in and note down how you can develop your style to be more like them.
- Call yourself a different name to a stranger and present yourself as that person.
- Think of a funny story in your personal life and determine how you could link it to a presentation on marketing, HR or accounting to make it more entertaining.

## 11.12 Our bookshelf

Steel, J. (2007) *Perfect pitch: the art of selling ideas and winning new business.* Hoboken, NJ: John Wiley.
This book gives a fascinating insight into how marketing agencies present in order to win new clients. The tips apply to all presentation styles as Chris learnt when he used the advice in his final year of university and the author is well acclaimed so offers a lot to take away.

Garr Reynolds (2008) *Presentation zen.* Berkeley, CA: New Riders.
A truly great book that takes the art of presenting from a different perspective, mainly a creative one. It provides solid advice and, as a lecturer, the author has a good understanding of both the academic and business world. We definitely recommend this as a worthwhile read for all students.

Davies, G. (2010) *The presentation coach: bare knuckle brilliance for every presenter.* Chichester: Capstone Publishing.
This book provides detailed advice on how to create an effective presentation from the world of business and provides some alternative viewpoints to topics such as body language, hence provides an interesting read.

## 11.13 Online

Conway, C., Fletcher, S., Russell, K. and Wilson, W. (2012) 'An evaluation of the potential use and impact of Prezi, the Zooming Editor Software, as a tool to facilitate learning in higher education', *Innovations in Practise*, 7: 32–46. Available online at: http://ljmu.ac.uk/ECL/ECL_docs/InnovationsMarch12.pdf#page=32 (accessed 20 May 2012).
Kellaway, L. (2011) 'Anti-PowerPoint revolutionaries unite'. Available online at: www.ft.com/cms/s/0/059e7092-af27-11e0-914e-00144feabdc0.html#axzz1tLhAm7dP (accessed 10 May 2012).
Nam, A. (2012) 'Coca Cola company'. Available online at: http://prezi.com/ftv9hvziwqi2/coca-cola-company (accessed 26 June 2012).
Perron, E.P. and Stearns, G.A. (2010) 'Research on social work practice'. Available online at: http://141.213.232.243/bitstream/2027.42/78306/1/Prezi.pdf (accessed 29 May 2012).
Prezi, www.prezi.com.
TED, www.ted.com.

## 11.14 References

Atkinson, C. (2005) *Beyond bullet points: using PowerPoint to create presentations that inform, motivate, & inspire*. Redmond, Washington: Microsoft Press.

Doumont, J-L. (2002) 'Verbal versus visual: a word is worth a thousand pictures, too', *Technical Communication*, 49 (2): 219–224.

Doumont, J-L. (2005) 'The cognitive style of PowerPoint: slides are not all evil', *Technical Communication*, 52 (1): 64–70.

Gabriel, Y. (2008) 'Against the tyranny of PowerPoint: technology-in-use and technology abuse', *Organization Studies*, 29 (2): 255–276.

Gershon, N. and Page, W. (2001) 'What storytelling can do for information visualization', *Communications of the ACM*, 44 (8): 31-37.

Jeary, T., Dower, K. and Fishman, E.J. (2004) *Life is a series of presentations: 8 ways to punch up your people skills at work, at home, anytime, anywhere*. New York: Fireside/ Simon & Schuster.

Jobs, S. (2005) Steve Jobs' Stanford Commencement Speech 2005. Available online at www.youtube/watch?v=D1R-jKKp3NA. (Accessed 7 November 2013).

Reynolds, G. (2008) *Presentation zen*. Berkeley, CA: New Riders.

Weissman, J. (2003) *Presenting to win: the art of telling your story*. Upper Saddle River, NJ: Financial Times Prentice Hall.

# 12

## Succeeding in exams

### 12.1 Chapter summary

Whilst there is a great deal of innovation in assessment methods, exams still form the backbone of assessment at university. This chapter will show you how to work out a strategy for your exams and also how to write concise, high quality answers. In some ways, this chapter brings together many tools and techniques from the book including using the reading, notes and relationships developed with lecturers to succeed in exams. It ends with specific tips regarding the actual day of exams and how to cope in order to be as effective as possible.

## 12.2 Planning – what exams and when

Key to success in exams is planning. You will know that we talk about this in practically every chapter in the book but, for exams, if you set out in a disorganised way to read up a bit on the topics for your exam, you are bound to do less well than you should and are very likely to fail.

So what do we mean by planning? There is a mindset that an exam is just a test of where you have got to in your understanding of the topic so, aside from a brief refresher, you should turn up and see what happens. Never *ever* do this! People who do well in exams do not do so by accident – incidentally many people pretend that they have done no revision and still get high marks. They are not telling the truth. People who do well in exams have planned, prepared and are ruthless in their approach to exams. It is especially true in the UK where it is unfashionable to admit trying hard. But it is always true. So what preparation have these successful people been doing? They know the answers to all the following key exam questions:

- What topics does the exam cover – and what does it not?
- What is the pattern of questions from the past papers?
- Which are the difficult topics to learn – and do they need to be learned for the exam?
- How many marks is each question worth?
- Which topics do you think you can get a really high mark in?
- Which topics do you need to really put extra effort in to get up to standard?

Once you know the answers to *all* these questions, you can plan where to direct your effort to the best effect. Lecturers may argue that you need to learn everything in the module so you have a rounded understanding of the topic. And we (especially Pat) have some sympathy for this view. But the truth is that you need to know how to play the game – and exams have rules in the same way that games do. Of course, the truth is that revision is an expandable activity which can fill all the time available. The rule is usually that the more you do the better you get. But that is not enough. You need to be focused on directing your effort into getting the most marks. At all times in your revision process, ask yourself, 'Is this activity going to gain me more marks in the exam?' If you don't know, then you need to find the answers to the key exam questions shown above.

## 12.3 Question spotting

For some lecturers, you can be almost certain of particular topics and even specific questions coming up in the exam. Talk to lecturers and try to find out what they are going to put in the exam – use the tactics we described in Chapter 4. Most will be evasive so one way round it is to show them the topics you are revising and say – have I missed anything crucial? Lecturers hate being asked about the exam but by all means push them for all the information you can. Pat's usual response is to say that he can't remember what is in the exam – and actually this is usually true since the exams are written months before they are taken. But you can always try to corner the lecturer and find out if a particular topic is definitely not going to be included. If you have managed your relationship with your lecturer properly then they should be willing to help, though do show you have made an attempt at beginning to revise first otherwise they could think you are looking for an easy way out. Some lecturers call this the 'what's going to be in the exam dance' where the students try to probe for what questions are going to be in the exam whilst the lecturer tries desperately to balance being helpful with keeping it secret.

Of course, if you have built a relationship with the lecturer over a period of time, you will be far more likely to get useful information at this stage. Lecturers can tell when a student only becomes interested in talking to them when exams are in the offing and are naturally less inclined to be helpful than to students who have shown genuine interest in the topic all term.

The most widely accepted method to know what will be in the exam is to find former exam papers and look for patterns. Many universities have these available through the library or via the Virtual Learning Environment. When using this technique, make sure that the past papers you are looking at were set by the same lecturer you have and that the course hasn't changed since the exam was set. These days very often there will be changes from year to year and if your exam has changed, looking at past papers might not help you all that much. But it is definitely worth trying. It isn't cheating and in fact looking through exam papers will focus your mind on the work you need to do – and knowing what work to do is so critical to success in exams. If you find that the course has changed or the style of exam is different to previous years, it is a good idea to ask your lecturer for examples of the questions which will be coming up so you can get a clear idea what is in the mind of the examiner. From the lecturer's point of view, this is sensible preparation and they are very likely to be able to provide examples for you.

## 12.4 Revision

The main thing is not to do any revision until you have been through the planning above. There will be topics covered in the module that will definitely not be in the exam. So ignore them for the moment – but you must be 100 per cent sure of your ground and only completely exclude topics from revision that you know for sure won't be examined.

The most successful students are ones who work together with groups of friends. For revision, you need to find motivated people who want to do well and with whom you can get on. Students who form this sort of group do better than those who don't – and it is also useful for all sorts of work at university.

> Revising with others can be the most beneficial way to revise. I do this through the use of a study buddy, essentially one person can revise one section of the module and the other can learn another. After you teach each other what you have learnt. However, I always ensure it is just two people as a group of more than three tends to end up in a chat and makes it very hard to get learning done.
>
> Victoria Saville, BSc Business and Sociology

Just getting together and discussing topics and how you have approached assignments really helps, as the example from Victoria highlights. These days universities have places where groups of students can work together so use these spaces for your meetings. It is better to have a small group – perhaps three or four people – so you can be organised and focused on revision rather than having a chat. It is best to agree with your group what topics need to be covered. For example, there are usually some topics that you need to know in detail and are 100 per cent certain to be in the exam. And there may be others you need only a little information about, for example, just knowing a couple of references. And of course there may be topics you can ignore completely (again, do be completely sure that these topics are definitely not going to be examined before you take this step!). The key to a successful study group is the right balance of work and socialising. By all means form a group with people you like but remember that the aim of the group is to prepare for the exams so choose your group members carefully – it can be frustrating if some members of the group appear to be more interested in chatting than working.

Having scoped out what topics are going to be in the exam, you can divide up the topics between the members of the group and agree which of you will learn a topic detail. Set yourself a deadline to come back to the group and each of you then presents back your own topic. Focus on the critical elements first then expand to the peripheral theories. It is best if you write a summary including key references for everyone to learn. One tip is to look for a recent academic paper on a topic and use the literature review section as the basis for your revision. In fact some journals carry review papers from time to time – these are papers solely setting out a systematic audit of the current state of thinking in the topic area.

Getting a study group to function properly takes planning, but if you should work out a series of meetings where you can go through the topics and stick to the timetable, it can pay back in a big way come exam time. If you plan enough in advance, you can spread this out so you gradually build up your knowledge. Last minute cramming is a very poor way of working. Absorbing information over an extended period is a much more effective way of making sure that you can remember all that you need to when you enter the exam hall.

> Once I feel I have a good grasp of the topic in hand, I will try to meet up with some of my course mates and we will test each other on the topic. I find being put on the spot and having to either explain my answer to a question, or test someone else's knowledge, really helps me to work out exactly what I need to go over again before the exam.
>
> Samuel Wilson, BSc International Business and Modern Languages

Some people prefer to work alone – maybe you have to for one reason or another. For example, Chris never really liked the idea of study groups as he found them to be too distracting, he much preferred to work on his own. Pat found groups extremely useful when he was at university. Most of all we recommend them as on the whole those who study in groups do better than those who don't.

The key to learning is repetition. In order to commit facts to memory, you need to have been through them many times and in different ways. In cognitive psychology, they talk about 'memory traces' which is the form that a particular fact takes in your brain. In order to make sure that you have committed something to memory in a way which you will be able to recall it, this memory trace needs to be as rich as possible. And by this, psychologists mean that you have thought about it in different ways. So, here is the process for committing a subject to memory:

- You begin by reading. Just reading without noting anything down. Do this quite quickly and skip anything you don't understand. Make sure you are only reading the material you will need in the exam though. This stage of the process is designed to lay down the first elements of the memory trace.
- You then read again taking notes. Look up anything you don't understand and follow up until you do understand. As always, make sure you are only learning the things you will need for the exam. The notes should be summaries of the key theories including the dates of the reference. In exams you are expected to remember the theories and the dates but not the full reference. So make sure this is in the notes. Your notes should be written by hand and not typed on a computer because when you write, you are actually forming the letters in your head and this is a more effective way of creating and then reinforcing a memory trace.
- You then put the books or journal papers to one side and just read the notes. Make sure that you can understand them on their own – going back to the text if anything doesn't quite make sense.
- Next, take a new sheet of paper and write a reduced summary of the notes by just using the key words.
- Then read through your reduced notes and check that they make sense on their own. Go back to your first notes or the original text if you need to.
- You then reduce your notes again – just the key theories and elements of them that you need to have in the exam. Think of what you might need to reproduce in the exam and have some key theories and maybe even diagrams that you can reproduce from memory exactly.
- Keep on reducing the notes until each topic can be summarised on a post card – just with the key theories, dates and diagrams. These are the notes you should have with you on your journey into the exam as prompts for last minute reminders of the material you will need. The notes on these cards should be committed to memory exactly so you need to make sure all the information is correct and relevant to the exam.
- Now you are ready to start testing yourself. Devise a test for yourself based on the longer notes with questions and full answers. It is another form of repetition to write this out in

full. Make sure you do this in such a way that anyone can test you. If you have done this properly, any member of your family will be able to act as your quiz master.

- Get someone to test you – or if not possible, write out the questions, hide the answers and write out the answers in exam conditions.
- Do it again.
- And again.
- And again.
- Only stop when you are getting it 100 per cent correct every time.
- Then try the questions in a different order. One way of doing this is to write the question on one side of a blank post card and the answer on the back. So you can shuffle the cards, then read the question. Write the answers down (don't just say it to yourself – the act of writing is an important part of committing things to memory) and mark yourself against the answers on the back. Give the cards to a friend and have them test you in the same way.
- Once you get all the answers right, leave it for a day and then come back to it and test yourself again.

> The revision techniques that I find work best for me are working through lecture slides, articles and any reading and making key notes in my own words. I then go on to rewrite the notes onto revision flash cards. Rewriting the notes helps the memorizing process of revision. I like to do this in a quiet space, which is usually my room. I am unable to work in noisy conditions and therefore require complete silence.
>
> Shivani Sharma, BSc Marketing

The example from Shivani highlights just how well this method can work. To get even more from this technique, we recommend that you undertake these methods using Mind Maps whenever possible. For example, write your notes using a Mind Map and then rewrite them. Test yourself using Mind Maps, for example, having the questions as one node and the answers as another. There are additional methods you can use which are particularly useful when perhaps a topic is complicated or you are struggling to remember it all.

### 12.4.1 Notes on the wall and flashcards

You can place notes on the wall all round your room. Pat used to buy a roll of lining paper from a DIY store and basically papered his bedroom with it and then wrote key theories up on the wall. It is also a good idea to gather your notes physically together by topic so when you are in the exam room you can close your eyes and think of the particular place in your room where the notes are. This often helps. You can then use them with a revision buddy to go through the topic. Pat used to have a fellow student teach him the theories from the notes and then they would swap roles. We know of people who would have particularly important notes taped to the bathroom mirror so they could look at them whilst brushing their teeth. Chris still remembers his law module where he plastered key acts and laws all around his bathroom so that every morning he would read them whilst brushing his teeth. The beauty with this technique is that even when you are not consciously revising, you subconsciously are every time you walk past the notes on the wall.

> Being a visual learner, all of my revision techniques involve a lot of colour! The first thing I always do is rewrite my lecture notes in a way that is a bit more memorable. The standard lecture slide is always quite boring in the way the information is communicated, I find. Therefore I have less chance of remembering it unless it is communicated in a way that is attention grabbing. Flash cards using different coloured paper and Mind Maps on large A3 sheets of paper are the main revision techniques I use to organise the information I need to know.
>
> In terms of actually learning the content, once I have organised it in a way that is best for me, I always do lots and lots of past exam papers and practise questions. Repetition is a great way of remembering things, and learning by actually doing them is a much more effective way of learning things than just reading! It works for me anyway!
>
> Devon Parker, BSc International Business and French

## 12.4.2 Diagrams

Using diagrams might also be a way of remembering a particular theory, much like the Mind Maps we described in Chapter 2. Sometimes you may need to memorise a diagram so you can reproduce it in the exam. Or maybe it acts as an aide memoire so in the exam you can jot the diagram down just in your notes section and then cross it out so it isn't marked.

> When I have to memorise things, for example in my Chinese module, I use images to help me remember words. I also try to associate certain words to images in my head, like making a script. For example, in Chinese the word for the colour 'blue' is 'lan'. In Romanian, 'lan' means 'field'. So, in my head, I have a picture of a field and a blue sky.
>
> Alexandra Cojanu, BSc Business and Management

### 12.4.3 Typing up notes

Having said that writing by hand is a far more effective means of revising, in fact you can take your notes and then type them up as part of the process of revisiting the notes yet again. We don't recommend you only use typed notes but it is a different way of going into your memory so will increase the memory trace. Clearly this is a good use of the Mind Mapping techniques we discussed in Chapter 2 and you might like to use one of the software packages to draw a Mind Map of the subject matter.

### 12.4.4 Creating a story

Creating a story can work wonders, especially when you have to remember lists of information. Remember the brain remembers unusual and quirky things but also things that are structured, which stories naturally are. For example, you may need to remember the four recommendations an author stated for creating a strategy:

1. vision
2. insight
3. mission
4. goals

Using a story, you could remember the list: a man once had a *vision*, to score four *goals* for Manchester United. One day he met a woman called *Insight* and she told him the key to success was to have a *mission*. The more creative you get here, the easier it becomes to remember, as you can see we are not that creative and we are sure you can do better than this.

### 12.4.5 Acronyms

Similar to the creation of a story to help your memory of a theory, you can create an acronym or an expression to help you remember the key elements of a theory. Pat always presents the five factor model of personality in such a the way that the first letters of the factors spell OCEAN. Pat's son can always remember the points of the compass through the expression Never Ever Support Wolves. This resonates with him as he is an avid Aston Villa supporter and it tickles him that it says something rude about a rival team (apologies to any readers who support Wolverhampton Wanderers!). But you should make up your own as they need to make sense to you and not other people. Pat remembers his father trying to teach him Morse code using the trick he (his father) had worked out. This made sense to his father but not to Pat who needed to work out his own in order to learn the code.

## 12.4.6 Different colour paper for different subjects

You can get different pastel shaded paper from a stationary store and use different colours for each topic in a module. This gives further cues to your memory so when you are in the exam room, you can think to yourself, 'Right this was written on the green paper', which will help you retrieve the facts from your memory. Post-it notes can work particularly well here by developing short notes that are on different pieces of coloured paper.

> When I was revising for my marketing exams, I found it difficult to remember all the different models. I played around with a few techniques and thought of some different ideas. In the end, I decided to write bullet points on a Post-it note for each model. The result was I had an A4 page for each model with a short Post-it note for each, allowing me to easily remember and recall each model in the exam.
>
> Silvia De Almeida, BSc International Business and Management

## 12.4.7 Where to revise

We know that the library becomes very busy in the run up to exams but it can be useful to have books and journals easily to hand. However, there is a danger that you become sucked into a sort of social group which will keep you away from your revision rather than helping. When we look around the group working space at revision time, we see many students clearly wasting their time. Our advice is to work with absolute focus and then make a clean break and socialise. If you are chatting when you should be revising, there will be a part of your brain which is telling you that you should be working. This means you are feeling guilt rather than pleasure. So we suggest you find a quiet place to revise and then make a clean break, put the books and notes away and socialise.

By all means work in a revision group but be careful that this doesn't become a social chat rather than a focused group helping each other to learn a topic. If this starts to happen, try to bring the group back on track. If this isn't possible, then be ruthless and leave to find a quiet place to work. You are only going to have one shot at doing well at university and you shouldn't let other people's lack of focus impact on your work.

When revising, I find that where I revise depends on what type of revision I am undertaking. When taking information out of either a book or lecture notes to make my own revision flash cards, I find it easier to sit in an environment which it is not totally silent but where I can easily sit in silence if there is a section that I find particularly difficult. Therefore, I am most likely to revise in my room with the radio on low so that I can alter the conditions as they suit me. When creating revision notes, I tend to read a section first without making notes and then reread the section, this time making notes so that I understand the topic I am revising. In contrast to this, when writing detailed notes, I prefer to do this with a group of people so that I can discuss points that I am writing about whilst checking that it makes sense.

Charlotte Voss, BSc English Language

Closely related to where to revise is the question of what time to revise. We don't really want to give any advice here as it comes down personal preference. Chris, for example, liked to wake up late and revise well into the night. Conversely, he had a close friend who liked to be in the library at 6 a.m., every day, without fail. As we said, it comes down to personal preference and what suits you best.

## 12.5 Dos and don'ts of revision

- Pretending to work but actually making yourself stressed – by this we mean sitting in a cafe or the social area of the library chatting with your friends with the work out on the table. The work on the table is telling you all the time that you should be working so you won't even be really enjoying the socialising. You need quiet to revise alone. Best not to do this in the library – do it in your room. In quiet.
- Music – some people seem to like to have music playing when they are revising. The psychology tells us that this is unlikely to be an effective way of working as it will be diverting your attention from the work in hand. If you find that you need to have headphones on to block out background noise, then find a quieter place to work
- Working alone can get tedious, so take a break. This is particularly important when revising at night which we know a lot of students do. Chris used to revise and go straight to bed and literally used to dream about the content he was learning and obviously didn't get much sleep. So even after revising it is important to take a break and switch off for a while before going to sleep. But make sure you have come to the end of a section of working before you do so and have planned what you are going to do next or else the short break can stretch into a longer one. You will feel worried that you should be working and not really enjoy yourself.
- Try and revise topics that span multiple exams. It is likely that you will undertake modules that have overlaps, particularly if you are conducting a specialised rather than general course such as Human Resource Management, Accounting, Marketing, Operations, etc. Look for topics that may possibly crop up in two or more exams and learn about them

inside out. Chris did this for the formulating a strategy topic, which came up in his marketing strategy and strategic management modules. He learned all the basics about the subject and a tonne of extra theories and journals. The topic came up in both of his exams and he was able to write advanced answers for both. Pat's first degree is in Psychology and he learned a great deal about the theories of Sigmund Freud in his first year, which he was able to draw on repeatedly in his degree.

- Have a set of well-understood examples, most business modules require you to link theory to practical examples, particularly in exams, so you should have many examples which you can draw upon. The key to doing this efficiently is to learn about three to five organisations that interest you. Learn about them inside out, buy books about them, follow them on social media and regularly research them. Then whenever you need an example for a module, draw upon your key organisations. Even without any extra research, you might be surprised to discover that you already know a lot of examples that you might be able to use from the goods you buy such as your iPhone, perhaps films you have watched or (more relevantly) the organisation where you conducted your work experience.
- Don't use the same revision technique over and over again. Revision can become extremely repetitive and boring so you need to use a range of different techniques. Of course, if you have something that works for you, then use it. But just remember to mix things up a bit to add some variety and help you remember information.

## 12.6 The big day – the exam

We all know what that big day feels like, we have experienced it at school and sixth form/college many times before. The nerves are rushing, thoughts are constantly being thrown around. Have I done enough revision? What questions are going to come up? What if I am delayed in traffic? Where is the exam? I can't remember *anything*! Friends are sending us text messages and writing their thoughts on Facebook. If you aren't careful, the time you put into careful revision can become lost in a whirlwind of panic and rush. So, we recommend some further careful planning which will enable you to reap the reward of all the preparations you have made and all the work you have done.

Remembering what we discussed in Chapter 5 on fear is key here: concentrate on what is in your control, not what isn't. In light of this, we want to run through some things we recommend you do before, during and after the exam.

### 12.6.1 Before

First and absolutely key is to eat something. In times of nerves, we seem to forget to eat, particularly during exams time. Eat something that will fill you up, such as a sandwich – especially made from wholemeal bread for slow releasing energy. This is particularly important if you are very nervous, without eating, you can leave yourself prone to dizziness and fainting.

Then make sure that you have all the necessary equipment with you. A few black and blue pens and maybe a pencil to quickly Mind Map with. It is amazing the number of students who turn up to an exam without a pen and then have to ask around or waste time in an exam if it runs out. Anything like this is distracting and can have a big impact on your ability to perform. In some exams, you may need extra equipment like a calculator. Make sure you have everything with you, it is usually best to do this the day beforehand. And make sure it is all in a see-through pencil case. If you haven't got one, use a food bag. Your university will usually require proof of ID, often your student card. Put it in your pencil case so you don't forget it. Finally, get a bottle of water, you will get thirsty due to all the nerves and it will help you to maintain concentration.

Arrive early, a good idea is to be near the exam room but not hanging around outside it as there is a sort of negative nervous energy around an exam room. Be early, go for a coffee and be 100 per cent sure that you know where the room is. Chris used to go an hour in advance to mentally prepare himself and not have to worry about turning up on time.

Around 10 minutes before the exam go to the exam room, find out where your seat is and sit yourself near enough to the door so you can get in easily but don't talk to people. They will confuse you! Just focus on your key notes. Don't be fazed by the other students outside the room. Pat used to not speak to anyone and just kept himself to himself, he even wore a baseball cap to avoid the gaze of anyone and wore earplugs so he wouldn't be distracted in the exam hall. Instead, have a few notes to look at on your way into the exam – Pat used post cards (as described above). We definitely don't recommend taking text books with you as we have seen some students do, there is nothing you could possibly learn just before the exam.

Just beforehand, sort out your mind with a quick exercise. A few positive affirmations said out loud can go a long way, 'I've got this', 'I can do this', 'I am ready', 'I will pass'. They may make you look slightly crazy but that isn't important, as Victoria highlights:

I personally believe going into an exam stressed and worried, stating 'I don't know enough' is the worst thing to do. I always tell myself 'I can do this! I can do this!'. After the third time of repeating this I eventually believe it and it comes across in the exam room. Sometimes confidence is the key! But being prepared with knowledge, prastise and all the equipment needed is the best confidence boost.

Victoria Saville, BSc Business and Sociology

Sort yourself out. Switch off your phone, put all your stuff away as instructed and head to your chair and desk. Check to see that the desk doesn't wobble or the chair squeak. If it isn't right complain immediately. This is no time to worry what people think about you. The invigilator is there to help you so make sure that you are diva-like in your requests. If there is a noise which is putting you off, complain.

## 12.6.2 During

Listen to the instructions given by the examiners. Normally they will run through the format of the exams and any particular rules. Listen to them to ensure you haven't missed anything important. If there is anything you are unsure of, ask. You do not want to waste time later on after the exam has begun.

When they say begin, whatever you do, *do not start to write immediately.* You will see other people doing this but they are writing rubbish. You need to read the whole paper first (OK – if it's multiple choice this isn't practical) but you can get a sense of the whole paper and see if there are questions where you can make some good points. If there is a tricky theory that you are not sure about remembering, write it down so it is out of your brain and you can use your thinking power to decide what questions to answer and in what order.

Make some plans – for the questions you are going to choose, can you really provide enough evidence to answer them? Make sure you take proper notice of the rubric. How many questions? How many marks for each? How long have you got? Make a rough plan for how long to spend on each question. You should know all this information before you enter the exam room.

When writing your answers be sure that you include the basics first before writing the more advanced material. In the rush of the exam, we want to make the best impression possible by writing everything we know but then forget to include basic things such as a plan of what we are going to discuss or defining the key terms. For his marketing communications exam, Chris spent a great deal of revision time reading extra journals and concentrated on discussing them in his exam answers. Everybody was certain he was going to achieve a first, including himself. He was then gutted when he got 62 per cent when others who told him they didn't read any extra journals got 70 per cent plus. After reviewing his paper with his lecturer it was clear that he skipped over the basics and thus he could not be awarded any marks for advanced understanding. Always get the basic material down first before try-ing to get clever!

And make sure you are constantly answering the question. Even when we make a plan, it can be so easy to go off topic. Constantly read back to yourself and ensure you are answering the question. This is one of the most common mistakes in exams yet can be so easily avoided. It is particularly important if you have sub-questions that need to be answered.

What if you look at the paper and you don't think you can answer any questions? If there looks like just one you can answer, work on that first. Then, once it's done, look for others. Most of the time there will be other questions you can answer. But don't spend all your time on the one that you can answer. Be ruthless in keeping to time – by all means allow a little more for the question you have more to say about but you should allow time to try to work out what a good answer for the other questions would be too. Remember you need to be tactical about how you deploy your time and the guidance is given to you in terms of the number of marks for questions.

Even though time is limited, you need to maintain a cool head and keep calm. Pat used to sometimes go to the toilet between each section just to make a clear break between topics. Take a moment to just sit and think. Chris would take a few minutes out between each section and just briefly look round the room.

When you have finished be sure to read your answers. You will be amazed at some of the mistakes you can make. Chris once had the opportunity to read one of his exam papers a few months later when he wasn't happy with his mark. He simply laughed because it really didn't make any sense and he understood why he didn't score the best of marks! Sometimes you will only have a minute or two to read over your answers but be sure you do it. Read through as fast as possible. Use absolutely every second you have in the exam. Don't worry about others leaving early, they clearly haven't used their time as wisely as they could. Once you have finished, make sure an invigilator picks up your paper and then stay seated until told you can leave. Remember not to talk just yet, you can still be penalised.

When I get my exam timetable the first thing I do is put the dates in to my phone, this allows me to calculate exactly how much time I have to prepare compared to how much time I estimate I will need to spend on each module. I find that knowing I am prepared is a big part of helping me stay calm in the days running up to the exam. During the exam, it is important to stay focused as time is always short. I give myself a time limit to spend on each question, in relation to the marks they are worth, this makes sure that I have enough time to answer all the questions without wasting time on ones I am stuck on. Finally, I find writing a brief plan before I start a question helps me get all the information down on paper which can then be organised in the actual answer. This allows me to concentrate on what is necessary and what to leave out.

Neil Kumar, BSc Business, Computing and IT

### 12.6.3 After

After the exam the most crucial thing you can do is to forget about it. Often we see students compare answers with each other but this really has no value whatsoever. It just ends up producing unnecessary worry about who took the best approach, developed the best answers and wrote the most pages. A note about quantity, it really doesn't matter all that much, 10 pages of waffle is nothing compared to two pages of concise and quality material.

To help forget, don't take the exam paper with you, you will end up going through it in loads of detail and thinking about what you should have done, could have done and shouldn't have done. This is one of those times where reflection isn't immediately valuable. Instead wait for the result and then discuss it with your lecturer for an objective viewpoint.

It is usually the case that you will have another exam coming up which furthers the importance of forgetting about the completed exam. It is not uncommon for business students to have six exams over a couple of weeks. You need to be able to move on quickly and concentrate on the next exam. The time you spend worrying about the previous exam could be much better used to score higher marks in the next exam.

Many people focus on what they should do before their exams – how to prepare, how to cram, how to make the most of the limited time we always have. What about post exam? How do we celebrate the success (or maybe try to forget the disappointments)? In my experience, I found that there was one thing that helped – going to the gym. Post exam, your brain is exhausted, you don't want to think, you would just like to relax. Your body? It's not in the same place. Exercise is scientifically proven to make you feel better, but for me, working out post exams made me feel like I managed to fatigue both my mind and my body. It made the post exam nap, party, or sometimes three parties, feel more deserved. What could be better than coupling your education with a healthy lifestyle?

Justyna Zybaczynska, BSc Marketing

## 12.7 Taking it to work

We doubt that your university exams will be the end for you. Many organisations now require their employees to undertake training courses that often come with formal assessments. This may particularly be the case if you are pursuing a finance/accounting career where extra qualifications are a must. Alternatively, you may wish to undertake a Masters course, which will most certainly have exams to complete. Rest assured that the techniques we have developed will be useful. The memory techniques we have discussed can work wonders for any times where you will need to remember things, even as simple as a shopping list.

> Whilst I was at university I also held down a part-time job, essentially now I have flipped the two. I now work full time and study part time. Currently I am studying CIMA which in essence can give you a number of qualifications. At university I would plan what I needed to learn, how I would learn it and then how long it would take. I would then factor in time for working my part-time job and start to plan how I would get the revision done. Now I try and follow the same plan but it becomes more difficult with additional responsibilities that come when you start a full-time job and a 'normal' life. When you have less free time, prioritising your tasks and working to targets becomes more important. Coming towards exam time the majority of my evenings and weekends will be focused on studying, if need be I'll also take time off from work as holiday. I now make a much more conscious effort during the taught phases of CIMA to understand the material more thoroughly to ensure it is imbedded and less difficult to dig out during revision.
>
> Daniel Platt, Retail Support and Marketing Analyst at Mitchells & Butlers

## 12.8 How to get started

### 12.8.1 Professional

- Choose a group of friends to revise with.
- Practise some of the techniques we have recommended by undertaking an extra qualification.
- Try to put all your notes for all your exams on one giant Mind Map.

### 12.8.2 A little more interesting

- Turn your next shopping list into a story.
- Pick three organisations and buy a book about each of them, learn everything you can about them to use for examples in multiple exams.
- After your next exam, try not to speak a single word about it until you receive the result. If anybody asks, just state that you plan to wait and see.

## 12.9 Our bookshelf

O'Brien, D. (2007) *How to pass exams: accelerate your learning – memorise key facts – revise effectively*. London: Duncan Baird Publishers.
Dominic O'Brien is well recognised in the field of revision and memorising techniques. He is even a world memory champion, whatever that is meant to be! He has a very direct writing style and so gives you the tips without messing around, just like we have done. The techniques are a little strange and out there but there is no doubt, they work.

O'Brien, D. (2011) *You can have an amazing memory: learn life-changing techniques and tips from the memory maestro*. London: Watkins Publishing.
This is another one from Dominic O'Brien but this guy really does know his stuff. The book is very in depth and again comes with many examples to help you practise and utilise the advice.

# 13

# Business communication

## 13.1 Chapter summary

This is a book about how to get a great business degree so it might seem odd including a chapter on communication at work. We include it with good reason though. Here we show you how to present yourself – particularly at interview – and then take you into the workplace with advice on what to do. And what not to do!

## 13.2 Why communication is important

The most employable graduates are those who have managed to pick up work experience along with their studies. In the UK, this is as many as 30 per cent of graduate hires (more information from High Fliers, 2012) and in some businesses they will *only* hire graduates they have had the chance to work with on some sort of internship or placement. So, we recommend that you find a way of picking up some good quality work experience as you study. In order to get this experience, you will need to communicate professionally with business people and there are some clear rules you need to be aware of. In common with most topics in this book, these are rules you may well eventually pick up yourself but without this book you are likely to make mistakes. This chapter sets out the rules – some of which are hard and fast, others less so. We will help you avoid making mistakes and make sure that you present yourself in a professional manner.

## 13.3 Listening

Perhaps the least practised skill Pat comes across in executives is that of listening. We are often so keen to get our own point across that we miss important information. And when you are setting out in your career, listening is far more important than speaking, which is why we put this section first. It sounds such an easy thing to do but all too often people do not listen in an effective manner. Commonly, people make the following mistakes:

- Talking too much – never an attractive trait.
- Not asking enough questions or asking too many questions – you end up misunderstanding.
- Not demonstrating that they are listening – people think you are ignoring them.

### 13.3.1 Talking the right amount

It is very easy to avoid these mistakes. Ensure you concentrate on what people are saying, if you have a point that you really want to say then note it down and wait until they are finished. Remember that you are learning and a great way of doing this is by listening to experienced people. People are always happy to talk about themselves and their experience so let them!

### 13.3.2 Asking questions

This is such an important skill. One of Pat's long-term contacts is a highly successful management consultant called Richard. Over the years, Pat has realised that Richard's main skill is asking questions. When they worked together, Pat noticed that Richard would simply keep on asking questions until he really understood what the situation was. But he didn't only ask questions, he would show that he had listened and understood. This way he would come away from a meeting with 100 per cent clarity about what he had to do. Clients *loved* this and Richard never put a foot wrong when it came to delivering what the client asked for. And this is such an important part of not only consulting but any job. Imagine that you are a manager and you know that one of your team will always deliver *exactly* what you wanted them to. Contrast that with a team member who hasn't taken the time to make sure that they know exactly what it is you want them to do – they will frequently do the wrong thing.

From my work experience at Marks and Spencer, the main thing I have learnt is to always be inquisitive. Asking questions is vital to ensure you get everything you could possibly want out of the experience; at the end of the day, it's only relevant experience if you have actually learnt something! The more questions you ask, the more you will know and the better you will understand it. It also means that you come across as being interested in what you are doing, which is important if looking for a future role in the particular organisation. Now, even in day to day life, I find myself asking questions all the time. I feel that this has made me a more effective communicator both in a professional sense as well as in social settings, and has also broadened my knowledge on a variety of subjects. The skills I have learnt from my work experience have been vital to my studies; I can now apply what I have learnt to my modules at university.

Grace Turner, BSc Business and Management

### 13.3.3 Showing that you are listening

This is something called 'active listening'. It is a massively important skill to have and the difference it makes to your life will be huge. We are not over-stating this – and it is incredibly easy to learn.

1. Really pay attention to what the other person is saying. We tend to start to mentally work out counter arguments or prepare what we are going to say whilst the other person is speaking. This means we frequently miss really important parts of what they are saying. So, try to empty your mind of everything apart from attending to what they are saying.
2. Use body language and non-word cues to show you are listening. Nodding, saying 'uh-uh', smiling all show the person you are listening. And maintain eye contact – but not staring at them because that will freak them out! Show them that they have your full attention.
3. Never interrupt – even if you are getting bored or it seems like the person is rambling. Let them finish what they have to say. It might seem like it takes ages, but so often you will find that you were jumping to conclusions and that your interruption would have led to misunderstanding. The one exception might be if you physically can't hear what they were saying and you might say, 'I'm terribly sorry to interrupt but I didn't hear that last point'. If you allow people time to say their piece, they will feel that you are listening more than if you interrupt all the time.
4. Feed back that you are listening. Now this is the important bit. Use phrases like, 'Can I check I have understood you correctly?' or 'So, I hear that …' or 'What I'm hearing is …'. You may well be corrected by the other person – but this is great! You have avoided making a mistake! Never be embarrassed to check as it will save you so much hassle and wasted time later. No one will mind at all – especially when you are new in a job. We all have to learn and if you show that you are listening and learning, this will go down really well with your boss.

## 13.4 Speaking

We think that speaking is pretty critical to your career but reckon that there are different skills when talking to a group as compared to talking one to one. What we are covering here is of course a different type of situation than the sort of thing we were talking about in Chapter 11 on presentations, which are more formalised and usually involve slides. By speaking we mean just that – how do you talk to individuals and groups in a business setting? The next sections describe what you should be thinking about in those circumstances.

### 13.4.1 Speaking to a group

When it comes to speaking within a group the common misconception is that you should speak as much as possible and make sure your viewpoint is heard. This again is fundamentally wrong. To ensure you are an effective speaker try to do the following:

- Ensure you do not dominate the conversation.
- Ask valuable questions but don't ask too many.
- Keep the group on topic.
- Use collective language, for example, instead of saying, 'We should do this' ask, 'What do you think about doing this?'.
- Include everyone in the group by making sure your gaze moves around all members of the group.
- Summarise what has been discussed to ensure clarification and a mutual understanding.
- Admit things when you are wrong, this is very difficult for many people to do but it goes a long way in moving on from mistakes.

Where we often go very wrong with speaking is when involved in an argument/confrontation. Often each person wants to express their view and not listen to what the other person has to say. In these situations, have respect for yourself and just as importantly have respect for the other person involved (Weeks, 2008).

### 13.4.2 Speaking one to one

Of course you will be speaking one to one perhaps more frequently than to groups. These might be meetings with your boss or speaking with people when networking. If you meet with someone who you think of as quite senior, you might feel nervous which sometimes makes people talk too much. Be careful not to just babble away – make sure that the person you are speaking with has time to speak too. Think about the active listening skills in the previous section. Have some stock phrases you can use to prompt the other person to speak more. Pat uses phrases such as:

That sounds really interesting.

Wow – that must have been challenging!

How did you manage to do that?

Also, have some short standard things that you will say in answer to frequently asked questions. For example, you will often be asked what your career ambitions are and it is good to have something succinct to say in response. People in business often talk about an 'elevator pitch'. This is an American expression which refers to an imaginary situation where you find yourself in a lift (or elevator) with a person you want to pitch an idea to. The trouble is you have only about 30 seconds to do this before they reach their floor and leave the lift. But for that time you have them to yourself. Pat once was invited to an annual party given by a large supermarket chain and suddenly found himself in a corner with four of the main board directors. He realised this was the moment for the elevator pitch about what the university could offer this massive business and fortunately had a quick pitch ready which he could deliver.

Think about what sort of questions people might ask you and also what are the messages you want to get across. Perhaps it is something like 'I am studying for a generalist business degree but have developed a keen interest in marketing so I'd really like to get some experience in a marketing department to see what the job is like in reality'. Whatever your pitch is, by all means practise a set form of words and never be embarrassed to use it. Pat has seen very senior people do this and have a standard way of introducing themselves so they can quickly convey the main points they want people to know.

Of course precisely what you prepare depends on what sort of meeting you are going to. We have advice on interviews and assessment centres in the final chapter so these are specific forms of preparation. But you might find yourself meeting with business people at careers fairs or at networking events on campus. Many businesses like to get involved with student activities so there will be opportunities to meet business people and make your pitch.

## 13.5 How to dress

Anyone who knows either of the authors will know we are in no position to advise on fashion! But we do know about the standards required at work.

TABLE 13.1   What to wear to work

| Men | Women |
|-----|-------|
| Dark, plain suit | Plain dark suit – either trouser or skirt |
| White/pastel coloured shirt | Matching blouse/top |
| Top button done up | Not too revealing (e.g. skirt/dresses not too far above the knee, tops not revealing) |
| Plain tie – that matches shirt | Simple makeup |
| Black formal shoes | Formal shoes – heels not ultra high |
| No visible piercing | Single earrings, no other piercings |
| Hair combed – 'sensible' style | Hair combed – 'sensible' style |

These days it has become rather unclear sometimes how formally one needs to dress. Our advice is that if you are ever unsure, always dress smarter than you think is necessary. In fact, Pat recently ran an assessment centre where one candidate probably lost the job because of the clothes he was wearing. The job was in a very old fashioned part of the insurance industry in the City of London and the candidate turned up wearing a very trendy suit. This was considered rather off the wall and the partners were worried that this showed the candidate hadn't understood what the job required of him. It might not have been 100 per cent why he lost the job offer, but it was certainly a factor. Of course the dress code rules vary from country to country and so we are working on what we see in the UK, which is probably true for Europe and the USA. Table 13.1 outlines what is required for an interview when you need to make a good impression.

After the interview, when you start work, each business has its own standards of dress. If you work in the City of London, for example, the above rules will probably hold every day. If you are working in a different sort of office, a more relaxed style might be the norm. Look around the office and see what the smartest person in the room is wearing and go for that as a model rather than the scruffiest or least formal person. Indeed, there is a view that you should always dress as smartly as a person who is at least one grade more senior than you. In that way people can think of you as promotable!

## 13.6 How to email

We all use email and of course everyone knows how to send an email. But the way you write emails to your friends is not at all appropriate for business.

Chris remembers the first time he had to send a business email at work as part of his industrial placement and he was very nervous. He told a colleague about his nerves and she gave him some pointers to write an effective business email. To help you avoid this situation, we want to give you some brief advice. Let's start from the top and work down.

At the very top is whether an email is needed. Depending on what you wish to achieve, would a call or meeting be more appropriate?

Always use a subject. Most business people look at email on mobile devices and they can sometimes use the subject line to decide whether to delete the email without reading. This is essentially the hook of an email, the thing that determines whether somebody reads or deletes the email. With such a short amount of time and attention span of most people it is crucial to get the hook perfect (Frank, 1987). Make sure it doesn't look like a phishing or spam email or one which comes from a mailing list. Keep it short – less than five words is ideal – but informative. Business people often receive over 100 emails a day so you need to help them manage this more easily by keeping everything as clear as possible.

The very first line of the email can be the most difficult to figure out – this is the address line. How do you address the person. Table 13.2 is our quick reference to work this out.

TABLE 13.2   Salutations in a business email

| Salutation | Use |
|---|---|
| Dear Mr/Mrs/Ms | Some formal businesses (e.g. banking, law)<br>Some nationalities (especially German)<br>If the person is very senior<br>When in doubt |
| Dear (first name) | Most businesses<br>Most nationalities |
| Hi (first name) | Only when you know them well<br>When they are at the same seniority level as you |
| (first name) | Some formal businesses (e.g. insurance, banking)<br>Military |
| No salutation | Only with someone you know very well indeed as part of a rapid exchange |
| Yo! Hiya! Hey! | Friends only |

The only caveat is about being too formal. This can look odd and might make the business person wonder if you really understand English, for example. When Pat sometimes receives emails addressed to 'My esteemed lecturer', he wonders if the person speaks English or if they are being sarcastic. Table 13.3 offers a few more email tips.

TABLE 13.3   The dos and don'ts of email

| Do | Don't |
|---|---|
| Write in full sentences | Use abbreviated 'text speak' |
| Write politely | Use emoticons like :) |
| Note how the person signs their own emails and address them that way | Be too familiar |
| Respond to emails within 24 hours – or leave an out of office message | If an incoming email annoys you, don't reply to it right away |
| cc people who do need to be in the loop | cc people into emails who don't need to know the contents |
| Read through important emails before sending. If in doubt, save a draft and come back to it | Wait too long – business people expect a reply within the day |
| Make sure you are being clear – many misunderstandings can happen over email | Be too long winded. If an email is more than a couple of paragraphs, it might be better to speak on the phone |

Having written your email, the last thing to check is the sign-off. Most business have a set way of doing this called the 'signature block'. It usually contains the formal job title of the person and all their contact details (incidentally a useful source of information). Yours should be the same. There isn't any need to include your address but you should have your email address there. Even though people can see where you have sent it from, if the email is forwarded on sometimes this gets lost in the system so it's important to have it written out. Also include a mobile phone number. This is especially important if you are writing about getting work experience or an internship. Perhaps a manager sees your email, is interested and decides to give you a call. Ensure all the information is to hand even if it is also included in a CV. Make it easy for people to get hold of you. And by the way, if you have included your mobile number on any formal business communication, remember this when you answer your phone! Always assume calls from unfamiliar numbers are from someone important and answer the call accordingly. Be prepared to take some ribbing if it's actually a call from a friend or family member. Far better that than sound unprofessional to a potential employer.

A note about security. Emails are so easy to forward on you need to be wary about what you write in them. It is also very easy for them to be sent to the wrong person by mistake. We know of one person who wrote a scathing email attack on his boss only to include her in the circulation of the email by mistake. He lost his job because of it. Our rule is to assume that everybody will read your email. Once an email is sent, there is nothing you can do about it. It looks like you can 'recall' an email once sent but all that does is alert people that you have made a mistake and they will all read it more closely. Never say anything about anyone in an email that you wouldn't be happy for them to read themselves. If you need to communicate something which would be embarrassing for you, never write it in any electronic communication. If you must, say it in a face to face conversation or over the phone. Then there is no chance of being caught out.

Finally, remember to proofread every email you send, once is not enough. Reread the email a couple of times, if it is particularly long or important, reread it a few times. If you have attached a document, make sure you have actually attached it – it is so easy not to do this and then you have to send another email that actually contains the attachment. We have all done this at some point. Just as importantly, when you have attached a document/file, question whether you actually need to. For example, could you just copy a certain part of the document or paraphrase it? This makes it much easier for your audience to consume and ensures you get the exact point across that you wish to. Edit the email to ensure it is as concise as possible, are there things you can remove which do not add much value? We receive so many emails nowadays that less equals more. Once done, cut the email into short distinct parts, the way people read online is in short bursts often omitting a lot of detail so be sure to play to this style (Canavor and Meirowitz, 2009).

## 13.7 How to speak on the phone

One of the major impacts of the extent of email usage is that most business people now get very few calls out of the blue. It used to be accepted that you would be interrupted many times in the day by unexpected phone calls, but this is no longer the case. If you need to speak on the phone, always arrange a time when it will be convenient. And if a potential employer has agreed to a time to speak to you, call them *exactly* at that time. Pat always uses Outlook to remind him of appointments and sets an alarm to warn him of the timing of calls. In fact, he often gives coaching over the phone so his diary consists of many appointment phone calls. Other managers will have conference calls that are also booked in and an unscheduled call could interrupt these. So, always check what the best form of communication is – and the initial contact should almost always be by email.

Do remember that employers, your university and contacts may need to ring you out of the blue and you should be prepared. As part of Chris's job, he frequently needs to ring and speak to students. He often ends up speaking to students at house parties, in a bar, at home with the TV/radio on loud, etc. When you do receive a call from an unrecognised number, think to yourself that this could be important and do some quick adjustments to prepare for it – turn down the music, go to a different room or tell your friend to shut up. Chris often laughs when it happens to him, for example, he has spoken to a student's mum, one student in a club and another who was sleeping. Chris laughs about it but an employer will not be as forgiving.

Having arranged to make a call, make sure you are somewhere quiet. Background noise can lead to misunderstandings and make it tough to understand what the other is saying. If in doubt, take the call and say you will call back once you are somewhere quieter. If you are going to need to make notes or write anything down (and you should always have a pen and paper to hand to take notes!), make sure you are somewhere that this is possible. Never take important calls on the train. Railway lines frequently go through cuttings and the mobile reception is very intermittent. The only sort of call to make is one which is only a few seconds – perhaps to say you are running slightly late. If it is to be a longer call, arrange to speak once you get off the train. Sometimes using a hands-free headset can help block out background noise but be careful if using a Bluetooth one as they can be temperamental.

Even if you have made an appointment to speak to someone on the phone, always check that it is convenient for them to speak to you. Say something like, 'Are you OK to speak?' or 'Is now a good time for us to discuss …?'. This shows that you are taking the call seriously and that you are going to concentrate on the call.

Your speech should be clear and remember that speaking on the phone is more difficult than face to face because you don't have any of the body language cues to help you. This means that other interference such as a poor line or background noise at either end can make communication even more difficult. Make sure that you have as good a chance as possible to make yourself understood. To help with this, stand up as you are talking, it helps to project your voice and prevents you from slouching.

### 13.7.1 Skype

There are many different systems for communicating by video over the internet but Skype is easily the most popular. Many people use Skype these days both at home and work and this can be a far better form of communication than telephone – especially mobile. Even without video, the audio quality is so much better than the phone network, it is much easier to understand people. However, actually Skype is most commonly used at work between people who know each other quite well. Pat has conducted job interviews on Skype but this is still quite unusual. If you are a Skype user, you can include your Skype name on your contact details at the bottom of your emails and your business contacts can decide whether or not to use this medium. If you are going to communicate this way, a possible question arises as to whether or not to have your video switched on. Sometimes there isn't sufficient band width for this but our advice is to have the video switched on and then the person you are speaking to has the option of having theirs on or not. This means you need to dress appropriately for the call and make sure you check where you are in terms of background noise – and also what is in the background on view! Of course if you are on the phone, you can speak from your bedroom in your pyjamas but this would not be appropriate on a video call!

## 13.8 Social media

It is now commonplace for businesses to check applicants' social media profile before interview and Pat has seen first-hand cases where potentially good applications have been turned down as a result of this. So be careful what photos and comments you leave on your Facebook site! Business is becoming far more savvy about using social media and many managers have their own Twitter feeds as well as more official corporate ones. It does make sense for you to have one – even if you only use it to learn what a business is about. If you are someone who tweets, use the same principal as the email rule: always assume that your boss is reading your tweets. There is no need for them to be censored as such, just ask yourself what your boss or a potential employer would think if they read what you are tweeting.

### 13.8.1 LinkedIn

This is another form of social media but we have a separate section for it because it has so much more importance for students and graduates today. You can think of LinkedIn as a Facebook for professionals and it is growing at a huge pace. Hence the first rule is this: you *must* have a LinkedIn profile. More and more businesses recruit using LinkedIn to advertise posts and those that don't will almost certainly look you up on LinkedIn before working with you in any way. It is such a brilliant way of presenting yourself to the world, that you cannot avoid having this. And as with all of the advice in this chapter, think formal and think of your audience. What impression do you want to make? Who will be reading your profile? So, even if you hate having your photo taken, have a decent head and shoulders picture to upload to your site. It looks odd if there is no photo these days. But never use one taken on a party night out. Just get a friend to take a simple head and shoulders shot on a camera phone. It doesn't need to be super formal but it really helps if you look friendly – so smile! Then all you need to do is make sure you have as much information as you possibly can on the site. As a student, there will be limits to the experience you have to showcase, but make the most of what you have. Don't write long stories but have sharp bullet points about your experience and what you are looking to do with your career. If you possibly can, ask your previous line managers to write a recommendation on your LinkedIn profile, these are very powerful in demonstrating what you say is true. Also get group members and fellow society members to write recommendations.

When adding somebody, be sure not to use the standard default message, instead personalise every request. Just like email, address the person with a suitable opener and close it off with the same level of formality. This also shows to anybody you are connecting with that you place value on them and you truly would like to connect.

Remember there is no spell checker on LinkedIn, so make sure to import any content into a word processor to proofread it.

The great thing about LinkedIn is the more you use it, the more powerful it becomes as you can potentially connect to more people. The general consensus is to connect to at least 50 people, this should provide a sufficiently wide network to expand with. Just as important is to keep it up to date, update your status every few days and be sure to update your content each month. Recruiters are using social media sites to check upon students and graduates which increases the importance of maintaining an up to date and professional profile (Bohnert and Ross, 2010).

The best tip we can give you when it comes to LinkedIn is to actually use it. Many students set up a profile and then leave it hoping one day an employer will turn up and offer them a job. It simply doesn't work like that. Use it in every way you can just like Joe did below to build a vast and valuable network.

LinkedIn is more than just my digital CV. It's a crucial networking tool that has gained me 500+ genuine connections and a place in the top 5 per cent most viewed profile list. Here's what worked for me:

- A complete profile: relevant job history and publications I've written, but omitted my cocktail experience.
- Make connections: personalise each and every connection request.
- Update regularly: recent blog posts, industry news and business developments.
- Engage and interact: comment, like and share other updates adding genuine insight where possible.
- Facilitate business opportunities: introduce connections to each other and expect nothing in return.
- Get recommendations: get as many as you can on your personal profile and give them where possible as well.
- Be proactive: upgrade your profile and use the advanced search to find new opportunities and introduce yourself via InMail.

Joe Bush, BSc Business and Management

## 13.9 Body language and non-verbal communication

We can show a lot about ourselves and what we are thinking through non-verbal cues. These are mostly to do with posture and how we arrange our limbs. For example, it is commonly understood that having one's arms folded is a negative or defensive stance. People will trust us less if we speak with arms folded and if you are sitting with arms folded, the person talking to you will think you don't like what they are saying.

A considerable amount of communication comes from our body language – how we stand or sit, gestures we make, how we arrange our limbs. When we are communicating face to face with someone, we can emphasise points we are making through gestures and sometimes we inadvertently give away what we are thinking through our body language – our posture might show that we are bored or that we are paying attention. It is important that you understand some core principles of body language but also that you don't become too obsessed by it. If you start worrying too much about how you are standing, you might forget to say the right things. But do remember that our posture and gestures do communicate a lot.

One of the most common signals from our body language comes from folded arms. Indeed Pat once had some feedback from a training session which only said, 'folded arms'. The audience had taken this as being defensive and negative. In fact, folded arms can indicate concentration and focus. But more usually it is interpreted as putting up some sort of barrier. In general, if you realise that you have folded your arms, it is probably better to unfold them as unfolded arms are generally regarded as being more positive. One drawback of knowing this is that it might make you self-conscious about what you are doing with your arms and legs.

A body language tip for presentations is to try to reduce the amount of gestures you make. This means when you do make a gesture, it has far more impact. Too many gestures and too much movement is interpreted as being shifty or that you have something to hide.

Moving on from the section on listening skills, a massively important part of listening is the feedback you are giving as you are listening. The body language element can be nodding and smiling. But most importantly, maintain eye contact. This shows you are paying attention to the other person. But do be careful – it can become unnerving if you stare too hard. Just show that you are really paying attention and not being distracted by other things going on. And never look at your watch! This is such an obvious gesture of impatience and boredom.

We have given some follow up reading on body language at the end of the chapter if you would like to know more. But if you master these basic ideas, you will be gaining a lot in your interactions.

A note of caution: these body language tips are not completely universal. Some cultures have different interpretations of gestures. In particular, eye contact might be inappropriate in some cultures especially between men and women. Some researchers also question whether all of the advice about body language is really true and we tend to see unqualified 'experts' talking about this on the TV. However, to be honest, to a certain extent it no longer matters whether this is true or not since it has entered the common psyche. So, have an open stance when talking – and indeed when listening.

Our advice is to find a posture which is comfortable because shifting in your seat also shows you to be less than riveted with what is being said. When delivering a talk, we discussed how less is more when it comes to movement and gestures and this is true in all forms of speaking and listening.

## 13.10 Taking it to work

Most of this chapter concerns students and new graduates presenting them-selves appropriately as they enter the world of work. As such, the advice applies beyond university and issues of dress code, how to write emails and so forth will become second nature. In terms of which areas you should refer back to when you have been at work for a while, we strongly recommend that you remember the ideas of active listening in this chapter. People who listen in this focused way find their career path is so much easier because they become known for this skill. It becomes even more important when you start to manage people. As a line manager, you are in effect being paid according to the produc-tivity of the people who work for you – so you have to get the best out of them. We know from over 100 years of study of people at work that the most impor-tant way of motivating people to work harder is to understand them. And you only understand through listening. But this isn't 'being nice'. Finding out what makes people tick will give you a huge advantage in the competitive world of work. When you know what people are motivated by – and what they are not, you can focus on the right levers to make this happen. And the curious thing is that people actually like to work hard. No, that's not quite right. People like to be successful and to think that they are doing a good job. By taking the time to understand and communicate properly, you will have made the most impor-tant step in bringing your team up to its optimum productivity.

Being in a customer facing role, I find the most important aspect of my role is to listen to clients in order to fully understand their banking needs. This is the most important part of the process to ensure that I fully understand their banking needs and deliver solutions that meet these to the best of my abilities. My job is to then communicate the solution in a manner they understand and through a channel that best speaks to them, be it email, face to face, email or social media. Often this is a blend of all these channels which each require a slightly different approach.

Tim Newman, Relationship Director at Lloyds Bank Commercial Banking – Mid Markets

## 13.11 How to get started

### 13.11.1 Professional

- Practise active listening by using one of the key phrases in a conversation ('Did I understand that …' or 'What I'm hearing is …').
- Catch yourself before you speak – when you have something you are waiting to say in a conversation, practise just not saying it.
- Body language – practise a posture for listening in which your arms are not folded.

### 13.11.2 A little more interesting

- Try having a conversation with a friend where your only input is to get the other person to speak. See if they notice – in fact afterwards ask them if they noticed anything different. And also ask if they enjoyed it!
- Without saying what you are doing, try mirroring someone's body language as they speak to you. See if they become more positive towards you. See if they notice!

## 13.12 Our bookshelf

Carnegie, D. (2006) *How to win friends and influence people*. New York; Vermilion.
This book was first published in 1936 but it remains just as popular today as it was then. It provides valuable principles that allow you to do exactly what it says on the tin – win friends and influence people. At first, we were put off this book as it sounds like it's for people who do not have any friends. That is not the case, it provides great advice that allows you to build relationships with team members.

Hargie, O. (ed.) (2006) *The handbook of communication skills*. London: Routledge.
This is the go-to resource for a complete academic summary of the latest research on communication. It is therefore less practical than some other

texts but great if you want to know whether practical advice has any scientific basis. Chapter 3 on non-verbal communication is particularly useful as there is a lot of nonsense talked about this stuff.

## 13.13 Online

www.youtube.com/watch?v=AQENwD-QlRA – great programme on body language.
www.emailreplies.com – great resource on everything to do with email.
www.dresscodeguide.com – masses of information on what to wear at work. American focused but it still applies widely.

## 13.14 References

Bohnert, D. and Ross, H.W. (2010) 'The influence of social networking web sites on the evaluation of job candidates', *Cyberpsychology, Behavior, and Social Networking*, 13 (3): 341–347.

Canavor, N. and Meirowitz, C. (2009) *The truth about the new rules of business writing.* London: FT Press.

Frank, O.M. (1987) *How to get your point across in 30 seconds or less.* New York: Simon & Schuster.

High Fliers (2012) *The graduate market in 2012.* Available online at: www.highfliers.co.uk/download/GMReport12.pdf (accessed 25 July 2012).

Weeks, H. (2008) *Failure to communicate: how conversations go wrong and what you can do to right them.* Boston, MA: Harvard Business School Press.

# 14

## Securing your career

### 14.1 Chapter summary

We debated whether to include this chapter because your career of course starts after you graduate. We decided to include it in the end because of the large number of enquiries we receive from students about your future career and finding the right job is clearly a measure of the success of the course for most business students. So we have pulled together a great deal of information to help you launch your career. We firmly believe that this should be something which you are working on throughout your time at university and not something you suddenly do in a panic as your final year draws to a close. So this chapter is about building towards being able to land the job you want in the career that really suits you. It includes applications of many of the skills we have discussed throughout the book and so is a good way of drawing the book to a close. Everything you have done to date reflects stages of your career including voluntary work, training and your degree. Now it is about extending this to achieve your long-term goals.

## 14.2 Careers advice – the best resource

Before we get into this, a word of advice. Our experience, which has been backed up by comments of the reviewers of this book (i.e. other academics), is that most universities have superb careers resources. But it is also true to say that careers professionals always say that all too often students do not make the best use of this resource. Our very strong advice is to go to your careers centre and tap into as much of their experience and resources as you can. All manner of value is to be had – especially from attending mock-interviews and meeting recruiters. So we really want you to go there and make full use of everything on offer. It's a good part of what your fees are for!

However, before you go there, you need to have done some preparation and, taking our advice from Chapter 1, let's begin with the end in mind.

## 14.3 Key question: what are you trying to achieve?

The important thing to establish before anything else is to decide where you want to go, i.e. your career goals. You are probably fed up of the word goals by now but we just can't emphasise enough how important they are. Without knowing your goals there is little chance of securing the right job as you will not know what type of CV to write, where to look for jobs, how to prepare for an interview – the list goes on. Most students tend to think long-term career goal setting is determining their graduate job but this is very short-term

TABLE 14.1   What do you want from your career?

| Aspect | Possible ingredients |
| --- | --- |
| Travel | Permanent location<br>Plenty of travelling |
| People | Work in isolation<br>In a team, opportunities to meet new people |
| Computer | Minimum exposure to IT<br>Every opportunity to learn IT tools |
| Financial security | High level of money<br>Enough to live on |
| Security | Permanent job<br>Always moving with opportunities to progress |
| Responsibility | High<br>Medium<br>Low |
| Entrepreneurial flair | Wish for none<br>Like to generate ideas and make them happen |
| Variety | In role projects<br>Set role and responsibilities |
| Work culture | Hard working, 9 to 5<br>Have some fun |
| Aims of Organisation | Profit driven<br>Government based<br>Charity/community |
| Size of Organisation | Large<br>Medium<br>Small<br>Start up |

thinking. We are aware that there are some students who fully understand what they want – if you are in this position then great. Your goals instead are to determine which exact positions you are seeking in the short, medium and long term.

However, we accept that at such a young age students do not know their career goals. To help, we want to provide an alternative approach that looks at the ideal ingredients of jobs in order to reveal possible options. The central idea behind this is to think of everything that will create the perfect job, and Table 14.1 lists some of the more common aspects.

By working through these aspects you can start to get an idea of the sort of job and career that you will be happy in. Hall (2002) refers to this as the protean career. 'The protean career is one that is driven by an individual in pursuit of their own values. Therefore it is defined more in terms of what motivates it, not what it look likes from the outside' (Arnold et al., 2010: 604). Schein (1993) refers to these as career anchors which are completely vital to a person. Feldman and Bolino (1996) showed that students should work hard to identify their anchors as part of their development of self-knowledge in order that they are sure that they are pursuing the right career. However, you will not get every anchor you wish in one 'perfect' job so it is really important to rank the anchors you desire most to determine what you are willing to sacrifice. A similar approach is to analyse jobs that you like and break down the elements to reveal what you like. The chances are that your anchors will change as you progress through your life and career. For example, financial security may not be that important at this time in life, but if you have a family, it will inevitably increase in importance. It is thus important to regularly review your anchors and pursue jobs that will support them. This is where the power of work experience really comes into play – it helps you to see work environments first hand and help identify your anchors. As Skillings (2008) puts it, people have many different possible career paths that could suit their needs and so you need to get some insight into them, just as Ben has done so well to discover what really motivates him and gets him up in the morning.

At an earlier age, money was certainly my main motivator in a career. This was the case throughout my degree and in fact following my graduation. This changed, however, after my first 'major' job in which I was a business strategy consultant. The money was good, although the hours were long and I didn't have the job satisfaction. Shortly after this time I decided to pursue my entrepreneurial passions and this is really when my career aims became clear.

Freedom, being able to use creativity rather than being restricted to set instructions and doing something I enjoy are certainly now my main motivators. This opinion was affirmed as I began to explore social enterprises and how business can be used to help others.

This meant that not only does freedom matter to me within my career, but also the sense of doing some social good if it is possible. I am also certainly of the opinion that if you work within a job you are passionate about, you will work harder and therefore the money will follow, so I believe that the factors can link.

Ben Smith, BSc International Business and Modern Languages

### 14.3.1 What you can offer?

Each employer will seek a mix of skills that are specific to its culture as well as the vacancy. However, generally speaking there are certain key skills that employers are seeking, it is important to learn about these to identify any gaps in your skill set and subsequently begin developing them.

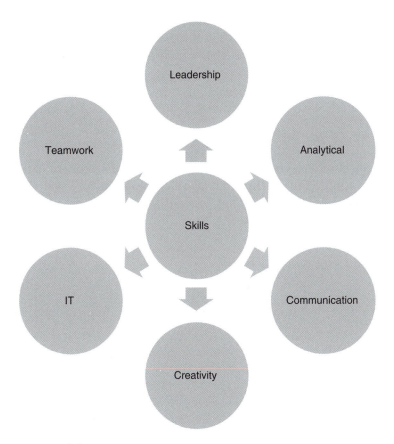

FIGURE 14.1   Your skill set

Generally speaking it is good to have a skill set that combines all of the skills in Figure 14.1 with a couple of speciality areas that allow you to stand out. Think hard about which of these you are best at and create some supporting evidence that you can use on application forms and in interviews. But remember, your skills are by no means static. If you find you have some real gaps in your skill set, then seek to develop those skills as quickly as possible. We know of many students who undertake society work, entrepreneurial ventures and community projects to quickly develop their skills and bolster their CV.

> During the start of my second year at Aston University, a flatmate and I recognised the great expense that textbooks were costing us and wanted to find a way of buying second hand books from other people around our university. We decided to start our own small project and set up an online web service which allows students to buy and sell items around university. Firstly, we had to teach ourselves a high level of web development skills, this took some time but with each other's support we managed to get the site created. Then we had to market the website to students to actually get them to use the service, this involved creating a real brand and an online identity, aspects which we had never dealt with before. The online service is now up and running successfully, I have used the technical skills in my academic work and also the business knowledge to move on to other ventures.
>
> Neil Kumar, BSc Business, Computing and IT

### 14.3.2 Where do you want to work?

You must select where you wish to work in terms of sector/industry and geographical location. Have a think about the type of culture you wish to work in, the type of people, etc. Try not to limit yourself by being open to many different locations and sectors.

### 14.3.3 Why do you want to work?

Finally, you have to determine why you want to work. At a simple level, most will say for money but it is about far more than this. For example, if you want to work to make a difference in the world then charities may be of high importance to you.

## 14.4 Preparing the plan

When you have an idea of what you want, it is important to articulate the plan. Going back to the chapter on goal setting, some of the key questions are:

- What are the benefits?
- What are the key blockers?
- How are the blockers going to be overcome?

The benefits are going to be personal to you and so we do not want to go over them. Instead, we want to concentrate on the blockers, two in particular, time and fear. Many students seem to think the recruitment process begins in September but it is actually continuous across many organisations and many employers are starting much earlier (High Fliers Research, 2013). This means you should begin earlier and complete steps without the pressures of academic work.

> I began my placement search in early August so I could begin making applications as soon as I started university and ensure I could dedicate enough time to achieve my goal of securing a first. The most important thing I did was to draft my CV and review it several times with the help of books and friends who work in recruitment. This gave me enough time to really perfect my CV and learn a lot about the job process. I also completed an application to familiarise myself with the process and identify areas I needed to improve on.
>
> Costa Pouzouris, BSc Accounting and Financial Management

Fear of failure is the most common fear when it comes to job hunting but 'failure' and rejection are an inevitable part of securing a job. As we highlighted in Chapter 5 on fear, if you fail a stage such as an interview you have learned something new and subsequently got closer to success. Failure is actually guaranteed in job applications as we have yet to hear of any student who has applied to just one organisation and succeeded. Chris personally knows this himself having been rejected over 45 times in his second year of university. Crucially, however, was that he learned so much that when he graduated it took him just three weeks to secure a job. Pat has been made redundant several times and each time he has learned new things – mostly that he had been in the wrong job! The key is to learn from your failures. A good technique to help desensitise yourself and reduce your fear is to apply to organisations that you have little interest in. This helps to familiarise yourself with the process and identify areas you need to improve on.

## 14.5 Opportunities

There are many opportunities out there for students even though it may not seem like it from the news. There are still vast numbers of jobs and

TABLE 14.2   Opportunities for experience

| Opportunity | Structure | Popular areas | Advantages |
|---|---|---|---|
| Part-time work | Undertake basic responsibilities for a day or two per week | Bar work, retail jobs and administration | Earn income whilst studying, develop basic skills |
| Volunteering | Help a local organisation or charity for free for a few hours to two days per week | Children, disability, drugs, education, employment, environment, families, museums, sport | Feel good factor, develop skills, discover career anchors |
| Internships and work experience | Spend a couple of days to a couple of months working for a business | Banking and Finance, Consultancy, HR, Marketing, Retail | Develop skills, discover anchors, sometimes paid |
| Industrial placement | Spend your third year working for 12–15 months | Banking, Consultancy, Finance, HR, Logistics and Supply Chain, Marketing, Retail and FMCG | Great opportunity to learn and often comes with a salary |
| Graduate job/ programme | A set structure consisting of different placements and training courses ranging from 2–5 years | Banking, Consultancy, Finance, HR, Logistics and Supply Chain, Marketing, Retail and FMCG | Number of training courses, opportunity to socialise with other graduates |

opportunities out there and we want to share what exactly these are, where you can find them and how to go about securing them.

Many students are just aiming for a graduate job but there are many opportunities before this, such as those listed in Table 14.2. We recommend any student to undertake volunteer work, internships and placements. These are all things Chris did and he received tremendous personal and professional benefits from doing so. Within all these experiences, there is a lot of scope to undertake different business roles from marketing, leading, admin, etc. The idea with most of them is to get a foot in the door and develop transferable skills. For example, Pat first came to Aston in 1998 to deliver three lectures as a visitor. At the time he wasn't at all sure it was a good use of his time but in 2000 he was offered a job – first part time then full time and he stayed there until 2013 eventually becoming a senior manager. We are aware that students can pay to undertake work experience but we believe this to be an unfair request and would advise students not to do so. Instead, volunteering can offer the same level of experience whilst being free and providing you with the opportunity to do something rewarding. The key to success is how you go about securing the job, which we will discuss next.

As part of my sandwich degree, I was successful in gaining a place on the National Grid Industrial Placement Scheme. These programmes are an excellent way to gain some initial experience of the working world, and allow students to put into practice some of their knowledge and skills that they have built up from secondary school, university and part-time work. Having responsibility of high profile projects and delivering key pieces of work to a real life business was very rewarding. The programme allowed me to gain a client for my final year dissertation, gain sponsorship for my last year at university, and I was also offered a great opportunity to progress onto the graduate development programme.

Kerrie Martin, BSc Business Information Technology

## 14.5.1 Entrepreneurial route

We know that many students actually wish to set up their own business upon graduation, an increasing percentage are even setting up businesses as they are studying. We want to provide some brief advice specifically for these students. There are generally two routes for students wishing to set up their own business:

1. Set up your own business straight out of university: this is the ideal route for any student wishing to start their own business. One determining factor with this seems to be having the 'big idea'. Many entrepreneurial students state they would set up their own business but say they haven't got an idea. First, you don't need to have a 'big idea' and second, an idea is not going to happen by chance.
2. Buy an existing business, i.e. franchise: this option supports the fact that you don't need an idea to start your own business. This is a route often overlooked by students, mainly because of the lack of finance to pursue it. However, if possible it is a great route to becoming an entrepreneur.

Due to the current recession, the government is offering a wealth of support to those wishing to set up their own business, particularly to younger people. We suggest you fully take advantage of these and suggest you research some of the following: Young Enterprise, Shell Livewire, NACUE, Unltd, BSEEN, New Entrepreneurs Foundation.

The desire to start your own business does not mean that you have to do so immediately after university. Many entrepreneurial people begin working life within other organisations in order to learn about the corporate world, develop their skills and discover new opportunities. Thus, we suggest that if you do not know where or what business you would like to establish then begin by working for another company. Starting your own business takes a lot of hard work, determination and commitment. Thus, we recommend you only pursue it if you are really passionate to do so. We say this as many students are setting up their own business as a last minute resort, mainly due to not being able to secure a job. In this case, we suggest that you carry on trying to secure a job and we hope the advice we have provided will allow you to do this. We suggest that if you really do want to set up your own business to go ahead and do it, action is the only key way to get going.

## 14.6 Types of organisations

We briefly want to touch on the type of companies all these opportunities can be found within as many students can have a somewhat limited mindset towards large organisations.

### 14.6.1 Large organisations

These are the focus by the majority of business students and we can fully understand why. They tend to offer the highest salaries, come with prestige and kudos of working for a well-known company and offer many employee benefits. We do wish to highlight some aspects of large organisations which seem to be omitted in students' considerations. They are extremely competitive as so many students apply to them. Because of this, they come with long and stressful assessment procedures. Moving away from the obvious, there can be limited responsibility given to graduates. The typical programme consists of mini-placements within different departments; this is good for exposure but can limit responsibility as line managers know that students will soon move on.

### 14.6.2 Small and mid-sized businesses

Small and medium sized enterprises (SMEs) are organisations that are classed by certain limits, often employees and/or turnover. The UK government has recently started to focus on a new grouping – mid-sized businesses (MSB) which are larger but not at the global size. For some reason, students seem to think of smaller companies as inferior, a second choice (Moy and Lee, 2002). The reason why is unknown to us though we believe it is due to the esteem and identity that come with larger organisations, for example, 'I work for Microsoft', and because of the higher salaries. The truth is that whilst the well-known firms may have some cachet in the name, the reality of the jobs in them is often quite limiting. Imagine the difference between being the only person in the business thinking about marketing compared to being one of many in a huge department. In the latter case you are likely to have very limited exposure to any real decision making whereas in the smaller business you could be carrying the whole business in terms of its marketing. You can get great experience that way. Maybe some students even want to work for SMEs but do not know how. Ahmadi and Helms (1997) view small firms as big opportunities, and so do we. Many small organisations have shown a desire to hire graduates (Woods and Dennis, 2009) and actually offer the attributes graduates find important in larger quantities than larger organisations (Moy and Lee, 2002) such as job security and opportunities to progress. Pat's experience in his current role involves reaching out to businesses and he is constantly approached by mid-sized businesses who struggle to attract good graduates. There are great opportunities in all manner of businesses that aren't household names but are nevertheless often great places to work.

Due to the limitation of time, no person can realise all the opportunities and overcome all the threats. It thus becomes very important to rank these in order to identify the best opportunities and concentrate your efforts towards them. This is where the summer term can prove very beneficial, be sure to make the most of it whilst you don't have academic work to complete.

## 14.7 Finding the job

Many students concentrate on the same websites and sources for jobs, which actually worsens the problem of competition. Websites are a great way to find a job but they are just one source of many. It is a simple case of statistics, the more methods you use the higher chance you have of securing your dream job.

### 14.7.1 Websites

Websites are undeniably students' favourite method in searching for opportunities and indeed they are powerful. Many, if not all, of the larger graduate recruiters now post their opportunities on one or more websites. Some of the main and most popular websites, just in case you have not heard of them, are:

- Target Jobs
- Times 100
- Rate My Placement
- Milkround
- Prospects

We don't really want to run through these, as we are sure you have heard of them, if not then you certainly will do. Instead, we want to run through some smaller and less well-known sites that are just as valuable, if not more so as many people are not aware of them.

- Escape the City – provides volunteering and jobs for those not seeking a corporate career.
- Enternships – entrepreneurial internships for students interested in becoming an entrepreneur or working in small start ups.
- Intern Avenue – a relatively new site that provides internships for students.
- Guardian Jobs – professional graduate level jobs across all different areas.
- BBC and Channel 4 – provides media related work experience and graduate opportunities.

### 14.7.2 University careers service

We mentioned this earlier but the careers service offers so much potential help to your career we wanted to mention it again. Spend time in careers centre be clear on what you want from them. Remember they are not there to do things for you, i.e. write your CV, but to provide guidance. Many careers officers have vast experience so listen to them! Also, your careers service will hold a network of companies with roles which may be specific to your university.

### 14.7.3 Mentoring

Mentoring can take many forms but essentially it is a way for you to gain access to the experience of other students or professionals. Many universities and business schools are now running business mentoring schemes, linking students with business professionals. These are amazing opportunities and we recommend that absolutely every student undertake them. Mentors can open their networks to you and provide you with job shadowing, maybe even work experience, a placement or a graduate programme.

### 14.7.4 Career exhibitions, presentations and open days

Rest assured these are not put on for the fun of it, recruiters attending these events maintain a keen eye in identifying possible students so we class them as a real opportunity. There are plenty of them lying around, from the smaller industry specific ones hosted at your university to the larger ones such as the National Graduate Recruitment Exhibition. Often, the graduate recruiters and even directors attend these and hence they present a valuable opportunity to create a good impression. Our tips for exhibitions and presentations are:

- Research the companies that are attending, particularly those you are interested in. If you stumble upon an exhibition whilst, for example, going to lectures see what time it ends and then spread your time doing some research, even if it is just a quick search on your phone.

- Dress smartly to ensure you create a good impression (see Chapter 13 for details).
- Think of some good questions that you wish to ask.
- Take a CV in case an employer wants your contact details, but only give it if asked. Even better is to take a business card which cost just a few pounds for 100 and they look very professional.
- If you have a positive conversation, ask for their contact details and follow it up.
- Be aware of how many freebies you take, if you do take something then initiate a conversation.

### 14.7.5 Networking

A network is a group of people that can help you achieve what you want. It is very powerful because of what's known as social capital, the ability to derive benefits from being involved in a certain group (Portes, 1998). Seibert et al., (2001) describe three key ways in which networks help: social capital,

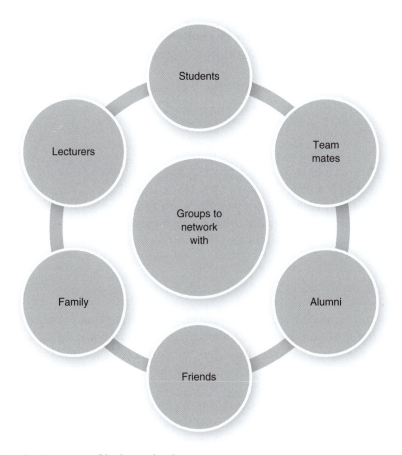

FIGURE 14.2   Sources of help and advice

access to information, resources and career sponsorship. Above this, social capital can help by being offered job opportunities, i.e. being headhunted (McDonald and Elder, 2006). This illustrates just how valuable your network can be. It really comes back to the old cliché, it is not what you know, but who you know. Have a think about who is in your network and how they can help you. Some groups you may wish to think about are shown in Figure 14.2.

Any one person in your network will be able to offer one or more types of advice depending on their relevant experience, skills, position and network. For example, alumni are a great source – people who have studied at the same university as you so they are usually keen to help. You can find them at events on campus as well as online databases where they have stated that they can be contacted.

Your network will probably already be larger then you thought and so you will need to be strategic. For example, Chris had a placement interview at National Grid, a company where a close family friend had worked for the last 30 years. By speaking to him for 30 minutes Chris was able to develop a vast level of knowledge about the company that allowed him to perform better at the assessment centre and secure the role. This is primarily concerning your current network but you can certainly take steps to expand yours:

- LinkedIn offers vast opportunities to network so be sure to follow our tips in Chapter 13 on communication and proactively use it.
- Attend events and conferences around areas that interest you.

As you can see, there are masses of opportunities to network, it is very beneficial for your career and it can provide you with great friends. In terms of how to network effectively be sure to create a specific goal for everybody you wish to network with but do not ask for a job as it creates the wrong impression. Finally, follow up every meeting and conversation by thanking them for their help, carrying out actions and seeking feedback when possible.

## 14.7.6 Employment agencies

There are an increasing number of employment agencies popping up which are attracting students in these tough times. Employment agencies do seem to attract some bad press, mainly due to there being so many of them and their pestering manner to win clients. They don't have a great reputation and in many cases this is justified. But we do recommend you go there because some businesses will only recruit through them. Just be aware that they are only interested in filling jobs and aren't really interested in your career or what is best for you as an individual.

### 14.7.7 Ringing an organisation

Essentially, what you are aiming for here is to talk with somebody valuable and discover opportunities. Yate (2002) is a big fan of this technique. If you can get past the receptionists and speak to somebody you can make anything happen. These days so much communication is carried out via email, it might be that you phoning up and speaking to someone in person could be a way of standing out from the crowd. Be careful with this technique though and do not pester people. If somebody cannot help you, thank him or her and move on. Often you will need a name of somebody specific to talk to and LinkedIn can be massively powerful for achieving this. If you do get through and they have nothing for you, ask them if they know anybody who does.

## 14.8 The job recruitment process

Different opportunities and organisations will encompass different processes, however, most share common elements which we want to share with you. Companies actually receive a significant number of bad applications and this is what we want to help you avoid.

### 14.8.1 The CV

The CV is an important tool in your armoury, it is essentially a summary of you and your life experience. Writing one is a task many students are scared and confused about but they are not that difficult. Essentially a CV needs to encompass education, work experience and your skills. All CVs encompass these elements in one way or another and the different types of CVs place a different emphasis on one or more of these. We are going to discuss the chronological CV as this is generally preferred by employers seeking business students and graduates. But first an example from a graduate who recently landed his dream job:

> Having graduated I applied for a lot of jobs mainly because a company, which I will leave unnamed, offered me a graduate job which they had to cancel due to recession driven HR cuts. Anyway, this experience changed the way I applied for jobs – I made changes to my thought process, which got me to much further stages and eventually a job at IBM (I don't mean to brag, but 300 jobs were given to 12,000 applicants, so I must have done something right).
>
> *(Continued)*

*(Continued)*

My thought shift was from me 'selling myself', to viewing myself as my own company. For example, the voluntary work I have done is my PR; my LinkedIn profile is my marketing; and my CV is sales literature to my sales pitch, which is my interview. What this has done is create a framework for applying for jobs. I now see it as selling a product rather than 'selling myself'. There are a number of benefits. The two key ones, to me, are:

1 To sell a product you have to understand the customer. So what does the customer want? How can I fulfill these needs? How can I develop my skills (product development) and solve problems that I couldn't solve before? What is the cost-benefit of training (R&D)? How do I assign personal expense for personal gain (finance), etc., etc.
2 It has allowed me to 'unattach' myself from the skills I am offering. It is difficult, particularly for a Brit, to talk-up my abilities – we see it as boastful. Unattaching myself from my skills, by seeing them as a service that I am trying to sell, makes it much easier to comfortably promote what I have done and what I can do.

Dan Turner, Technology Consultant, IBM

So, to learn how to write a CV you must first understand its purpose, which is to generate enough interest to be invited to the next stage of the process. It can also form the basis of an interview where an employer questions different elements. Combining this with the fact there is a competitive job market there are three key implications for writing a CV:

1. Make each point distinct – there is little room on a CV so none of it should be wasted.
2. Ensure every line adds value – every line needs to be valuable in the eyes of an employer, be it from a specific duty in a job to your phone number which allows them to contact you.
3. Presentation – it needs to be easy to read and consistent fonts and formatting will ensure this.

Include your basic contact details: name, address, email address and phone number. However, make sure these take up the minimal amount of space possible apart from your name, as they are not things that generate interest. Be mindful as to what email address to include, if you have a university address include it as opposed to your personal address. Immediately after, include a personal profile which will act as a summary of your CV, be sure to make it strong enough to make an employer want to read your CV. Where many students go wrong here is being too artistic. For example, you can often find lines like, 'I am a determined, hard-working, charismatic and charming student'. What does this say about somebody? Nothing! Instead you need to present how you can solve the problems of the organisation (Covey and Colosimo, 2009). For example, 'With my experience of digital marketing, I will be able to help ABC Ltd improve its marketing strategy by generating creative ideas, leveraging social media and creating attention grabbing emails to reach its aim of X profit'. Your CV then goes on to prove that you are indeed capable of doing this.

As a student, your education section is important and it needs to include your time at university, college/sixth form and school. Start with the present/most recent and work backwards so your degree will be first – your university name, degree title and expected grade. As you progress you generally want to decrease the level of detail, for example, for GCSEs just state how many you gained and the grades you received, e.g. nine GCSEs A–C. The education section also provides an opportunity to personalise your CV by highlighting relevant topics you have studied which an organisation may find important. Don't expect them to know what is in your degree – you have to tell them.

Work experience is the key section that can allow you to stand out and so it should be the largest section. Again, the job title, organisation and dates of employment are important to include but are not going to make you stand out. It is advisable to include a brief sentence that describes the role as this can sometimes be unclear with the variety of roles students undertake. Then include some bullet points on what you did in the organisation, i.e. what projects you worked on, what your daily duties were and what results you produced. Similar to education, start from the most recent and work down from there, decreasing the level of detail as you progress. As a general rule of thumb, include three or four achievements for each role. This ensures that you have something to surprise the employer with at a later stage. Writing your work experience section well enough means you should not need a skills section, for example, stating you successfully negotiated a discount for the prom party illustrates that you have negotiation skills. To help achieve this, you need to be specific with your achievements and responsibilities. For example, many students have worked in a retail job and might therefore say things like, 'I served customers, dealt with customer complaints and stocked the shelves'. These sorts of points do not really say much, yet can do with the inclusion of specific numbers and details (Fox, 2001):

- Served over 50 customers a day.
- Dealt with five customer complaints a week which helped to manage frustrated customers.
- Stocked the shelves to ensure demand was constantly met.

It is important to include an interests section as this helps to describe you on a more personal note. It also provides an opportunity to stand out, particularly with interests that might be of value to the organisation/role. In an example of how not to do it, Chris had a keen interest in poker in his second year and included this on his CV. He was swiftly told to remove it due to its negative connotations. Try to be specific when discussing your interests, for example, thousands of students state they like to exercise/keep fit but this doesn't say much, state what you actually do, like biking or jogging.

Include an additional skills section where you can explain other relevant details such as what languages you speak, whether or not you have a driving licence, IT skills and how mobile you are. There is no need to include references on a CV so they can be a waste of vital space. Instead, just include a line saying that references are available upon request. Writing references in this way helps to protect the details of your referees.

In terms of presentation, keeping it simple is more effective than trying to be too creative. Remember the person reading your CV will be reading dozens if not hundreds of CVs so make it easy for them to read it and make the key points stand out. Don't make it too crowded though – having sufficient amounts of white space as well as clear headings will make it easy to scan read. Also, be sure that it is no longer than two pages and no less than one (unless you are a mature student – Pat's CV is about 12 pages long these days – and even longer if he includes all his publications!).

A final note about writing a CV, it is not a static document and you should regularly update it, this also helps to motivate you as you reflect on what you have achieved. The fact it always changes also means it will never be perfect. Referring to the time management chapter, perfectionism can prove a waste of time and a CV is a good example of this. You can never get a CV to be perfect as every person that looks at it will give you a different opinion. You need to eventually stop and send it out.

### 14.8.2 Covering letter

The general structure of a cover letter should have four paragraphs:

- Introduction.
- Why you want to undertake the role.
- The skills you can offer.
- Why you want to work in the organisation.

Include your name, address, email address and phone number but again ensure these take up the minimal amount of space. 'Dear sir/madam' is the best way to say to an employer that you have not bothered to put effort into an application. It is crucial to include a name whenever possible, to find a name scan the website, ring the HR department or ask at an exhibition. Then state the job/scheme you are applying for and where you discovered the opportunity. This is the first paragraph and thus where an employer is going to start forming their opinion.

Immediately after, discuss why you want to undertake the role. For example, what is it about marketing or finance that makes you so determined to secure a job in it. Again be specific and really think through your answer. If you can speak to somebody who currently does the role or one similar, discuss it as it shows you actually know what the role is like in practice. For example, many students wish to work in HR because they like meeting new people but in reality HR is a far cry from this, particularly when it comes to performance management or disciplinary procedures. Show that you really know what the job is about and what you can bring to it.

Why you want to work in the organisation is perhaps the best way to personalise a cover letter. Many mistakes are made here where students talk on a general basis, for example, I wish to work in the organisation as it provides excellent training opportunities. Instead, a student would be better to discuss the specific training opportunities an organisation offers. You don't have to make it sound like it has been your ambition from the age of five to be (for example) a chartered accountant but employers need to know that you have seriously considered what the job is all about and why it is the right fit for you personally. End the cover letter by finishing on a positive open note, thanking them for taking their precious time to read your application and state that you are free anytime for the next stage. Finally, sign the letter off by stating 'yours sincerely' assuming that you included the employer's name, otherwise use 'yours faithfully'.

### 14.8.3 Application forms

Many larger organisations are now switching from cover letters to online application forms which usually include a list of simple questions such as education, contact details and references. The crucial aspect is the competency based questions where the STAR framework is the most widely used method: situation, task, action, result. Many of the questions asked in application forms are also used in interviews so we will explore specific questions later in the chapter. With any cover letter, CV and application form, it is crucial to review it multiple times yourself, by your friends and others. Specifically, ensure there are no grammatical or spelling errors and that it is personalised to the role and organisation. Finally, ensure it tells the truth, lies will only come back to haunt you.

### 14.8.4 Assessment centres

Employers are increasingly using assessment centres in order to give students the chance to illustrate their skills and allow the employer to select the most capable candidates. They typically encompass many exercises, some of which will be generic whilst some are more specific to the role. They are certainly not easy, they can last anything from half a day to two or even three days which can prove mentally draining. The best advice we can give you is by breaking down each element.

### 14.8.5 Interview

There have been many changes in the recruitment process but interviews still remain at the core of nearly all. They have become so universal that students could face as many as three interviews before being offered a job. An interview is essentially an interactive presentation of yourself, from the moment you walk in to the moment you leave. There are three key stages that you need to prepare for.

### 14.8.5.1 Pre-interview

Before the interview, you need to discover when and where the interview will be conducted, whether you can learn from other people who may have attended and the interview style and agenda. It is crucial to research the company. How do you actually go about doing this? The key is to use as many sources of information as possible to discover all the information needed, such as those listed in Table 14.3.

Talking to employees is a crucial source of information and this is where LinkedIn can be used. Just send a message to people explaining the fact you have an interview and are seeking information about the company, you may be surprised at the positive response you receive, just like Alexandra did in the next example.

TABLE 14.3   Sources of business information

| Sources | Information found |
| --- | --- |
| Company website | Mission and vision, Values, Company structure, Clients, Products and services, Training offered |
| Business sites | Business environment |
| Annual review | Competition |
| Internal magazines | Latest projects |
| Employees | Company culture<br>Expectations of the role |
| Trade magazines | Sector trends |

I started using LinkedIn to get in touch with people who work for the companies I was applying for when searching a placement. I used to send messages to people I did not know asking about the company culture, the assessment process and so forth. Amazingly enough, 3 out of 10 people usually respond. Then, I would mention in my interviews that I had contacted people from the company in question and that impressed the interviewer.

What is more, nowadays you can even apply for jobs directly on LinkedIn, exporting your profile as a CV. That just goes to show how important it is to have a professional and impressive LinkedIn profile. Employers, I have heard, search employees on LinkedIn so you need to make a good impression.

Alexandra Cojanu, BSc Business and Management

### 14.8.5.2 During the interview

When you meet the employer, remember to give a firm handshake and maintain eye contact. When answering questions, take a minute to think through

TABLE 14.4   Commonly asked questions

| Questions | Your answer |
| --- | --- |
| Why do you want to work for this company? | This is your chance to shine and research is the key to success. You can end up with a lot of information and so it can be useful to combine it and tell a story. For example, starting at the top like the vision and mission and then working your way down. |
| Tell me about yourself and your experience | Be specific and keep your answer concise. It's generally good practice to follow the format of your CV. |
| What was the most difficult part of your last job? | Do not be negative or talk badly of others. Instead focus on specific challenges and explain how you overcame them. |
| Where can you see yourself in 2, 5 and 10 years? | Be realistic with this one and don't give the standard answer – I want to be the CEO. Realistically it takes ages and there can only be one CEO. |
| What is your greatest weakness? | Do not say you have no weaknesses – nobody is perfect. Instead, be honest but do not say anything that may be detrimental to your ability to do the job. |
| Tell us about your greatest achievement | Try not to default to your degree, instead try to use a work or personal example that proves you are a bit different. |
| Tell us about a time when you worked with somebody you didn't like | Some people try to knock this question off by saying that it has never happened. However, chances are it has. Talk about it and explain what you did. |
| What would you like to earn? | Flip the question round and ask what is usually paid for this role. Then negotiate from there. |

your answers and if you did not quite understand then ask the interviewer to repeat/clarify the question. Remember that it is not just you talking, listen by using the tips we discussed in Chapter 13 on business communication. In terms of how to answer the questions, some of the most common questions are listed in Table 14.4.

The key themes from these questions are be honest, give concise answers, focus on proven results and use positive language. These tips can also be applied to competency-based questions used on application forms but in that case, you also need to ensure that you stick to the word count, never go over it, as it will be dismissed. The only way to achieve all this and be successful in an interview is to listen. All too often, we hear from recruiters that students and graduates simply don't listen to what is being asked of them, either they answer the wrong question or don't hear key information and then ask a question that has already been answered. If you haven't read the business communication chapter, we strongly suggest you do so.

> Listening skills have always been an important aspect in anyone's academic career especially when you are starting to have interviews. In my interview for Mattel Europa, I had to ensure I was paying full attention to detail and listening to every question I was asked, otherwise I risked replying with an insufficient answer. One of the questions I got asked was, 'Why do you want to work with Mattel' which could have been interpreted in two different ways. I had originally seen it as which parts of the roles do I like the sound of, but after taking a second to think about the question in more detail I realised they were asking me why I wanted this placement. From this I was then able to talk about my passion for the company by backing it up with examples of further reading and research into the company, which they responded to by stating 'a perfect answer'.
>
> Lewis Boot, BSc International Business and Management

### 14.8.5.3 After the interview

Be sure to ask questions, which you should have prepared. Some you may wish to ask are:

- Who carried out the job last and what happened?
- Where have graduates who took on the role previously ended up?
- Can you tell me more about the role?
- If successful, what would the next stage entail and whom would it be with?
- Do you have any concerns about my application? (Beshara, 2008)

Be careful not to interview the interviewer by asking too many questions, three to five questions are more than enough. Beshara (2008) recommends never ending with, 'What else would you like to know about me?' and we agree as it prompts the thought 'Is there anything else I should know?'. Finally, avoid questions on the benefits or salary as it can look like you are solely motivated by money.

### 14.8.6 Group tasks

Group tasks come in many formats from business case to fictitious plane crashes, at the core of all these is measuring how well somebody can work within a group. Remembering the roles we discussed earlier in Chapter 8 on group work, it is key to select a role for each group member. Typically for an assessment centre, roles needed are a leader and a time keeper. Conflict is going to be inevitable with people you have never met and worked with, especially as you are all competing against each other. However, so long as it is functional conflict then it is fine. If somebody does begin to create dysfunctional conflict then try to end it and steer the group back on track. Be sure to listen, it will look very bad if you constantly disrupt others or passively don't listen to what they say. At the same time, it is important to talk, if you don't say anything then the employer has nothing to mark you on. Just make sure you do not just talk for the sake of doing so, only talk if you have something that adds value even if it is simply clarifying what somebody has said for the benefit of the group.

### 14.8.7 In-tray exercise

An in-tray exercise involves being an employee within a fictitious or real organisation and completing a practical task. It is usually designed to be quite difficult by giving you a number of things that need to be completed. The trick is to remember that they are not expecting you to complete everything. They are really seeking to understand your decision making process and more importantly why you chose the actions you did. As part of the task, you will normally be given a brief that could include information on role and responsibilities, goals and priorities of the organisation, key staff members/ structure chart and a calendar including future tasks and meetings. Be sure to read all of these in detail and if something is not explicitly stated then by all means make an assumption and make these clear later on.

Also, make some brief notes so you can remember your decisions. When completing the exercise, remember that the idea is to pick the most important tasks. Thus remembering some of the tips from time management think about what you may be able to eradicate, delegate, put off and prioritise – use the time matrix grid if it helps. When justifying your decisions, be sure to include information on the organisation. When Pat uses these exercises in assessment centres he designs it usually to see how the candidates prioritise things. So, it is really important to show what the criteria are that you are using. You may have a different set of criteria from the ones the assessors are expecting but if you at least show what they are, you may still score well.

### 14.8.8 Role play

These are typically linked to the type of role being undertaken. The important thing to remember here is that role play is often taken to the extreme to see how you react. Chris will never forget the role play he had where he had to act as a manager and tell an employee that people said she needed to improve at her job and work longer hours. Everything Chris said, she took it to the extreme by saying she was already under stress and working more hours would result in her husband leaving. It got to the point where Chris just ended up laughing as he didn't know what to say. What this highlights is that they are not realistic and are designed to test you. Maintain a professional mind and do the best you can.

### 14.8.9 Psychometric testing

Psychometric tests are often conducted online with a follow up in person to ensure a student is not cheating the test. The typical areas tested are numerical reasoning, verbal reasoning, spatial awareness, diagrammatical reasoning and personality traits. In broad terms, for the first four, there are correct answers where as for the final one there is not. For these, try and get some practise – the careers service will be a help and you might find some useful websites too. Remember good exam technique – pace yourself, keep an eye on the time, don't rush, don't get hung up on one question, answer in the order you are confident, make sure all your multiple choice answers are against the right question. With the personality test, the important thing is never try to guess what they want you to answer. Good tests will pick this up and it looks to the assessor like you are trying to cheat or have something to hide. Just answer honestly. There is no such thing as a personality profile which recruiters are looking for in a particular role so whatever you answer it is essentially right.

### 14.8.10 Presentation

The tips we provided in Chapter 11 on presentations should provide you with all the information to deliver a presentation at an assessment centre. The only difference is that you may not get that much time to think everything through, for example, you could get half an hour to assemble and deliver a presentation. The key is to remember that you are not expected to deliver a world class presentation. We recommend you follow our steps by thinking about your target audience, generating the key theme with three supporting points and developing some supporting materials like flipchart papers if possible. You may be lucky enough to discover the presentation topic in advance, in this case, you would be expected to deliver a very good presentation so be sure to put the time in.

### 14.8.11 Social events

Some assessment centres will encompass a social event which can be anything from meeting employees to having lunch. Often employers will state these are not formally assessed which is true but remember that in every minute an employer is forming an opinion of you. Thus when it comes to social events, relax and do enjoy them but just be sure to remain professional by not drinking too much, being aware of your actions and watching your choice of words. In one assessment centre Pat ran, the candidates went for a drink after the testing was over with some members of staff. One of the candidates made a series of racist comments at this gathering which posed an interesting dilemma. In the end it was reported back to the CEO who (rightly) ruled out hiring that individual.

## 14.9 Things to remember for interviews and assessment centres

There are some quick tips that are crucial to remember when it comes to assessment centres:

- Prepare what you are going to wear and dress smartly even when it is not a formal interview.
- Be on time and make extreme allowances to ensure you are not late. Once you get there, relax at a local cafe and then arrive exactly when scheduled.
- Never treat the word informal as a chance to relax. Always be formal and prepare for it just as if you would for anything else, the same goes for internet-based interviews.

- If asked for feedback like, 'If you were doing this exercise again would you do anything differently?' give an honest reply. If you state anything that you would have done differently, be prepared for the next question, 'Why didn't you do it this way in the exercise?'
- If asked what you thought of the task itself then respond in a positive manner.
- Time is crucial with all the exercises, particularly in group tasks, as it is so easy to run away with a conversation and not complete the task.
- Always listen carefully to what is being asked of you, if you are unsure at any point, then say so and ask the assessor to clarify things.
- Do not be alarmed by assessors, they are there to ensure you are fairly assessed.
- Once you return home, it is crucial to email the assessors to thank them for the opportunity. Make it personal, did you enjoy learning about a part of the role or seeing the office?
- If possible, ask for feedback as it will provide vital learnings if you do not succeed.
- Write down notes at the earliest opportunity to reflect on your performance – what you did and didn't do well, what they asked you and what would you do differently.

## 14.10 Taking it to work

As you have come to realise, career management is not just about getting a graduate job. It is much more long term than this and something that you will need to continually monitor, review and practise. The average person goes through the job hunting process at least seven times in their lifetime thus career management is a skill well worth learning.

## 14.11 How to get started

### 14.11.1 Professional

- Make a list of everybody you know and how they could help you towards your aims, rank them and take some actions towards the top five.
- Critically review your CV line by line.
- Make a practise application to an organisation you are interested in.

### 14.11.2 A little more interesting

- Go to a local networking event in an area that interests you such as marketing or HR.
- With a friend, take it in turns to interview each other and be very critical of how each other did.
- Undertake an entrepreneurial project or a role within a society to develop your skills.

## 14.12 Our bookshelf

Rath, T. (2005) *Strengths finder*. New York: Gallup.
This book provides a great insight into what skills you are good at, in turn it gives sound advice in terms of what jobs to aim for and how to ensure you use your key skills to the maximum each day in whatever role you undertake.

Bolles, N.R. (2013) *What color is your parachute?* Berkeley, CA: Ten Speed Press.
This book has become a worldwide seller and provides advice that every student should learn about. It is written in an informal style which makes it very easy to understand, entertaining to read and easy to put into practice.

Williams, J. (2010) *Screw work, let's play*. London: Pearson.
A great book to help discover what you enjoy and more importantly how to turn that enjoyment into a profitable business. It provides a rather different stance to the whole concept of work so it is definitely worth reading.

## 14.13 References

Ahmadi, M. and Helms, M.M. (1997) 'Small firm, big opportunities: the potential of career for business graduates in SMEs', *Education + Training*, 39 (2): 52–57.

Arnold, J. and Randall, R. with Patterson, F., Silvester, J., Robertson, I., Cooper, C., Burnes, B., Swailes, S., Harris, D., Axtell, C. and Hartog, D.D. (2010) *Work psychology: understanding human behaviour in the workplace*. Harlow: Pearson Education.

Beshara, T. (2008) *Acting the interview – how to ask and answer the questions that will get you the job!* New York: AMACOM.

Covey, R.S. and Colosimo, J. (2009) *Great work, great career: how to create your ultimate job and make an extraordinary contribution*. New York: FranklinCovey Publishing.

Feldman, C.D. and Bolino, C.M. (1996) 'Careers within careers: reconceptualizing the nature of career anchors and their consequences', *Human Resource Management Review*, 6 (2): 89–112.

Fox, J.J. (2001) *Don't send a resume: and other contrarian rules to help land a great job*. New York: Hyperion.

Hall, D.T. (2002) Careers in and out of organizations. Thousand Oaks, CA: Sage Publications.

High Fliers Research (2013) *The graduate market in 2013: annual review of graduate vacancies & starting salaries at Britain's leading employers*. Available online at: www.highfliers.co.uk/download/GMReport13.pdf (accessed 4 February 2013).

McDonald, S. and Elder, H.G. (2006) 'When does social capital matter? Non-searching for jobs across the life course', *Social Force*, 85 (1): 521–549.

Moy, J.W. and Lee, S.M. (2002) 'The career choice of business graduates: SMEs or MNCs?', *Career Development International*, 7 (6): 339–347.

Portes, A. (1998) 'Social capital: its origins and applications in modern sociology', *Annual Review of Sociology*, 24: 1–24.

Schein, E. (1993) *Career survival: strategic job/role planning*. San Diego: Pfeiffer & Co.

Seibert, E.S., Kraimer, L.M. and Liden, C.R. (2001) 'Social capital theory of career success', *The Academy of Management Journal*, 44 (2): 219–237.

Skillings, P. (2008) *Escape from corporate America: a practical guide to creating the career of your dreams*. New York: Ballantine Books.

Woods, A. and Dennis, C. (2009) 'What do UK small and medium sized enterprises think about employing graduates?', *Journal of Small Business and Enterprise Development*, 16 (4): 642–659.

Yate, M. (2002) *Knock 'em dead*. Avon, MA: Adams Media.

# Index

NOTE: Page numbers in *italic type* refer to tables and figures.

# HOW TO WRITE SUCCESSFUL BUSINESS AND MANAGEMENT ESSAYS

**Patrick Tissington**, *Birkbeck, University of London* **Markus Hasel**, *Management Consultant,* and **Jane Matthiesen**, *Sydney University*

**How to Write Successful Business and Management Essays** is a systematic guide to successfully producing written work for business and management degrees. The authors address the all too common pitfalls of essay assignments, as well as providing students with a step-by-step programme to approach essay questions, both in coursework and exam contexts.

Starting with the basics this book helps develop skills through the use of examples, exercises and checklists.

Helpful features include:

- Annotated essay examples, showing both good and bad points
- Tips on time management and motivation, note taking and effective reading
- Final checklists to use before you hand in
- Explanation of what the markers are looking for – and how to give it to them

Many students find referencing particularly confusing so the book provides detailed but easy-to-use information on what referencing is and how to do it properly.

**SAGE STUDY SKILLS SERIES**

2009 • 160 pages
Hardback (978-1-84-787590-7) • £62.00
Paperback (978-1-84-787591-4) • £16.99

## ALSO FROM SAGE